SECOND EDITION   SECOND EDITION   SECOND EDITION

MATH ACTIVITIES FOR CHILD INVOLVEMENT

Enoch Dumas

C. W. Schminke
UNIVERSITY OF OREGON

Allyn and Bacon, Inc.   Boston   London   Sydney

LIBRARY OF CONGRESS CATALOGING IN PUBLICATION DATA

Dumas, Enoch.
  Math activities for child involvement.

  Includes bibliographical references.
  1. Mathematics—Study and teaching (Elementary)
I. Schminke, Clarence W., joint author. II. Title.
QA135.5.D85 1977   510'.7   76-26872

ISBN 0-205-05592-3
ISBN 0-205-05577-X pbk.

CONTENTS   CONTENTS   CONTENTS   CONTENTS   CONTEN

In this book can be found hundreds of suggested projects, manipulative materials, games, puzzles, riddles, and other resource items that can spark children's learning. This is not intended to be a book of explanations of mathematics or of methods of teaching it, but a book of ideas to draw from as you involve children in their own learning.

Children do best what they like to do. What they like to do may be hard work, but that, too, may be part of the fun—to be stimulated, excited, surprised, spurred to competition, amused by ridiculous rewards for success. The purpose of this book is to suggest a variety of activities that will bring that kind of mental and emotional involvement into the learning of mathematics.

No attempt is made to be exhaustive with regard to either the extent or the variety of possibilities. Creative teachers may find many ways of modifying or adding to what is presented in this book. But if the ideas suggested on the pages that follow can assist teachers or parents in helping children gain appreciation for and develop competence in elementary mathematics, then the purpose of the author will have been achieved.

The Preface is intact from the first edition and is dedicated to the memory of the late Professor Dumas. It is timeless.

C.W.S.

The author is indebted to many who have directly or indirectly made this volume possible. Among all of our acquaintances, however, there are always a few who stand out. Thus, the writer acknowledges with gratitude those educators who have had a special or unique influence upon his view of the educational enterprise. Most notably this includes Paul B. Jacobson, Dean Emeritus of the College of Education, University of Oregon, and Professor Herbert F. Spitzer, retired, University of Iowa. More immediate appreciation is due Mr. William Sutherlin, whose generous assistance was given throughout the development of this second edition.

*Numbers following game titles refer to the activity number.

SKILL OR TOPIC	ACTIVITY NUMBER
Statistics	381–384, 446, 448
Subtraction	
algorithms	57, 134, 138
concepts	59, 120, 130, 137
facts	74, 87, 121, 123–129, 131–133, 135, 136, 139, 140, 226, 227, 229, 232, 234, 237, 409
Topology	244, 249, 263, 273–279
Trichotomy	45, 46, 229
Vocabulary	9, 11, 46–48
Writing numerals	36, 37, 282, 328

MATH ACTIVITIES AND YOU

RATIONALE

Whether you are a student teacher, a first- or second-year teacher, a seasoned practitioner, or a parent, the search for fresh ideas to utilize when helping children learn mathematics never ceases. Once an appropriate resource of ideas has been discovered, your philosophy of teaching must be brought to bear on that resource. In short, you must make decisions related to (a) the purpose or desired outcome; (b) the selection of an activity or activities most likely to generate that outcome; and (c) the requirements for interaction that will promote the greatest efficacy among the desired outcome, the activity, and the learner.

After reading Chapter 1 you should be able to:

1. Enunciate a personal teaching philosophy that embraces active teaching as well as active learning.

2. Discuss the detrimental effects upon children of undesirable conditions during mathematics instruction.
3. Describe the organization of this book.
4. List the dominant features of a laboratory approach for the mathematics period.
5. Describe an activity card and state two principles for its design.
6. Identify five advantages for activity cards in facilitating active learning and active teaching.
7. State at least five practical teaching suggestions for planning and implementing mathematics instruction in the elementary school.

DYNAMICS OF THE CLASSROOM

Mathematics is an increasingly fascinating and important study. Many children are excited by the orderliness of mathematics, by the sheer fun of manipulating numbers, by the scientific achievements possible through the use of mathematics, by the discovery of a surprise relationship, or by the solution of a puzzling problem.

The negative attitudes that children and adults may hold about mathematics are learned. Usually they can be traced to prior pressure to learn something that was either incomprehensible or boring or both. When children are frustrated or bored, changes need to be made.

From the beginning, mathematics should be made understandable to the learner. With the materials and activities described in this and other books, ways can be found whereby all children can understand the concepts and principles suitable to their levels of development.[1] Much of the mystifying element can be taken out of mathematics, and children can learn to appreciate the logic and order on which mathematical facts and computational procedures are based. While all learning in mathematics cannot be enjoyable for all children at all times, appropriate emphasis can be placed on inquiry, exploration, pleasure, and interest rather than the amount of work to be done. Believe in this and then act upon it. If children enjoy their work, they will learn a great deal and, more importantly, they will develop an abiding interest in mathematics.

Children learn if they are expected to learn. Over the years a great deal of evidence,[2] both formal and informal, has accumulated to support the thesis that when parents and teachers expect high levels of performance from children, the tendency is for them to fulfill those expectations. And the opposite seems to be true also—when little is expected, little is likely to be achieved.

Of course, one may set expectations too high and so discourage the learner, particularly if he has little confidence in his own abilities.[3] Comparing a child of moderate ability with one who made unusual achievement may have serious negative effects. Remember, although engaged in mathematics during the mathematics period, children learn a great deal more than mathematics. They learn to like or dislike mathematics and they may learn to like or dislike school; they develop acceptable or unacceptable behavior patterns; and they can learn the frustration of conflict, competition, and failure or they may learn the gratification of exploration, cooperation, competence, and success.

CONTENTS OF THE BOOK

Organization

The reader will note that the book is organized around major curricular topics from the mathematics of elementary school classrooms. Further, the chapters may be seen to constitute a sequential order closely paralleling topics from the most widely used professional texts on teaching elementary school mathematics. Throughout the text activities are simply identified by consecutive numbers, and a functional cross-index of activities by concept or skill is provided at the end of the book. The latter is for locating quickly a concept or skill and a concomitant activity or activities.

The final organizational feature of importance lies in the specific behavioral outcomes for children. These are appropriately placed with each major topical subhead within the separate chapters. In addition, a more general statement of purpose is usually provided with each activity and each activity is self-contained; that is, the materials, circumstances, procedures, and so forth that are necessary to carry out the activity are also found (explicit or implicit) with each activity.

Purpose

The focus of teaching is the student. The objective of instruction is causing children to learn. The purpose of this book is to help you "cause children to learn" mathematics under conditions that are mathematically, psychologically, and pedagogically sound. To do so, the dynamics of the mathematics period must foster an alert, receptive, and responsive attitude in children with respect to mathematics. Because of the historical antecedents with which we are all too familiar, the conditions of an alert, receptive, and responsive environment are particularly crucial for the mathematics period. The activities in this book will be especially useful to you in establishing that desirable conditioned learning environment.

The activities, procedures, games, puzzles, projects, charts, and displays that form the recommendations of subsequent chapters are intended to captivate children's interest and increase their enthusiasm for the mathematics program in your classroom and in your school. The activities are condensed, functional, and specific, and they have been tested with children in classrooms. To be chosen for inclusion, each activity had to meet the following criteria:

1. A clear purpose in terms of the educational objectives of an elementary school mathematics program.
2. Truly interesting and enjoyable to children at their developmental level.
3. Ease of implementation related to directions and materials.
4. Variety as well as practice for reinforcement of a skill or extended understanding of a concept.

The principal purpose of this book was aptly set forth nearly a half-century ago when A. N. Whitehead wrote: "One main idea runs through the various chapters, and is illustrated in them from many points of view. It can be stated briefly thus: The students are alive, and the purpose of education is to stimulate and guide their self-development."[4]

Use

A major assumption underlying thoughtful utilization of the material in this book is that teachers and children can form a partnership to become actively engaged in the process of teaching and learning mathematics. A hallmark of active teaching and its consequence, active learning, is a laboratory approach to the mathematics period. The dominant features of a mathematics period that effectively utilizes a laboratory approach may be summarized in the following way:

1. There is ample opportunity for children to communicate with the teacher and with their peers.
2. Feelings of inadequacy, frustration, and fear in relation to mathematics are kept at a minimum.
3. There is a dominant aura of inquiry and exploration as the teacher and children approach mathematics.
4. There is planned structuring and developmental modification of the immediate learning environment by the teacher through providing activities, suggesting problems, posing new questions, and making a variety of materials easily accessible.

It will be instructive to examine several specific examples of *one* approach to the enrichment of your mathematics teaching. It is an approach that encompasses the previous philosophy while promoting unique utilization of a variety of the activities from subsequent chapters. The approach lies in teacher-made activity cards. Variously termed "assignment cards," "task cards," or "job cards," an activity card is simply a sensibly sized card upon which a particular activity is portrayed. One good source for blank cards is a media or materials center where durable cardboard is punched out in the process of framing material for projection. The unused portion is ideal for an activity card. Biggs and Maclean suggest that all activity cards incorporate two important principles.[5] First, they must require children to do something, that is, measure, construct, design, organize, compare, or whatever. Second, the children must record or otherwise communicate their solutions through writing, drawing, or speaking.

Examine the illustrative cards that follow and carefully compare the card to its source. The comparison can be accomplished by finding the numbered activity in the text that corresponds to the number on the activity card. This procedure will enable you to see the ease with which many activities throughout the book may be translated to functional, active learning experiences for children. You should also observe that activity cards afford a flexible approach to instruction that can take account of the varying interests and abilities of your class. Related to this, it must be noted that although these illustrative cards carry the gross designations of primary and intermediate levels, it is true that intermediate-grade children can often profit from activities originally designed for lesser levels. Conversely, some primary-grade children can work with cards originally designed for intermediate levels. Of course, all activity cards must be written in the simplest language appropriate to the content.

Illustrative Activity Card (A)

ACTIVITY 1   SET RELATIONS   LEVEL: PRIMARY

Materials Bag of familiar objects; a table; a friend; and a piece of paper for recording.

1. Empty the bag on the table.
2. Place the objects into sets that are alike. How many sets did you get? Which set has the most objects? The least?
3. Have your friend place the objects into different sets that are alike. How many sets did your friend get? Which set has the most objects? The least?
4. See in how many ways you and your friend can group the objects that are alike. Record the number of ways you discovered.
5. Record, in as many ways as you can, the ways in which the groups are alike.

Illustrative Activity Card (B)

ACTIVITY 330   METRIC SYSTEM   LEVEL: PRIMARY

Materials Model of centimeter piece; decimeter strip; scissors; oaktag; and a piece of paper for recording.

1. Cut five 1-centimeter pieces like this.
2. Make a decimeter strip.

3. Is your finger wider than 1 centimeter?
4. Are your buttons wider than 1 centimeter?
5. Find the width of your hand in centimeters.
6. What is the length of your arm in decimeters?
7. Measure three things around your desk that are shorter than 1 decimeter. Record them.
8. Measure three things around your desk that are longer than 1 decimeter. Record them.

Illustrative Activity Card (C)

ACTIVITY 74　　　　　　　NUMERATION　　　LEVEL: INTERMEDIATE

Materials Seventeen counters (paper clips, chips, disks, or beans); a die; and a friend.

1. Place the counters into a single pile and roll the die to see who begins.
2. Now take turns removing one, two, or three counters from the pile.
3. You win when you force your friend to take the last counter.
4. Can you find a sure way to win?
5. Write your way on a piece of paper.

Illustrative Activity Card (D)

ACTIVITY 256　　　　　　PLANE REGIONS　　LEVEL: INTERMEDIATE

Materials Geoboard with a rubber band on the perimeter; and some additional rubber bands.

1. Place a rubber band at a slight diagonal across the upper region of your geoboard. Count the number of regions formed.
2. Use a second rubber band as a diagonal from the lower left corner to the upper corner. Record the number of regions you now have.
3. Place a third rubber band so that it intersects the other two rubber bands and creates a maximum number of regions. Now count the regions.
4. Repeat with a fourth rubber band. Did you count again the number of regions formed?
5. Can you place a fifth rubber band? (It must not pass through the intersection of any two other rubber bands.) Count the regions you have.
6. Write a discovered rule about the relationship between the number of line segments and the regions in a plane.

The advantages of activity cards may be summarized as follows:

1. They constitute a format that permits convenient and inexpensive translation of mathematical topics and concepts from their original source into functional instructional settings for children.
2. Activity cards may be utilized with individual pupils, with children in pairs or small groups, or, when appropriate, in large-group instruction.

3. They may be used in the introduction of a topic for original study, to reinforce a skill or concept through additional problem-solving practice, or in the reintroduction of a previously studied concept when extended understanding is desirable.
4. Activity cards afford flexibility in accounting for varying interests and abilities of children.
5. They provide for systematic and orderly implementation of the active teaching/active learning philosophy.

Considerations for Teaching

Clearly, the nature of this book does not lend itself to an exhaustive discussion of teaching strategies. It is further recognized there is no unique set of activities or procedures that is best for all teachers and all children. Your own personal teaching style will always play the single most important role in success with children. Still, the list of teaching suggestions that follows can form a practical guide in planning and executing mathematics instruction for children.

1. Gear tasks to children's developmental levels.[6] For example, kindergartners learning to count may profit by an activity such as number 41, while sixth graders who have reached a stage of abstract thinking may be encouraged to select for investigation from the list in Activity 455.
2. Proceed from concrete to abstract experiences. Most elementary school children learn mathematics first by manipulating real things, such as learning the meaning of 3 + 2 by joining a set of three buttons and a set of two buttons to make a set of five buttons. A next step may involve representations of real things (semiconcrete—pictures of things, dots, short line segments, geometric figures, "tickets" in a pocket chart, etc.), such as drawing a mark around a set of three dots and a set of two dots to show a set of five dots. More abstract would be filling the square in 3 + 2 = □ with the numeral for five. In this book will be found items illustrative of each step, e.g., concrete, number 4; semiconcrete, number 8; and abstract, number 21. If children have difficulty understanding an abstract number problem, help them grasp it by illustrating with semiconcrete or concrete representations.
3. Be sure that understanding precedes practice for mastery. A place-value chart (see Activity 224) may be used to illustrate regrouping in subtraction, but only when the concept is understood should the child practice subtraction computations that involve regrouping.
4. Encourage children to verbalize as they discover concepts or facts. Sometimes discovery comes through exploration as when a child manipulates Cuisenaire rods (see Activity 5) and discovers that all those of a given color are the same length. At other times a problem is posed

and questions raised, often by the teacher, until pupils find a solution; Pascal's triangle (Activity 443) lends itself to such a procedure.

5. Provide open-ended activities as well as closed. Because to the children so much of the school day seems filled with the search for "right answers," they easily grow wary during the mathematics period. If, however, inquiry and tasks are framed in a manner that challenges children to think, they are motivated to determine what is correct. Illustrative activity cards C and D are representative of desirable balance.

6. Alternate active and passive activities. Children should not be kept sitting for long periods of time with no opportunity to move about; the younger the pupils, the shorter should be the sedentary periods. If children have been doing "seatwork," play a game such as Going to the City, Activity 126.

7. Help children feel secure with their classmates and their teacher. Make it possible for *all* children to experience some success. When employing activities, weigh the competitive aspect carefully against individual self-confidence. If an activity or process has the potential for intimidation of certain children, its use will not increase motivation or enhance confidence and self-esteem.

8. Loosen the reins on children by giving them some choice of activities and materials. A teacher not confident of class control may wish to limit choices of activities, but choice should be provided. Accomplish this through a detailed examination of this book to familiarize yourself with the great opportunities to provide that choice.

9. The final practical teaching suggestion is, in reality, a caution. Ideally, of course, enrichment is an integral part of each daily mathematics period. Yet it is possible to become so enamored with "tricks," "puzzles," "oddities," and so forth that systematic learning of skills and concepts may be obscured. Remember, although children may be intrigued by the unusual, they prefer "real" things, things they can "figure out." In short, although the mathematics period should be enjoyable, it is inappropriate to consistently lose sight of the skill, purpose, or substantive mathematics of the activities or tasks undertaken.

NOTES

1. One such book is E. Williams and H. Shuard, *Elementary Mathematics Today: A Resource for Teachers Grades 1–8* (Menlo Park, Calif.: Addison-Wesley Publishing Company, Inc., 1970).

2. See R. Rosenthal and L. Jacobson, *Pygmalion in the Classroom* (New York: Holt, Rinehart and Winston, Inc., 1968).

3. See W. D. LaBenne and B. I. Greene, *Educational Implications of Self-Concept Theory* (Pacific Palisades, Calif.: Goodyear Publishing Company, Inc., 1969), especially Chapter 10.

4. A. N. Whitehead, *The Aims of Education and Other Essays* (New York: Macmillan Publishing Co., Inc., 1929), p. v (preface).

5. Edith Biggs and James Maclean, *Freedom to Learn* (Ontario: Addison-Wesley Ltd. Canada, 1969), p. 14.

6. An excellent account of child development levels relevant to learning mathematics may be found in C. W. Schminke, N. Maertens, and W. R. Arnold, *Teaching the Child Mathematics* (Hinsdale, Ill.: The Dryden Press, Inc., 1973), Chapter 1, pp. 5–30. See also Klaas Kramer, *Teaching Elementary School Mathematics*, 3rd ed. (Boston: Allyn and Bacon, Inc., 1975), Part One, pp. 3–45.

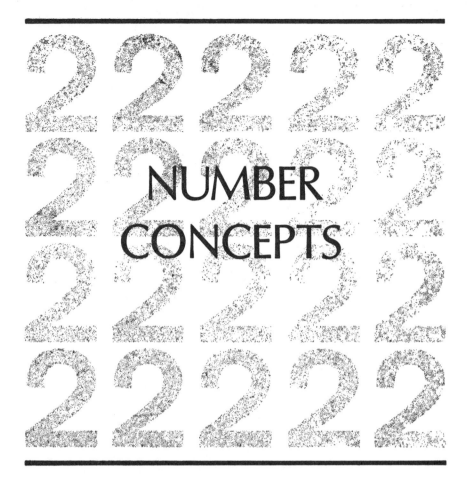

NUMBER CONCEPTS

❀ PART ONE ❀ FOUNDATION EXPERIENCES

RATIONALE

Probably nothing is so fundamental for children and so closely allied to later enjoyment and success in mathematics than those first quantitative experiences planned for children in the formal setting of the early years in school. Since these experiences and the child's feelings about them provide the foundation for study of all other mathematics and all sciences for that matter, the importance is self-evident.

Fortunately, when children enter school they are already familiar with rote counting. Many children can say the number names through ten or twenty or even one hundred, which is to say, they often display a degree of skill and confidence with number in the ordinal sense. Further, some children may even exhibit proficiency with the first few numbers in a cardinal sense;

that is, they recognize sets of one, two, three, and so forth. All this prior knowledge is based upon the child's everyday encounter with quantity from informal experience in the environment. This should say something to us as teachers and we need only to capitalize on it in the school setting.

Unfortunately, the environments from which children come are extremely diverse, and there remains a great unevenness in the quantitative development of any group of five- or six-year-olds, an unevenness that is often difficult to detect. The matter is further complicated because it is so easy to overestimate the conceptual development of those children who appear to have facility by virtue of *apparent* prowess with the uses of number.

The activities provided in the first part of Chapter 2 focus on number concepts, counting, and one-to-one correspondence and order relations. They are intended to develop and reinforce these important fundamental concepts. Ideally, of course, foundation experiences are an integral part of the mathematics program of each succeeding year in school.

As a result of utilizing the subsequent activities, the child will learn:

1. To classify groups of objects by their unique qualitative characteristics.
2. To specify cardinal values associated with groups of objects.
3. To recognize the sequential order of numerals.
4. To develop an understanding of the numeral representation of quantity.
5. To estimate and compare numbers by relative size.
6. To form numerals and write their corresponding word names.
7. To utilize the language of mathematics for communication.

SETS

For initial teaching about the characteristics of sets you should assemble several collections of familiar objects that reflect various physical characteristics (size, weight, shape, color, etc.) which may be conveniently utilized and easily stored. Buttons, bottle caps, stones, dried corn, spools, beans, disks, paper clips, and miniature toys, as well as felt, paper, wood, and tagboard cutouts, are proven examples.

A Bring a bag that contains a variety of familiar objects (spools, cans, blocks, silverware, dolls, etc.). Ask children to sort the objects into sets, first according to criteria you give (short, long, heavy, unpainted, metal, wood, etc.), then according to descriptions they give. Encourage discussions aimed at identifying "well-defined" sets when such an attribute as "heavy" is assigned; children might conclude that one item could be identified as the standard by which other items are judged as "heavier" or "lighter."

Variation   See if children can arrange sets by negative characteristics, e.g., not round, not red, small and not square, not thick and not triangular, and so forth. You can also transfer set selection to science and social studies by sorting, according to given criteria, such things as seashells, seeds, leaves, rocks, people (as by occupations), states, television programs, transportation carriers, and goods (as by ownership).

B   Compare sets by discussing how they are alike and how they are different; e.g., how does the set of children on the school patrol compare with the set of teachers in the school?

Name a universal set, e.g., children, and ask pupils to name subsets. At first, use concrete materials that can be moved about; later introduce sets and subsets of items that can be thought about and listed on the chalkboard but not manipulated, e.g., buildings, occupations, or smells.

C   Let pupils take turns dividing the members of a group into sets by placing each person in a spot designated for those children who meet given criteria. Children should suggest the criteria (sex, color of shoes or other clothing, color of eyes, etc.). Do not overlook the empty set (such as children with lavender polka-dot shoes—of which there are probably none).

Variation   Try to get children to suggest sets of items that require the use of senses other than vision (loud and soft sounds, rough and smooth surfaces, sweet and sour foods, etc.).

D   Find the number of various sets and then the number of the union of certain sets.

E   Compare sets by one-to-one correspondence; can one tell which has the largest number without determining the number of either set?

F   Lead children to discover interesting sets such as the set of pupils in the band and the set of children who are room monitors.

❀ 2 ❀ CIRCLE SETS

Purpose   To learn to recognize cardinal values.
Level   K to 1.

Number of players   10 or more.

Materials needed   None.

Procedure   Arrange the players in a circle. Call out a number, e.g., "Four. Begin with Mary." Children then form themselves into sets of four; leftover players drop out. The sets of children circle clockwise. At a signal, all stop and those who dropped out rejoin the circle. Call another number and a new starting place.

Circle sets could be adapted to provide practice in reading numerals by having the teacher show a numeral rather than calling it out.

❀ 3 ❀ CIRCUS

Purpose   To practice with cardinal value.

Level   K to 1.

Number of players   2 or more.

Materials needed   Cards with a numeral on each card.

Procedure   Distribute the cards, one to each player. Select a ringmaster and then have the other pupils stand in a circle and pretend that they are trained circus animals. When the ringmaster calls a number, the "pony" who has the appropriate card steps to the center of the ring and taps his foot as many times as the number indicates. If he is correct, the ringmaster permits the pony to run once around the circle.

❀ 4 ❀

Practice in establishing cardinal concepts related to order can be achieved through the use of clean plastic pillboxes (obtainable from a pharmacy) in which varying numbers of small objects, such as corn, beans, peas, peanuts, paper clips, brass fasteners, and buttons, are placed. The children are to count the objects in each box and place the boxes in order by numbers, or they may record the numbers on a sheet of paper.

Variation   Write a numeral on each of several pillboxes. The children may place the appropriate number of small objects in each box. The objects may be different from each other—to avoid developing a concept of number as being related only to things of the same kind.

❀ 5 ❀ MATCH IT

Purpose   To discover relationships.

The King's Library

Level   K to 2.

Number of players   Variable.

Materials needed   Cuisenaire rods[1] or facsimile. Some dice. An inexpensive set of "rods" can be constructed from tagboard or other durable material for use with a group of children (see the diagram for what to include).

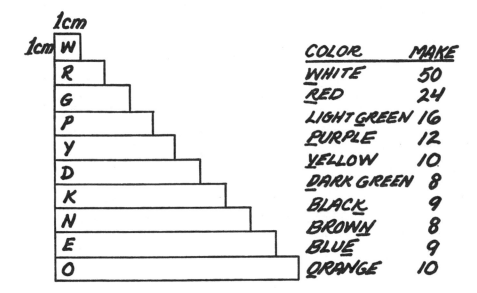

COLOR	MAKE
WHITE	50
RED	24
LIGHT GREEN	16
PURPLE	12
YELLOW	10
DARK GREEN	8
BLACK	9
BROWN	8
BLUE	9
ORANGE	10

Procedure   Children need the opportunity to explore before attempting to discern advanced concepts with manipulative materials. This activity may be implemented in whatever grouping or physical arrangements seem appropriate. This activity is readily transferable to an activity-card format if a more independent activity is desired. Opportunity for exploration and discovery may include asking the child (children) to:

(a) Make a staircase.

(b) Make some trains.

(c) Make a picture.

(d) Compare the lengths.

(e) Make a map.

(f) Assign a number to each rod.

(g) Compare a red train with a dark green one.

(h) Make a red and a yellow train of the same length.

(i) Invent a game using the rods, some dice, and a friend.

(j) Solve some addition problems from your book with the rods.

❀ 6 ❀ POCKET MATCH

Purpose To provide practice in recognizing cardinal values.
Level K to 1.
Number of players 1 or more.
Materials needed Pocket chart. Two sets of cards, one with numerals and one with pictures of sets of objects.
Procedure Players take turns placing numeral cards in proper order in the pocket chart. Then continue turns as they place pictures over corresponding numerals to indicate the number property of the sets.

Variation When teaching numerals and their meanings, place into a pocket chart cards on which numerals appear. Permit a child to match each card with one on which semiconcrete representations (such as dots in domino arrangements) or basic facts appear.

❀ 7 ❀ DOTS AND NUMBERS

Purpose To learn to associate cardinal values.
Level K to 1.
Number of players 2 or more.
Materials needed Two sets of cards— on one set write numerals on which the children need practice and on the other show spots in characteristic patterns.

Procedure Place the numeral cards face down in a box and place the corresponding pattern cards in the chalk tray. Call on a child to get a card from the box and place it over the equivalent card in the chalk tray. If correct, the child may choose the next player.

❀ 8 ❀ MATCH ME

Purpose To provide practice in associating cardinal-value word names.
Level K to 1.

Number of players   4 or more.

Materials needed   A set of cards consisting of subsets of three—one set
with numerals, another with corresponding number words, and the third

with spots in the characteristic pattern to show how many.

Procedure   Distribute cards among players (some may have more than one
card). Call on a child to come before the group and tell the number that is
indicated by his card. He says, "Who can match me?" Players with corresponding cards come to the front and stand beside the first. All hold cards
in full view of other players. If the latter agree that the cards match, the trio
return to their seats. The first child called on now selects the next player.

Variation   Play a simple variety of rummy. Use two sets of cards. The cards
may be dealt one at a time until each player has six. The rest of the deck is
placed face down on the playing surface; the top card is turned face up beside
the deck (this will be the discard pile). The object of the game is to meld (lay
down, face up) sets of three matching cards. Each player in turn draws one
top card from the deck or from the discard pile. If the player can meld, he
does so, and then he discards one card. When a player discards his last card,
the game is over. The score might be the number of cards left in each player's
hand; low score wins.

❀ 9 ❀ WORD RUMMY

Purpose   To provide practice on mathematical vocabulary.

Level   3 to 6.

Number of players   2 to 4.

Materials needed   A deck of cards, each card with a mathematics vocabulary
word on it from the following list or similar important words. The number of
cards in the deck will vary depending upon the level at which the game is
played.

    class, collection, set, group;
    addition, plus, sum, addend;
    both, two, couple, pair;
    circle, rectangle, triangle, square;
    liter, half-liter, kiloliter, milliliter;
    difference, subtraction, take-away, minus;
    division, divisor, dividend, quotient;
    duet, solo, trio, quartet;

ones, tens, hundreds, thousands;
ordinal, first, second, third;
principle, commutative, associative, distributive;
second, minute, hour, day;
set, crowd, bunch, flock;
meter, millimeter, centimeter, kilometer

Procedure   Shuffle the cards and deal five to each player. Place the balance of the deck face down on the table. Turn up the top card. Each player in turn tries to make a "book" of four related cards. He may take a card from the deck or he may take the turned-up card. As he finishes his turn, he discards one card face up. Succeeding players may take all turned-up cards or one from the deck. The winner is the first player to have an empty hand.

❀ 10 ❀

To provide practice in recognizing numerals and their sequence when count-ing, distribute numeral cards to each member of the group. On each card should be a numeral—1 to 9 at first, later 11 and up. Suggest that, in turn, children place their cards in the chalk tray in proper sequence.

❀ 11 ❀ MISCHIEVOUS KITTEN

Level   K to 1.
Number of players   1 or more.
Materials needed   Vocabulary cards containing number words or ordinal words.
Procedure   Place the word cards at random in the chalk tray. Ask the pupils to say each word with you. Then ask the children to help you place them in correct sequence. Next, say that while the children "hide their eyes" a mischievous kitten will come and change the order of the cards. The children cover their eyes and lower their heads to their desks or laps. The teacher switches cards and then calls on a pupil to return them to the correct places. Repeat with a child as the mischievous kitten.

❀ 12 ❀ WHAT IS IT?

To give practice in learning the whole-number sequence, make a simple outline of an animal such as a cat, or other familiar object, on a piece of paper. Then, using a duplicator carbon, write on the outline the 15 to 25 numerals on which recognition practice is needed. Run off copies. Suggest that the pupils draw lines from one numeral to the next, beginning with the one naming the least number and progressing to the greatest. The result should be the outline with which you started.

❀ 13 ❀ AIRPLANE RIDE

Purpose   To learn to use ordinal numbers.
Level   K to 2.
Number of players   2 or more.
Materials needed   Chairs placed as seats in an airliner.
Procedure   Select a hostess who directs passengers to their seats by using ordinal numbers, e.g., "Mr. Smith, your seat is the fourth one." When Mr. Smith is seated, the hostess asks other players, "Did Mr. Smith find the right seat?" If the children answer "Yes," the next passenger is seated. When all seats are filled, the hostess says, "We will now fly to San Francisco." Soon she says, "We are now in San Francisco." As each player leaves the plane, he comments to the hostess on his trip, as, for example, "I enjoyed the view from the fourth seat."

❀ 14 ❀ HOT OR COLD

Purpose   To learn to recognize relative position and to gain experience in reading numerals.
Level   2 to 3.
Number of players   2 or more.
Materials needed   A number line. A pointer.
Procedure   Select a child to be "It." He "hides his eyes" while another child points to a numeral on the number line. When all players except "It" have noted which numeral was selected, "It" may uncover his eyes and guess the "burning" number. The leader gives "It" hints by saying "cold" if the guess is far off the mark, "hot" if he is close, and "burning" when he guesses correctly. Repeat with other leaders and guessers.
Variations   Inequalities, such as "greater than," "less than," and so forth, can be used, with the leader giving clues by holding up relation flash cards of $>$, $=$, or $<$.

❀ 15 ❀ STAIRSTEPS

Purpose   To name rods in order of relative lengths.
Level   K to 2.
Number of players   1 or more.
Materials needed   Cuisenaire rods (see Activity 6).
Procedure   The leader asks the players to select the shortest rod, then add other rods to form steps—white, red, light green, purple, and so on. Ask pupils, one at a time, to "go up the stairs" by naming the rods from shortest to longest, then "go downstairs" by naming from longest to shortest. Next, have children discover the "one more" principle of natural numbers by numbering the rods from 1 to 10. Ask how many white rods need to be added to the white step to make it the height of red, how many white rods to make red the same height as light green, and so on.

NUMERALS AND NUMBER

❀ 16 ❀ VERSE

Purpose   To provide practice in rhyme, rhythm, and counting. For young children, practice in counting may be made a more pleasant experience if rhyme is used occasionally.[2]

A   One, two, three, four, five,
   Catching fishes all alive.
   "Why did you let them go?"
   "Because they bit my finger so."
   "Which finger did they bite?"
   "The little finger on the right."

B   Brother, brother, help me, do,
   Pick up sticks and kindling too,
   If we work, the pile will grow;
   Come, let's count them row by row:
   1, 2, 3, 4, 5, 6, 7, 8, 9, 10.

C   Fireman, fireman, we can't wait;
   There's a fire in Apartment Eight.
   Up the stairs he'll drag the hose;

Count the steps as up he goes—
1, 2, 3, 4, 5, 6, 7, 8, 9, 10.

❀ 17 ❀ FINGER COUNT

Purpose To provide practice in counting.
Level   K to 1.
Number of players   2 or more.
Materials needed   None.
Procedure   Seat the players in a semicircle. Have the children repeat with you:

Fish, cats, puppies, look at me.
How many fingers do you see?

Hold up one or both hands with a selected number of fingers raised and call on a child to tell you. If he is correct, praise him; if not correct, help him count the raised fingers.

❀ 18 ❀ TRICK OR TREAT

To provide practice in counting.
Level   K to 1.
Number of players   2 or more.
Materials needed   Small objects, such as seeds or plastic disks.
Procedure   Distribute a selected number of objects to each player. The leader carries a paper bag and knocks on the "door" (desk) of a player and asks for a certain number of items, which must be counted. The person visited must also tell how many objects he has left. If correct, the visitor moves on to another place.

❀ 19 ❀ FISH IN A BOWL

Purpose   To provide practice in counting estimation.
Level   Variable.
Number of players   Pairs or small groups.
Materials needed   An activity sheet with a picture of a large fishbowl, as illustrated.
Procedure   The activity sheet is distributed to the children. Working in pairs, they should estimate the number of fish and each record a separate guess.

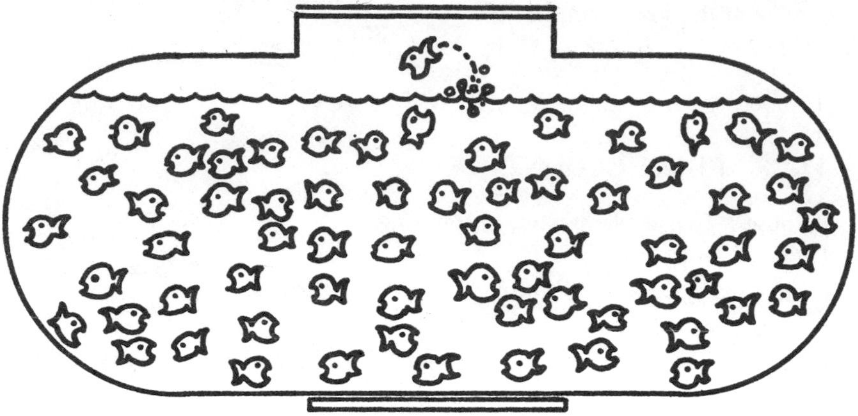

Then they may discuss with their partner and write down a team guess (they should agree on the team guess). Then each person counts the fish and records an individual count. They compare counts by **conferring** and recount if in disagreement. They may record a team count. Individual and team guesses and counts may be recorded on the board. Ensuing discussion may highlight highs, lows, cases where guesses were close, and pupils' methods of estimating.

❀ 20 ❀ COUNTING PARTY

Purpose To provide practice in counting.
Level K to 1.
Number of players 4 or more.
Materials needed None.
Procedure Give each player a number name. Select a party host or hostess, who sits in a corner of the room. Each player in turn goes to the corner and knocks on the wall as many times as is indicated by his number name. The host or hostess says, "Hello. Is your name __________?" If the guest says, "Yes, my name is __________," his reply indicates that he knocked correctly, and that the host counted correctly; so the host says, "Then you may come to my party." The guest then sits in the corner and helps the host or hostess count the knocks of other guests. If the guest makes a mistake, he is told, "You were not invited." And he must go back; he may try again after all others have had a turn. If the host makes a mistake, he is replaced by the guest.

✻ 21 ✻ BUZZ

Purpose   To provide oral reinforcement in counting.
Level   1 to 6.
Number of players   2 or more.
Materials needed   None.
Procedure   Players form a circle. Vary the directions according to the ability of the players. First and second graders might count by turns except that when a given digit is part of a numeral, the person whose turn it is says, "Buzz"; e.g., if the digit is three: 1, 2, buzz, 4, 5, . . . , 12, buzz, 14, 15, ... At grade three, "buzz" may be substituted for all even numbers; at fourth and fifth grades, all multiples of four; at sixth grade, all multiples of six and all numerals in which the digit six occurs (6, 12, 16, . . .), or all multiples of four and seven—"buzz" for the former and "tizz" for the latter. If a number is a multiple of both four and seven, say "buzz, tizz." Vary the selection of digits.

✻ 22 ✻ JUMP BOARD

Purpose   To provide practice in a variety of counting activities and in reading and following directions.
Level   1 to 3.
Number of players   2.
Materials needed   A playing board about 1 foot square with a circle of stepping stones numbered from 1 to 100. Two buttons or other markers. A set of direction cards; e.g., make two jumps by threes. Make five jumps by twos. Go back to 1. Jump to 100 and win. Go back three jumps by fours.

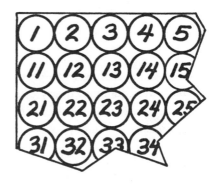

Procedure   Shuffle the cards and place them face down. The players take turns drawing the cards and following the directions. The winner is the player who gets to 100 first. (*Note*: If a player gets a card that would take him farther back than 1, he moves only to 1.)

❀ 23 ❀ DO I MEASURE UP?

Purpose To provide practice in counting and estimation.
Level Variable.
Number of players Small groups of children.
Materials needed A sealed 1-liter jar filled with beans. A ½-liter jar about two-thirds filled with beans. A set of metric measuring cups:

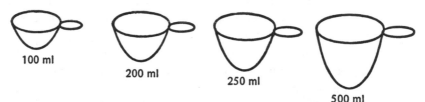

100 ml
200 ml
250 ml
500 ml

Procedure Each student in the group may guess how many beans are in the sealed jar and record his guess. All recorded guesses are examined and a group guess is recorded. Next, using the beans from the ½-liter jar and the measuring cups (counting is permissible), the group determines a more sophisticated "estimate," and this is recorded. The other groups follow the same procedure. Ultimately the beans in the sealed jar are counted and the group whose guess and estimate were closest to the actual number is declared the winner. Discussion of the winner's (and others') procedure is crucial at this time.
Variation Containers different from those in the example may be used. Also, same containers may be used but a different filler, e.g., marbles. Would a pan balance be seen as useful in this activity?

❀ 24 ❀

Purposeful counting experiences throughout the elementary grades provide pupils with the opportunity to see the need to know about numbers through providing a functional use for numbers. Following are several suggestions for capitalizing upon that potential. These may cause you to think of others.

A When pumpkins are brought to the classroom to carve for jack-o-lanterns, children can be encouraged to "guess" or "estimate" the number of seeds in each. Later the seeds may be dried and the nearness of the "guess" or "estimate" determined by counting.

B Count the number of treats needed for a birthday party in relation to the number of members in the class.

C Oral counting in unison to see "how long it takes us to get ready to recess"; "whether we can count to 60 before the bell rings"; or "how well we can measure a minute."

D Silent and oral multiple counting both forward and backward. For example:

1. Count backward from 23 to 6 by ones.
2. Count forward from 22 to 48 by twos.
3. Count forward from 36 to the last number you would say before 60.
4. Count backward from 63 to 14 by sevens.

❀ 25 ❀ TAPS

Purpose To provide practice in counting and one-to-one correspondence.
Level K to 1.
Number of players 1 or more.
Materials needed Beans or other markers.
Procedure Distribute a number of markers to each player with instructions to lay out as many as he hears tapped when you strike a table with a pencil or ruler. Check quickly and have each child return his markers to his pile so as to be ready for the next series of taps.

❀ 26 ❀ TEETER TOTTER

Purpose To provide experience with one-to-one correspondence.
Level K to 2.
Number of players 2 to 6.
Materials needed Small objects to be used as counterweights (washers, nuts, buttons). A simple balance mechanism upon which small containers may be hung. There should be sufficient counterweights, both uniform and variable.
Procedure Children take turns, under the teacher's guidance, placing objects in the containers. Developmental inquiry from the teacher may include:

"What happens when you place an object in one container and not in the other?" "Is there a washer in this container for every washer in this container?" Focus on one-to-one is ultimately provided when children achieve "balance" and remove objects from both containers, arranging them in a visual display of one-to-one correspondence.

 27

When teaching the recognition of numerals, their sequence when counting, and their number values, make a board marked off in rectangles. Paste on slips of paper showing numerals 1 to 10 in order. Drive a small nail near the lower edge of each division. Place in the chalk tray or hang at an easy level for kindergarten children. Make numeral cards with holes punched to correspond to the nails. Pupils match cards until they know the sequence; then pictures showing semiconcrete representations should be substituted for the children's numeral cards.

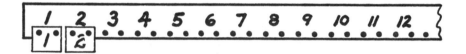

 28 ONE-TO-ONE CORRESPONDENCE

Purpose   To be used as a bulletin board activity.
Level   K to 1.
Materials needed   Variable. For example, a set of people (cutouts) whose occupations are easily identified by the clothing they wear and a set of pictures depicting tools commonly associated with the occupations.
Procedure   Pin the pictures at random on a bulletin board with the caption: "Is there a tool for every worker?" "Is there a worker for every tool?" Place the pictures of the tools and an assortment of pins in a manila envelope attached to a bulletin board accessible to children. The problem is solved by a child when all of the tools are correctly attached to the pictures representing occupations. From day to day the number of tools available in the manila envelope may be varied or a career depicted on the bulletin board may be changed so that there is no implement available to associate with it.

❋ 29 ❋ TUNE MY TV

Purpose   To associate numbers and numerals.
Level   K to 1.
Number of players   2 or more.
Materials needed   An outline of a television set on the chalkboard.
Procedure   Invite a player to come to the board to "tune" the TV set by writing a channel number. He says, "I have selected Channel _____."
If his statement corresponds to what he has written, he may choose the next player.
Variation   For more advanced pupils, have them write on the "screen" as many combinations as they can, the answer to which is the channel number. Include those operations which the children can manage.

❋ 30 ❋ RACE TO UNCLE JACK'S HOUSE

Purpose   To recognize numerals and values associated with them.
Level   K to 1.
Number of players   2 to 4.
Materials needed   A playing board with a route from home to Uncle Jack's shown in a chain of 40 squares. Tiny cars (paper will do) of different colors, one for each player. A set of 50 cards on each of which is a numeral from 0 to 9.
Procedure   Shuffle the cards and place them face down. Each player selects a car. In turn, each child draws a card and moves his car as many squares as the numeral indicates. The first one who gets to Uncle Jack's house wins.
Variations   Rather than use a playing board, make large squares from contact paper, place the chain of squares on the classroom floor, and have children actually "race" to Uncle Jack's house. If your classroom floor is tile, they could simply be numbered consecutively, forming an interesting movement pattern about the room.

❋ 31 ❋ ROD NUMBERS

Purpose   To provide experience in matching, in counting, and in seeing relationships.
Level   K to 2.
Number of players   1 or more.

Materials needed   Set of rods as utilized in Activities 5 and 15.

Procedure   Ask players to call the white rod by the name 1. Then find number names for each color by checking to see how many white rods are needed to measure the same as each other rod.

Now find out how many combinations of rods named by their number names can be found to match a given rod, also named by number, e.g., five (yellow): 1 and 4; 2 and 3; 2, 1, and 2; 1, 1, 2, and 1; and so on. See who has found the most matching series. Change the base rod and proceed as before.

Variations   If Rod Numbers is played orally, children might describe their findings in words before using equations; i.e., four red rods and one white rod are the same length as one blue rod. If children can write, they should be encouraged to record their findings like this: "4 red rods and 1 white rod are the same length as 1 blue rod"; later, like this, "4 r and 1 w are the same length as 1 e." When players get proficient at this game, see if they can play it by writing down the numbers of each series without manipulating rods. Plus signs may be used, as $2 + 2 + 2 + 2 + 1 = 9$. If a series named by one player is challenged by another, rods may be used to check.

❀ 32 ❀

When teaching the concept of one-to-one correspondence between the items of one set and those of another, suggest that children see how many items they can think of which represent a one-to-one correspondence: 1 to 2; 1 to 3; 1 to 4. Examples follow:

1 TO 1	1 TO 2	1 TO 3	1 TO 4
1 boy	1 boy	1 tricycle	1 car
1 head	2 hands	3 wheels	4 wheels

A committee might consolidate lists and display them on the bulletin board. (See Activity 28.)

❀ 33 ❀ PARTNERS

Purpose   To recognize numerals.

Level   K to 1.

Number of players   4 or more.
Materials needed   Two sets of cards—one with numerals and one with corresponding pictures of sets.
Procedure   Distribute cards among players. Select a player to come to the front, to show his card, and to say, "Who will be my partner?" The one who has the corresponding card will join the first player. All check to see if the pairing is correct; if it is, the second player may call on the next one.

❀ 34 ❀ NUMBER BINGO

Purpose   To recognize numerals.
Level   K to 1.
Number of players   2 or more.
Materials needed   Duplicated grids. Flat beans or other markers.

G	I	A	N	T
7	5	4	8	6
6	7	5	4	8
8	4	7	6	5
4	6	6	7	4
5	8	8	5	7

Procedure   Help the children choose a five-letter word or name, perhaps a child's name (all different letters), and write it in the top area. Select five digits on which practice is needed and suggest that the series be whatever order appeals to the child. (For beginners, prepare the playing boards in advance.) Call letters and numbers at random, as "N, 8." Pupils place beans on proper digits. The leader must keep a record of what has been called by writing numerals called on a card of his own. (The leader's card is blank except for the name at the top.) When a player has five in a row either vertically or horizontally, he calls "Giant," or whatever word is on the card. He is the winner.

❀ 35 ❀ NUMBER MATCH

Purpose   To recognize word names.
Level   1 to 2.
Number of players   2 or more.
Materials needed   Two sets of cards—on one write Hindu–Arabic numerals and on the other write number names. Select those on which the players need practice.

Procedure Place the cards on which Hindu–Arabic numerals are marked in the chalk tray. Place the other cards in a paper bag. Divide the group into teams, each to alternate in sending a player to take a card from the paper bag and match it with the proper one in the chalk tray. One point is scored for each successful pairing. The team with the most points at the end of play wins. If the group is large, return the cards to their places from time to time; mix the cards in the paper bag.

Number Match may be played noncompetitively. The children take turns drawing a card from the paper bag and matching it with its mate in the chalk tray.

❀ 36 ❀

Correct formation of numerals (writing) is an important foundation experience. To give children practice in counting and forming numerals properly, place interesting pictures, cutouts, and patterns on the bulletin board daily or weekly. At the base place a scratch pad and pencil and have the child write the numeral that tells how many. Change the number of objects on the bulletin board daily, and each time a child does the task, have him deposit the numeral he has written (with his name) in a special place. Later, at any appropriate time, the written numerals may be retrieved and analyzed by teacher-directed discussion and individual pupil comparison of the numerals they have written to a model chart. (The model chart may also be continually in sight at the base of the bulletin board.)

37 ❄

Some children need tactile reinforcement in order to learn to recognize or to write numerals. Try cards on which sandpaper numerals have been glued. (Do not use your best scissors!) Touch sensations can be varied through choice of materials. Sandpaper comes in many grades, from very fine to very coarse. Flocked paper or cloth such as felt, velvet, canvas, or worsted wool provide additional choices.

❄ 38 ❄ GENERAL DELIVERY

Purpose   To recognize numerals.
Level   K to 1.
Number of players   2 or more.
Materials needed   Cards about the size of letter envelopes, on each side of which is a numeral children need to practice reading. A facsimile of a post office.
Procedure   Select a postmaster and give him a set of "letters." Other players line up at the post office and as each gets to the window he asks, "Is there any mail for me?" The postmaster selects a letter and says, "Is this your name?" If the player correctly reads the numeral on the letter he says, "Yes, my name is ____," and takes his letter to his "home."

INEQUALITIES

 39 ❄

To practice numeral recognition and the concept of one more and of one less, distribute numeral cards to each member of a group. On each card should be a numeral—1 to 9 or more. Call a number. The pupil with the corresponding numeral card is invited to stand. His "Neighbors," those with numbers one less and one more, are then invited to join him.

❀ **40** ❀

To provide practice in the use of terms of comparison, suggest that each child name items that are taller or shorter than himself, heavier or lighter. Make other comparisons according to the children's sophistication.

❀ **41** ❀ **MY NEIGHBORS**

Purpose   To apply the concepts of "one more than" and "one less than."
Level   K to 1.
Number of players   2 or more.
Materials needed   Chalk and chalkboard.
Procedure   Write a numeral on the chalkboard and say, "I am 28. Who can write the names of my neighbors?" Call on a child who will write the numerals 27 and 29 on either side of your 28. Continue with other numbers on which the children need practice.

❀ **42** ❀ **BEAT IT**

Purpose   To compare relative size.
Level   Variable.
Number of players   2 or more.
Materials needed   Several decks of cards containing the numerals 1 to 20. A die.
Procedure   The cards are shuffled and a die is rolled to determine who goes first. Play is initiated when the first player turns over a card in his deck. Next the opponent turns over a card in his deck and continues to turn cards until he turns one "larger than" the initial card. Play shifts to the original player, who turns cards until he has one "larger than" his opponent. Play is halted the first time either player turns a card containing the numeral 20. The winner is the player with the most unused cards.
Variation   Use the same procedure as above, but the object is to turn a card "less than" the opponent. In this case, play is halted when either player turns a 1. The game is equally adaptable to fractions, integers, and so forth.

❀ 43 ❀ WHICH IS IT?

Purpose   To provide foundation concepts for odd and even.
Level   1 to 2.
Number of players   Sets of 2.
Materials needed   Beans or other small markers.
Procedure   Each player takes a number (less than 20) of beans, which he holds in a closed hand. His opponent must guess the number. He may ask, "Is it odd or even?" "Is it more or less than ____?" No other clues are permitted. If he guesses the correct amount in three attempts, he scores a point. When the correct answer is given, or after three tries, play goes to the second player. When both have played, the players should change the number of beans.

❀ 44 ❀ DISCOVER

Purpose   To provide oral practice for greater than and less than.
Level   Variable.
Number of players   Variable.
Materials needed   A "caller." Some pieces of paper. A pencil.
Procedure   A pupil is chosen to be caller. The caller selects a whole number between 1 and 100, records it on a piece of paper, and gives the paper to the teacher. The caller proceeds to call on a student or students, who may ask him questions about the number. A student may ask only three questions in a turn, and the caller may answer only yes or no. The student who guesses the number may be "caller." Students will discover efficient methods for determining the number as several games are played. For example, the number above might have been 43, and the guess could go:

Is it > 50?	(between 1 and 100)	no
Is it < 25?	(between 1 and 50)	no
Is it > 37?	(between 25 and 50)	yes
Is it > 46?	(between 37 and 50)	no
Is it > 41?	(between 37 and 46)	yes
Is it 43?	(range = 5 numbers)	yes

Variation   Teams may be formed and appropriate rules relative to number of guesses and "passing" to a team member can be established. Teams may compete against each other or a caller. Ten "no's" and the caller would win.

❀ 45 ❀ WHAT RELATION?

Purpose To illustrate the trichotomy of relation.
Level K to 6.
Number of players 2 or more.
Materials needed Chalk and chalkboard or a set of cards that contains relations signs.
Procedure Write on chalkboard:

$$> \text{greater than}$$
$$= \text{equal to}$$
$$< \text{less than}$$

Then write two numerals with a space between them. Call a pupil to the board to write one of the relation signs between the two numerals. If the group agrees that he is correct, let him choose the next player while you write two other numerals.

Variation Place in the hands of each of three pupils a card with a relation sign ($>$, $<$, $=$). When two numbers are called, the two children who have the appropriate numeral cards come to the front of the room and the person who has the correct relation card comes to stand between them.

❀ 46 ❀ SYMBOL BINGO

Level Variable.
Number of players 2 or more.
Materials needed Bingo-type cards for each player. Arrange symbols in a different order on each card. Beans or other markers for each player. A set of flash cards with the definition or an example of each symbol shown on the bingo cards. Some samples are shown.
Procedure Select a "caller" and distribute cards and markers to players. The

$\in$	$\emptyset$	$\cup$
$>$	$\cap$	$<$
$\cap$	$\overleftrightarrow{AB}$	$\neq$

is a member of	greater than	intersection
empty set	number	line A B
union	less than	not equal to

caller displays a flash card for a count of five. Each player who recognizes the definition of a symbol on his card covers it with a marker. When a player gets three markers in a row, horizontally, vertically, or diagonally, he calls out "Bingo!" Cards should be checked before writing the winner's name on the chalkboard.

 47

To provide practice on defining mathematical terms or relationships, young children can pretend to explain the meaning over the telephone (i.e., without gestures) to someone who speaks English but does not know the meanings of certain pairs of words, such as tall—short, near—far, greater than—less than, left—right, up—down, inner region—outer region, and the like.

48 WHAT'S THE GOOD WORD?

Purpose   To provide a mathematics vocabulary.[3]
Level   1 to 4.
Number of players   2 or more.
Materials needed   Set of word cards or a list of words written on the chalkboard. The vocabulary selected should include items on which practice is needed. A first- or second-grade list might include the following:

1. addition	14. longest	27. spent
2. altogether	15. lower	28. subtract
3. by fives	16. more	29. sum
4. by twos	17. next	30. take away
5. cents	18. nickel	31. taller
6. combination	19. number	32. thicker
7. counting	20. older	33. third
8. each	21. one	34. top
9. first	22. penny	35. upper
10. fourth	23. remainder	36. wider
11. have left	24. second	37. younger
12. heavier	25. shorter	38. zero
13. less	26. shortest	

Procedure   Divide the group into two or three teams; call them Eggheads, Wizards, and/or Geniuses. The teacher or leader selects a word card, holds it up (or gives the number of the word on the chalkboard), and asks the first player on the team of Eggheads to pronounce the word. Then, to show that he knows the meaning, he gives a definition, makes a drawing on the chalkboard, acts out the meaning, or uses some other acceptable procedure. If he succeeds, he scores a point for his team. If he fails, the Wizards may try. The team with the most points wins.

🌼 PART TWO 🌼 NUMERATION

RATIONALE

The concept of place value is basic at all levels of mathematical proficiency and fundamental to most systems of numeration. Unless children clearly recognize its manifestation, skill in basic operations is virtually impossible. Further, without conceptual recognition that our Hindu–Arabic system groups by tens and multiples of 10, the child cannot grasp a full understanding of the order, the simplicity, the utility, and the beauty of our decimal system of numeration.

Several simple examples may be used to demonstrate the importance of the fundamental concept of numeration. Consider, for example, placing 12 objects into one-to-one correspondence with our familiar numbers. After 9 objects have been so arranged, whether physically or in the mind, the process cannot be continued without invoking the first rudimentary notion of grouping by tens. This grouping notion is of increasing cruciality. Consider the notation for one hundred twenty-four. Clearly, the separate symbols, that is, 1, 2, and 4, have no common meaning beyond the fact that they belong to the conventional symbol system that we use to express number. It is only through conceptualization of their individual value by virtue of position in the number expression that they take on unique significance.

For most adults the previous examples may seem simple, but they are as elusive to children as they are powerful. To gain a principle-level understanding of 10 as our grouping number, children need many experiences that require their active participation. Subsequent to those experiences, it can be rewarding and reinforcing to engage in activities that center on the grouping principle when the collection point is other than 10. Additional activities resulting in appreciation of numeration can come from engagement with the historical antecedents of contemporary mathematics.

From the following activities the children will learn:

1. To recognize the significance of 10 and multiples of 10 as our basic grouping number.
2. To identify decimal numerals in expanded notation form.
3. To apply the basic principles of positional values with increasing skill.
4. To be familiar with grouping numbers other than 10.
5. To compare the merits of selected nondecimal systems of numeration.

6. To evaluate the contributions of early systems of numeration and notation.

PLACE VALUE

❀ 49 ❀

Early successful conceptualization of 10 as our grouping number will only follow children's active involvement with concrete representations of the grouping notion. Simply arrange the children in groups of 10. Each group of 10 children may stand or sit inside a chalk boundary on the floor. The number of sets of 10 children may be recorded as well as the number remaining. Variations include grouping the children's pencils, the workbooks of the class, only the girls, only the boys, and so forth. Each time the total group may be counted to verify the outcome.

❀ 50 ❀ MYSTERY CAN

Level   K to 3.
Number of players   2 or more.
Materials needed   Several open cans, each filled with tongue depressors, pipe cleaners, pencils, or some other, preferably uniform, counters. Each can should have only one type of material in it, but the cans should contain varying amounts.

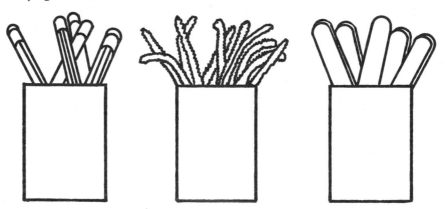

Procedure   In groups of 2, children are given a mystery can. They are asked to guess how many objects are in the can and to record their guess. They may then count to determine the "closeness" of their guess. Then children, using rubber bands, are instructed to bundle the contents of the can in groups of 10. Have them count the groups of 10. Discuss the advantages of groups of 10 with such inquiries as: "Would the pipe cleaners have been easier to count if they had been placed in the cans in groups?" Verify by returning the contents to the cans in groups of 10.

❀ 51 ❀

When teaching about the principle of grouping and place value, use a reading pocket chart. Make cards for the top pocket that read *hundreds, tens, ones.* Pin or tape a piece of dark-colored yarn vertically between the pockets for each place. Cut "tickets" from construction paper to use as markers.

With beginners, bundle 10 tickets and bind with a rubber band to place in the tens' pocket. Ten bundles of 10 tickets can be hung in the hundreds' pocket by placing only part of them in the fold and resting the balance outside. Later one ticket in the tens' place can stand for one bundle of 10 tickets. Similarly, a single ticket in the hundreds' pocket will suffice.

Care should be taken not to give children the impression that a bundle of 10 tickets placed in the tens' place of the chart means 10 tens. To avoid this possibility, the chart may be used with bundles but without the place-value identification cards until it is time to substitute single tickets for bundles.

❀ 52 ❀

To teach grouping with circle strips and chips, let the children make circle strips and circle chips by using a paper punch, some scissors, and lightweight tagboard. (Discarded manila folders are easily adaptable.) With very young children, you may want to prepare the strips prior to asking them to punch them. After children have punched holes, 10 per strip, they may be engaged in a variety of grouping activities, such as forming sets of strips and chips that show:

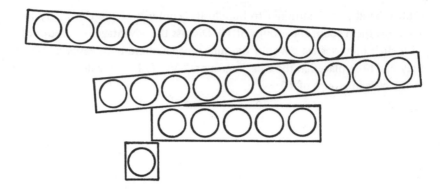

(a) The number of children in our room.
(b) What day it is.
(c) Strips and chips worth 43, 78, 65, and so forth.
Of course, the circle chips are obtained by cutting them from a circle strip. The strips and chips activities above may be made even more visually dramatic by providing children with a colored background upon which to do their experimenting.

❀ 53 ❀ SPILL THE BEANS

Level   K to 3.
Number of players Any number of pairs.
Materials One, two, or three beans. A can. Some ruled tagboard with nine cells. A die.
Procedure Children play the game in pairs. After rolling the die to see who starts, they take turns spilling the beans from the can onto the board. Scoring or winning may be set up several ways, depending upon the purpose and level. With one bean, the largest number wins; with two beans, the object can be to land on two numerals whose sum is 10. Also with two beans, it could be to record the largest number possible from the squares where the beans landed. Later this may be extended using three beans.

5	3	7
9	4	6
8	1	2

❀ 54 ❀

To illustrate the value of decimal normed numbers, make a peg-type abacus. Select a board and drill holes in three columns to represent ones, tens, and hundreds. Make three short, loose-fitting pieces of doweling to use as pegs. The illustration shows how the number 265 would be represented. Use as you would an abacus. (If this device is used with beginners, more pegs should be made so that they may be used as are the beads on an abacus. Thus, for the number 265, two pegs would be placed in the tens' column, and five in the ones' column.) Common peg board will adapt for this and other uses.

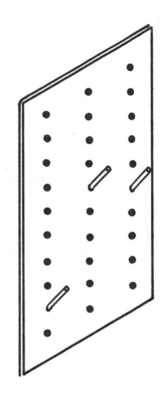

❀ 55 ❀

A chart for showing numerals from 0 to 100 by tens is useful to supplement pocket charts, number lines, and other graphic devices for relating the decimal numeration system to the system of whole numbers. For some purposes, a chart of natural numbers may be useful. Each position on the board is associated with one of the numbers from 1 to 100 or from 0 to 99. Both purposes may be accomplished with a permanent hundreds' board that contains rows of small finish nails upon which removable disks may be placed. A piece of plywood or chipboard will suffice.

❀ 56 ❀ SPLITTING CAPS

Level   K to 2.
Number of players   Pairs of children or small groups.
Materials needed   A divided box. Some bottle caps. Sheets of paper for recording results.

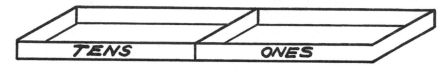

Procedure   Have the children count out 10 bottle caps and take turns holding them above the divided box, dropping the caps, and recording the number of caps that fall into each side. After doing this five times each, increase the number of bottle caps to 15 and repeat.

Variation   Use a box with three sections, labeled hundreds, tens, and ones. Egg cartons or small paper cups glued to a base are also useful and are adaptable to this and other grouping and sorting activities that you may devise.

❀ 57 ❀ FILL 'EM UP

Purpose   To mentally manipulate the concept of place value.
Level   1 to 3.
Number of players   2 or more.
Materials needed   Pencil and paper.
Procedure   On the chalkboard draw a pattern such as the one shown and have the students copy it on their papers. Call off random digits, one at a time. Ask the students to place the first digit in any box of their choice as 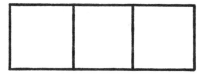 it is called. Repeat until the pattern is full. Ask the students to read their completed numerals and then announce a winner (the largest). Repeat until the rules for choosing the winner are discovered and then increase the pattern's length to four or more digits, using the smallest number as a variation.

❀ 58 ❀ PLACE RACE

Level   1 to 4.

Number of players   4 to 20.

Materials needed   Two sets of cards, each set containing one card for each digit, 0 to 9. (Games to show decimal numerals require two additional cards, each with a decimal point.)

Procedure   Select teams and distribute cards so that each team has one card for each of the numerals 0 to 9. Teacher or leader reads a numeral and pupils race to see which team can get to the front of the room first and line up with the correct cards for the numeral given. For example, if the numeral is 10, cards 1 and 0 must line up. After five plays, team members exchange cards.

Variation   An extension of this for expanded notation may be achieved with a similar set of cards (three cards for each numeral) which contain, in addition to the numeral, the printed words naming place values. The three cards for 2 would look like the illustration. In this variation, numbers whose names are "three-digit numerals" are called for.

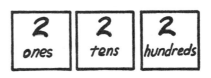

❀ 59 ❀

To teach number representations, make for yourself a simple abacus of heavy cardboard, elastic string, and short macaroni pieces soaked in food

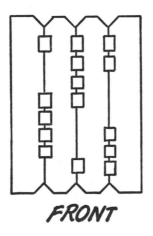

FRONT

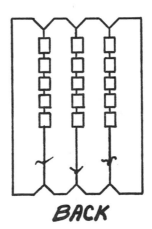

BACK

coloring. With yours as a model, help the children make their own. Knots are tied on the back. Because of the elastic, spare pieces can be brought to the front if one is broken. Also it is easy to have only as many beads in front as are needed for the numeral base being illustrated. Wooden beads will substitute for the colored macaroni.

❀ 60 ❀ SPIN A PLACE

Purpose   To provide practice in using the principle of place value.
Level   K to 2.
Number of players   1 to 4.
Materials needed   A spinner to select numerals 1 to 9. A pocket chart with as many pockets as there are players and with places marked for hundreds, tens, and ones. A supply of construction paper "tickets." Rubber bands.

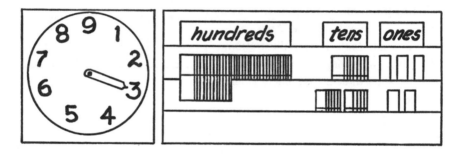

Procedure   Each player spins and places the indicated number of tickets in the ones' place of his pocket. On succeeding turns, as a player accumulates 10 tickets in his pocket, he secures them with a rubber band and places the bundle in the tens' place. *After* children fully understand that the tens' place indicates the number of sets of 10 ones, a single ticket may be used for each bundle of 10 tickets from the ones' place. (*Note*: If the bundle is too large, place only part of the tickets in the pocket, with the remainder hanging outside.)
Variation   The same procedure can be followed for work with nondecimal numeration. Merely change the place-value cards and the spinner.

❀ 61 ❀

To give pupils practice in various ways of expressing a given numeral, suggest to them that they find out how many ways they can rewrite a numeral in variations of expanded notation. Choose different numerals for each occasion or for each child. Example: $26 = 20 + 6 = 10 + 16 = 2 + 24 = 18 + 8 = 21 + 5 = \ldots$; or, if desired, maintain the tens by including $30 - 4 = 40 - 14 = 50 - 24 = \ldots$; or $482 = 400 + 80 + 2 = 300 + 180 + 2 = 200 + 280 + 2 = \ldots$.

❀ 62 ❀ EXPANDO RELAY

Purpose To provide practice in using the principle of expanded notation.
Level 2 to 4.
Number of players 2 or more.
Materials needed Chalk and chalkboard. Write on cards those numerals on which expanded-notation practice is needed. Two paper bags.
Procedure Place an equal number of cards in each paper bag. Select teams from among the players. (If a group is large, make several teams of 4 to 6 players each. In such a case, a bag of cards is needed for each team.) Designate space on the chalkboard for each team and place the bag of cards nearby. At a signal the first player of each team goes to the bag, pulls out a card, and writes high on the board the numeral and an expanded-notation form; e.g., $46 = 40 + 6 = 4(10^1) + 6(10^0)$, depending on the kind of practice desired. When finished, he touches the hand of the second player on his team, who proceeds in the same way. Continue until all the players have had a turn. Note the order in which the teams finish. Disqualify a team with an incorrect numeral expansion.

❀ 63 ❀ LARGE NUMBERS

Children, young and not so young, are fascinated by large numbers. Bulletin board activities, unusual projects, and large-number facts are ways of making large numbers meaningful. Role play or student explanations will verify concept development.

A Verse.   Big fleas have little fleas on their backs
            to bite 'em,
        And little fleas have little fleas and so
            on ad infinitum.

B Number facts.

1. You probably have more than 100,000 hairs on your head.
2. If you spent $1 million per day for 1000 days (a little over 3 years), you would spend $1 billion dollars.
3. (a) One million seconds is about 11 days.
   (b) One billion seconds is about 32 years.
   (c) One trillion seconds is about 32,000 years.
4. One million $1 bills laid end to end would be about 1000 miles long. How many dollar bills would it take to go around the earth at the equator? (25 million) How many dollar bills is the moon from the earth? (225 million) The sun? (93 billion)
5. A train traveling nonstop at 100 km per hour would take 1140 years to travel 1 billion km.

C Class project or activity.

1. Collect 1 million bottle caps. (If you have 30 students in your class and each student brings 100 per day, it will take about 8 weeks to collect them. If each student brings 100 per week, it will take about 35 weeks to collect them.) Design a place to display them as they are accumulated.
2. Make a wall display of 1 million zeros on butcher paper.

D For practice in writing numerals for large numbers, suggest that children write a numeral for a number larger than 5000; between 150,000 and 300,000; less than 1,000,000 but greater than 500,000; greater than 10,000 but containing no zeros; and so on.

E Period names for large numbers.

NAME	RELATIVE SIZE	ZEROS REQUIRED
Million	1000 thousands	6
Billion	1000 millions	9
Trillion	1000 billions	12
Quadrillion	1000 trillions	15
Quintillion	1000 quadrillions	18
Sextillion	1000 quintillions	21
Septillion	1000 sextillions	24
Octillion	1000 septillions	27
Nonillion	1000 octillions	30
Decillion	1000 nonillions	33
Undecillion	1000 decillions	36
Duodecillion	1000 undecillions	39

❀ 64 ❀ NUMBERS ALL AROUND US

Level   Variable.
Number of players   Small-group projects or a class project.
Materials needed   Resources and references appropriate to the investigation.
Procedure   Engage the class in a discussion focusing on number or quantity in our daily lives. Initiate the discussion through inquiry regarding how teachers may be identified by numbers and how students may be identified by numbers. A poster, as a continuing class activity, can be started containing a list of how people are identified and described. Examples follow that may be used in individualized, small-group, or class projects.

People Numbers

Social Security number	Date of birth
License number (bike or car)	Phone number
Street or avenue number	Zip code number
House number	Credit card numbers
Military service number	Bank account numbers
Height	Seat in class
Weight	Seat number at sporting event
Sport records	

Home Numbers

How are the houses on your street numbered?
Is there a pattern?
Is this pattern followed on other streets?
Could you come up with a better pattern?

Thing Numbers

How are cars numbered?
Why are cars numbered?
Do cameras, radios, bicycles, and motors have number names? Why?
How are streets numbered?
Is there a pattern?
How are highways numbered?
Is there a pattern?

NONDECIMAL NUMERATION

❀ 65 ❀ BODY COUNTING[4]

Numeration systems have all arisen primarily through a concern for counting. Systems of numeration with collection points other than 10 can be used to create a lively interest in children. Have children use a "hand" system and the decimal numerals 0, 1, 2, 3, and 4 for recording numbers formed with two-digit numerals. Count "one, two, three, four, hand; hand—one, hand—two," and so forth. For the illustration, children would record 13.

hand and three

How would they record three hands? Four hands? Two hands?

❀ 66 ❀ BEAN-CUP COMPUTING

Level   Variable.
Materials needed   Several sets of bean-cup computers. Some beans. Sheets of paper for recording results.

BASE 3   BASE 2   BASE 1   UNITS

Procedure   Children may use the collection point (base) of their choice. A four-cup computer such as the one shown is sufficient. Have them count familiar objects in the room by placing the appropriate number of beans in corresponding column values of the computer and record the results. Have pairs of children count the same objects but record them in different bases. See if they can figure out the corresponding decimal numeral.

❀ 67 ❀

To provide an activity in which numerals do not name numbers, suggest that the children make up a code that substitutes numerals for letters. Then write short messages for others to decode. The simplest such code assigns natural numbers to the letters, such as: 1, a; 2, b; 3, c; and so forth. Encourage children to devise their own symbol system without reliance upon the familiar alphabet letters. Cut a strip of tagboard for each child. Let each one record his name and birthday, writing all numerals in a base of his own choice and symbols of his choice. Mount on a bulletin board with a heading such as "Can You Translate?" Scratch pad and pencil may be provided if desired for other children to attempt to figure them out.

❀ 68 ❀ BANKER

Purpose   To provide pleasant practice in using various nondecimal numeration systems.

Level   1 to 4.

Number of players   2 to 4.

Materials needed   A die (singular of dice). A maximum of 20 small squares; 20 strips representing a multiple of the squares depending on the base selected; 10 large squares, called "flats," representing as many strips as the base indicates, e.g., 25. The strip is 5 times the size of the small square; the large square, or flat, is 5 times the size of the strip, or 25 times the size of the small square. The game may be played in any base, provided the correct materials are available.

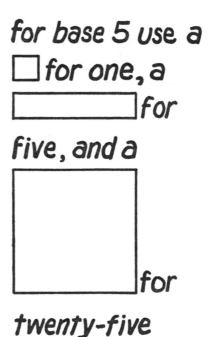

for base 5 use a ☐ for one, a ▭ for five, and a ▢ for twenty-five

Procedure   Place the squares, strips, and flats to one side. Players roll the die in turn. The one getting the largest number becomes banker. The first player is to the banker's left. He rolls the die and gets from the banker as many squares as there are dots on the top surface of the die. If the base for the game is five and a player accumulates this number of squares, he trades them in to the banker for a strip. When five strips have been accumulated, they are exchanged for a flat. When play ends, the players note what number their materials represent. The one with the largest number wins.

Variation   Many extensions and variations of this activity are possible through use of Dienes Multibase Arithmetic Blocks (MAB).[5]

❀ 69 ❀ GEOBOARD NUMERATION

Level   Variable.
Number of players   Small-group or whole-group activity.
Materials needed   Geoboards (5 X 5, 4 X 4, 6 X 6), one for each child. Rubber bands. Sheets of paper for recording results.
Procedure   Give each child a geoboard and some rubber bands. Decide upon a grouping number, call out an appropriate number using the base-10 numeration system, and have the children form the groups (according to grouping number) and record the result. Here are some examples of grouping numbers, the base-10 numerals, and the results.

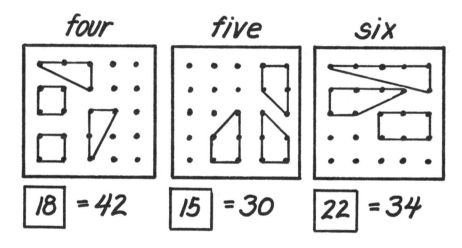

four   five   six

$\boxed{18}$ = 42 $\boxed{15}$ = 30 $\boxed{22}$ = 34

❀ 70 ❀

Since electronic computers as well as hand calculators have become a part of modern life, some children may be interested in computer mathematics. Base-2 (binary) is used because only two symbols are needed, 1 and 0; an electric circuit in the machine can be either on (1) or off (0) or a substance can be magnetized in either of two directions. Hence, for digital computers, numbers are translated from decimal to binary notation. For certain purposes, a less unwieldy notation is useful; and since changing between binary and decimal is time consuming, octonal (base 8, generally called octal by computer programmers) is often used.

To translate a binary numeral to octonal, "bits" (short for "bigits," which is the binary equivalent of "digits") are grouped in sets of three, beginning at the right. The reason bits are grouped into sets of three is seen when the binary and octonal notations are compared. With only three binary bits one can name numbers 0 through 7; with three more bits, one can name numbers through 63; with nine bits, numbers through 511. Note that the next number in each case (8, 64, 512) indicates place value in octonal notation; this is evident from the following table:

DECIMAL	OCTONAL	BINARY
1	1	1
2	2	10
3	3	11
4	4	100
5	5	101
6	6	110
7	7	111
8	10	1000
.	.	.
.	.	.
64	100	1000000
.	.	.
.	.	.
512	1000	1000000000
.	.	.
.	.	.
.	.	.

If each set of three bits is converted to octonal notation, these sets will name the same number. Example: 1001011100_{two} grouped in sets of three would be 1 001 011 100; translating each set to base 8, we have

Base 2:   1   001   011   100

Base 8:   1   1   3   4   or 1134_{eight}

The number named in both cases is 604 in decimal notation.

The binary-to-octonal conversion procedure may be reversed to convert a base-8 numeral to one in base 2. Example: 351_{eight} is 11101001_{two}; 3 becomes 11, 5 becomes 101, and 1 becomes 001 (prefix zeros to make a set of three bits); 351_{eight} names the same number as does 11101001_{two}.

Encourage interested students to experiment with converting number names of their own choosing from decimal notation to binary and octonal.

Some digital computers are programmed to accept words. To do this, the letters of the alphabet are divided into three groups; each letter in a group is assigned a number, as follows:

	B	A	BA
1	a	j	(skip)
2	b	k	s
3	c	l	t
4	d	m	u
5	e	n	v
6	f	o	w
7	g	p	x
8	h	q	y
9	i	r	z

The word *cat* would be represented as:

c	a	t
B3	B1	BA3

These symbols are converted to binary notation as follows:

B	1	1	1
A	0	0	1
8	0	0	0
4	0	0	0
2	1	0	1
1	1	1	1
	c	a	t

Note that B is indicated by 1 in its row, A by 1 in its row, and BA by 1 in each of the B and A rows. Below the representations of B and A, numerals are

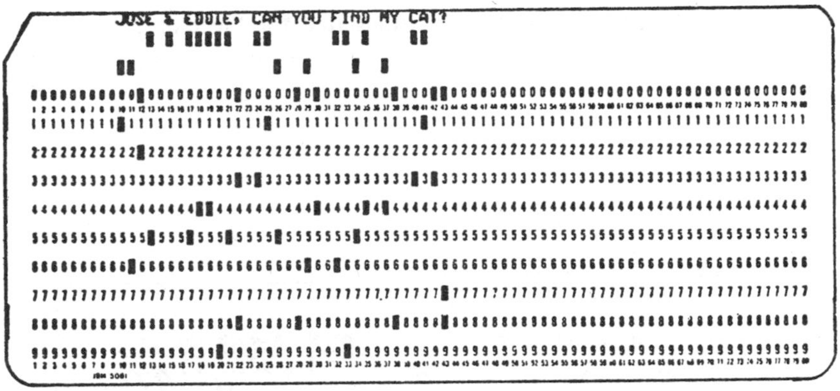

JOSE & EDDIE, CAN YOU FIND MY CAT?

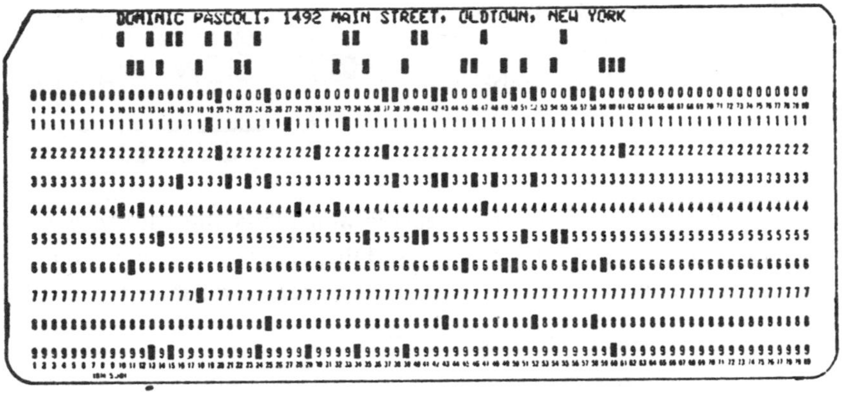

DOMINIC PASCOLI, 1492 MAIN STREET, OLDTOWN, NEW YORK

found for the position of a letter in its groups; the binary place values are shown in the left column.

The standard IBM card has bit positions in 12 rows and 80 columns. The rows are numbered from top to bottom in the order 12, 11, 0, 1, 2, 3, 4, 5, 6, 7, 8, 9. In transferring from the accompanying alphabet chart, B is punched in row 12, A in row 11, and BA in row 0, as in the cards shown here.

Some children may learn about a part of the process of programming computers through the construction of a chart showing the representations of all the letters in the alphabet. A part of such a chart is the following:

	a	b	c	d	$\cdots$	p	$\cdots$	z
B	1	1	1	1		0		1
A	0	0	0	0		1		1
8	0	0	0	0		0		1
4	0	0	0	1		1		0
2	0	1	1	0		1		0
1	1	0	1	0		1		1

With the letters of the alphabet translated for "feeding a computer," children now have a code in which they can write messages for others to decipher.

❁ 71 ❁

To stimulate interest in digital computers, help children make a "machine" to translate numerals from one base to another. Encourage them to invent one, or at least to make suggestions for the construction of one; or, better yet, to invent *and* construct a machine.

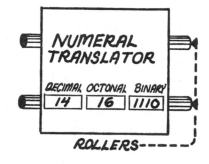

One type of numeral translator can be made from a box simulating a TV set. Cover the front with a piece of paper in which three slits have been made, one for each notation. On the roller, record the numeral equivalents so that as one numeral shows in a slit, the equivalent numerals will show in the other slits.

❁ 72 ❁

A device similar to the one described in Activity 71 can be made to illustrate the "computer language" for the letters of the alphabet as shown. Turn the "machine" so that slits are vertical. The information needed is described in Activity 70.

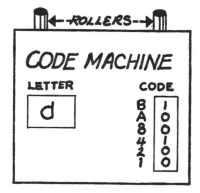

❁ 73 ❁

To further children's interest in computer mathematics, prepare a bulletin board announcing some interesting fact, such as, "No school on February 22," using the computer code described in Activity 70.

✽ 74 ✽ HIM

Purpose To challenge children of all levels of intellectual ability in an interesting game, and the most capable in an application of the binary numeration system.

Level 1 to 6.

Number of players 2.

Materials needed A handful of beans or other markers.

Procedure Place markers in two or more piles, each with a random number of markers. Flip a coin, roll a die, or in some other way decide who shall begin. The first player may remove any number (but at least one) of the markers from one and only one of the piles. His opponent then has the same option. Alternate in this way until one player takes the last marker. He is the winner.

At first the children will play without recognizing a pattern by which they can assure victory. Eventually, they may discover that if player *A* can play in such a way as to leave but two equal piles, he can win. His opponent can only make the piles unequal. Player *A* can then make them equal again. Continuing in this way, *A* will take the last marker. For example:

Bill leaves piles	00	00
Joe leaves piles	0	00
Bill leaves piles	0	0
Joe leaves piles	0	
Bill wins.		

When pupils have learned about nondecimal numeration, they should be told that the key to winning lies in the proper use of base 2. To win, one should (early in the game) place his opponent at a disadvantage by playing so that if the number of markers in each pile were written in the binary system and the 1s totaled, there would be an even number of 1s at each place-value position. For example:

NUMBER IN EACH PILE	
DECIMAL	BINARY
5	101
3	11
6	110
	222

Note that there are two 1s (an even number) in each place.

If one can play so as to leave the number of markers in each pile such that, were they enumerated in the binary system, the total of the 1s in each place-value position would always be an even number, he cannot lose.

 75

Practice on nondecimal numeration may be encouraged if one marks off on ruled paper 11 columns, making the left-hand columns wider than those on the right and numbering them from 2 to 12. In each column the children should write the numerals from 1 to 12 (or more) in bases to coincide with the numbering of the column; e.g., in column 2, write the numerals in the binary system.

2	3	4	5	6	7	8	9	10	11	12
1	1	1	1	1	1	1	1	1	1	1
10	2	2	2	2	2	2	2	2	2	2
11	10	3	3	3	3	3	3	3	3	3
100	11	10	4	4	4	4	4	4	4	4
101	12	11	10	5	5	5	5	5	5	5
110	20	12	11	10	6	6	6	6	6	6
111	21	13	12	11	10	7	7	7	7	7
1000	22	20	13	12	11	10	8	8	8	8
1001	100	21	14	13	12	11	10	9	9	9
1010	101	22	20	14	13	12	11	10	T	T
1011	102	23	21	15	14	13	12	11	10	E
1100	110	30	22	20	15	14	13	12	11	10

 76

A few pupils may be interested in learning of the advantages claimed for the duodecimal numeration system (base 12). If so, they should write to the Duodecimal Society of America, 20 Carlton Place, Staten Island, New York 10304. Qualifying for full membership in the Society requires such skill in the use of duodecimal numeration that it is unlikely that an elementary school child will succeed, but a budding young genius may be found here and there who is both able and interested.

❀ 77 ❀

Modular arithmetic, more often called clock arithmetic, comes from the Latin word *modulus*, meaning small measure. Because it is a finite number system, it can provide new insights into structural properties, such as closure, commutation, and association, as well as a sense of accomplishment in the search for order and pattern. Develop a simple example of modular arithmetic using a chart or a simple drawing on the chalkboard such as the one shown. Ask the children to get answers to such questions as: "Today is Monday. Imagine that you have a birthday 12 days from today. On what day of the

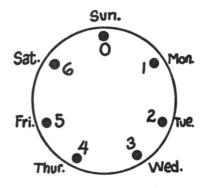

week will it occur?" "Tomorrow is Tuesday. Six days later we get our report cards. On what day of the week will we get them?" "What day of the week comes 9 days after Friday?" "If it takes you 20 days to write your book report and you begin on Wednesday, on what day of the week will you finish?" Later ask children to solve simple all-number problems. Have them make an addition matrix in mod 7. Compare it to a decimal addition matrix and record observations about similarities and differences. Is subtraction possible? Explore the other operations.

EARLY NUMERATION SYSTEMS

❀ 78 ❀

Many children will be interested in numeration systems of long ago.[6] One of the values to be achieved should be a recognition of the mathematical principles employed and how these affected the ease of use and hence influenced the development of mathematics. Especially note the elusiveness of the use of zero, discovered by the Mayans several centuries before it was known to the Hindus. The primitive Aztec numeration system will be seen to be similar to that of the Egyptians. Pupils may wonder that the Greeks achieved greatness in mathematics despite a clumsy system of numerals, but will have little difficulty in understanding the Romans' slow progress, encumbered as they were by their numerals, to which they and their Latin followers clung all too long.

Use bulletin boards to combine mathematics and social studies. For example, in a study of Central America, post illustrations of Aztec and Mayan numeration with the caption, "What are Hindu–Arabic equivalents?" Provide scratch pad and pencil. Adjust the activity and employ it with Roman, Egyptian, and Chinese numeration systems.

A *Egyptian numeration.* Principles employed are repetition, use of a base (10), and addition. Note the similarity to the Aztec system.

B *Mayan numeration.* Principles employed are repetition, use of a base (20), use of zero, use of place value, and addition. Except for repetition, these are the same principles as for our familiar Hindu–Arabic system. Numerals are

written upward, the ones' place being at the bottom with a space between it and the twenties. The third place value was 400 for commercial purposes but 360 for calendar calculations.

C *Aztec numeration.* Principles employed are repetition, use of a base (20), and addition (in thise sense referring to the addition of ones, twenties, four hundreds, etc.—often called the additive principle).

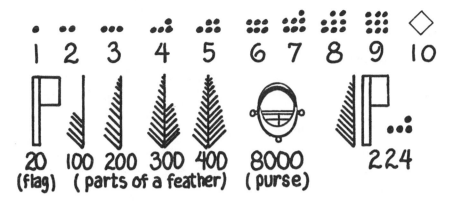

1	2	3	4	5	6	7	8	9	10

20	100	200	300	400	8000	224
(flag)	(parts of a feather)	(purse)	

D *Chinese numeration.* Principles employed are repetition, use of a base (10), addition (here ones, tens, hundreds, etc.), and multiplication (note that a lesser digit placed to the left of another digit implied that the second was to be multiplied by the first, e.g., $\equiv +$ means 3×10).

1	2	3	4	5	6	7	8	9	10	100	1000

$(5 \times 100) + (2 \times 10) + 4 = 524$

E *Greek numeration.* Principles employed are use of a base (10), addition, and multiplication (for large numbers only). The first letters of the alphabet represented the first nine natural numbers, the next nine letters represented the tens, and the next nine represented the hundreds.

α	β	γ	δ	ε	ς	ζ	η	θ	ι	κ	λ	μ	ν	ξ
1	2	3	4	5	6	7	8	9	10	20	30	40	50	60

ο	π	ϟ	ρ	σ	τ	υ	φ	χ	ψ
70	80	90	100	200	300	400	500	600	700

ω	ϡ	͵α	͵β	͵βφλε
800	900	1000	2000	2535
		(1000 × 1)	(1000 × 2)	

❀ 79 ❀ SIEVE OF ERATOSTHENES

A Greek mathematician, Eratosthenes, devised a method of determining prime numbers which became known as the Sieve of Eratosthenes.[7] Essentially, it consisted of crossing out all multiples of each prime number as it was located. All remaining numbers were primes (except the number 1, which is neither prime nor a composite number).

1 2 3 4̸ 5 6̸ 7 8̸ 9̸ 1̸0̸

11 1̸2̸ 13 1̸4̸ 1̸5̸ 1̸6̸ 17 1̸8̸ 19 2̸0̸

2̸1̸ 2̸2̸ 23 ···

Use the hundreds boards again by placing translucent chips or counters on the multiples as they are eliminated. Are any patterns seen when different colors are used?

❀ 80 ❀ ROMAN BINGO

Purpose   To provide practice in recognizing Roman numeral equivalents to Hindu–Arabic numerals.

Level   3 to 6.

Number of players   2 or more.

Materials needed   A spinner or other device for random selection of one of the following numerals: 1, 2, 3, 4, 5, 6, 7, 8, 9, 10, 14, 19, 40, 50, 55, 60, 90, 100, 105, 500, 1000. A set of bingo-type cards of 16 squares on which appear Roman numeral equivalents to the foregoing Hindu–Arabic numerals; arrange items differently on each card and omit different numerals on each. Beans or other markers.

C	II	IX	M
IV	VI	XIV	III
LX	D	VII	CV
V	XC	I	L

Procedure   Distribute the cards and markers. The leader operates the spinner and calls out the numeral indicated. He records this on paper or a chalkboard. The players place markers on the Roman numeral equivalent if it is on their cards.   The first to get four markers in a row horizontally, vertically, or diagonally calls out "Roman

Bingo." Leader checks to see if he called the numerals in the winner's bingo.
Variation Wtih only surface alterations, this game could be used in other historical systems.

 81

Numerology can provide interesting mathematics instruction through combining mathematics history with some basic arithmetic in an exciting and highly motivating manner. Reproduce the information below and have children determine their Life Cycle Numbers. Then direct them to the paragraph that describes the characteristics for their life cycle. Have them do it for a friend, for parents, brothers and sisters, and so forth. Have them do it for their full name.

A   Determine your Life Cycle Number.

  1. Write the name by which you are commonly known.
  2. Find the number value of each letter in the table.
  3. Place the proper number under each letter and sum the numbers found in both names for one answer.
  4. Sum the digits of your answer until you have a one-digit number.
  5. Compare your Life Cycle Number to the corresponding number on the chart.

1	2	3	4	5	6	7	8	9
A	B	C	D	E	F	G	H	I
J	K	L	M	N	O	P	Q	R
S	T	U	V	W	X	Y	Z	

For example:

B   i   l   l   i   e   J   e   a   n   K   i   n   g
$2 + 9 + 3 + 3 + 9 + 5$ $1 + 5 + 1 + 5$ $2 + 9 + 5 + 7 = 66$
$66 \rightarrow 6 + 6 = 12 \rightarrow 1 + 2 = 3$

Ms. King's Life Cycle Number is **3**.

B   Life Cycle Number Characteristics

  1. Capable, unchanging, and dignified. They are pioneers and innovators who are determined and independent people. They are born leaders

and organizers. Usually they have an outgoing personality. They are destined to work hard and attain their goals.

2. Helpful, adaptable, and considerate. They are reserved pepople who sometimes let their emotions interfere with making decisions. They make friends easily and other people turn to them in time of trouble. They are destined to be compelled to enjoy life through personal happiness.

3. Talented, popular, and ambitious, they are enthusiastic people who are full of energy. They are popular and dynamic individuals who enjoy the finer things of life. They arc destined to achieve success by learning to accept the good with the bad as a philosophy for living.

4. Responsible, studious, and agile, they are dependable workers and organizers who get things done. They are usually quiet, straight-forward, honest people. They enjoy sports and bodily activity. They are destined to seek security and achieve success in a slow and patient way.

5. Independent, bold, and ambitious; adventuresome, they treasure their freedom. They are enthusiastic people who enjoy doing things on impulse and dislike advance plans. They are destined to seek fame and fortune, although they will not always succeed. They will never stop being thrilled by trying to find it.

6. Patient, soft-spoken, and dependable, they have a strong sense of fair play and a deep love of beauty. They are frequently active in school or community affairs. They are destined to search for beauty and, when they do not find it, try to create it themselves.

7. Thoughtful, reliable, and analytical, they are original thinkers who enjoy traveling. They are frequently quiet people who are interested in the arts. They are destined to use their abilities for the good of mankind rather than for their own gain.

8. Strong, intense, and tolerant, they have great powers of self-discipline and individuality. They are energetic and active both physically and mentally. They are destined to be energetic workers and leaders who offer help and courage to those with whom they work.

9. Sensitive, perceptive, and compassionate, they frequently devote themselves to worthy causes. They are passionate, emotional people who are sometimes highly reserved. They are destined to work hard to seek perfection in an imperfect world.

❀ 82 ❀ BUILD A MATHEMATICS DICTIONARY[8]

To add interest to mathematical terms and to stimulate the use of reference books, pupils at any level may be asked to make a dictionary of terms and their sources. If the information is written on cards and arranged alphabetically in a file, the project could be cumulative. The following historical facts may be of help to parents and teachers for early cards.

acre from the Anglo-Saxon *aecer,* 1 furrow (about $\frac{1}{8}$ mile) long by 1 rod wide (as much as a farmer with oxen could plow in 1 day).

algebra from the Arabic *al-jabr,* meaning reunion of broken parts.

algorithm from the Arabic name al-Khuwarizmi, author of books on arithmetic written in the early ninth century. The Latin translation of these books was known as *algorismus.*

area from a Latin term meaning a broad piece of level ground.

arithmetic from a Greek word meaning to number.

baker's dozen 13, from English bakers' attempts to avoid being accused of short weight.

barleycorn $\frac{1}{3}$ inch, from an early English unit of that name. Shoe sizes are based on barleycorns; the largest size was once 13 (39 barleycorns, 13 inches), then each smaller size was 3 barleycorns less and each half-size was $1\frac{1}{2}$ barleycorns less.

carat from the Arab *carob,* meaning bean.

Celsius or *centigrade* attributed to Anders Celsius, a Swedish astronomer; Fahrenheit temperature minus 32 degrees times $\frac{5}{9}$.

center from the Greek *kentron,* a sharp point.

circle from the Latin *circulus,* a little ring.

counter (as in a store) from the habit of placing an abacus, or counting frame, on a table where the cost of goods sold was computed.

cubit the best known of ancient units of length, from the Latin *cubitum,* elbow. The distance from the tip of the elbow to the end of the middle finger.

decimeter in the metric system, 0.1 meter.

digit from a Greek word meaning a finger.

factor from a Latin word meaning to make.

Fahrenheit named for German physicist Gabriel Daniel Fahreheit: $\frac{9}{5}$ times degrees Celsius plus 32 degrees.

fathom the distance between the tips of outstretched hands, 6 feet.

foot the length of the foot from the big toe to the heel.

fraction from a Latin word meaning to break.

furlong from two Anglo-Saxon words meaning furrow and long, $\frac{1}{8}$ mile.

gram a unit of weight in the metric system; one thousandth of a kilogram. It was intended to be the weight of 1 cubic centimeter of pure water at 4° Celsius.

inch from the Latin *uncia,* twelfth.

light year the distance light travels in 1 year at the rate of 186,000 miles per second or about 6,000,000,000,000 miles.

liter from the Greek *litra,* meaning pound, a metric unit of capacity defined as 1000 cubic centimeters.

lug 25 to 30 pounds, considered a reasonable load for a person to lug or carry.

meter from the Greek *metron,* meaning measure, a metric unit of length, once calculated as one ten-millionth of the distance between the equator and the north pole. It was later changed to the distance (at the temperature of melting ice) between the centers of two marks on a platinum–iridium bar deposited at the International Bureau of Weights and Measures near Paris. The meter is now defined as 1,650,763.73 times the wavelength of orange light from krypton 86.

metric system the system of measurement whose common units are meter and kilogram. The former is length and the latter is mass. First adopted in France, it is in general use in most civilized cultures. It has nearly universal use for scientific measurement. Plane regions are measured by the are (100 square meters) and the unit of volume is the stere (1 cubic meter), although the liter (1 cubic decimeter) is usually more functional. The prefixes deca-, hecto-, and kilo- are invoked to designate 10^1, 10^2, and 10^3 times the common units. The prefixes deci-, centi-, and milli- designate 1/10, 1/100, and 1/1000 parts of the basic units.

mile from the Latin *mille*, a thousand; 1 mile is about 1000 paces.

notation from the Latin *notare*, to mark.

palm the width of the palm of the hand; four palms equal 1 foot.

per cent (or *percent*) from the Latin *per centum*, per hundred.

pound from the Latin *pondo*, meaning pound. The abbreviation, *lb*, comes from the Latin *libra*, also meaning pound.

quart from the Latin *quartus*, meaning fourth.

ratio from the same Latin root as reason.

rod from the Anglo-Saxon *rodd*, and derived from the combined length of the feet of 16 men.

span from the Anglo-Saxon *spann*, the distance from the tip of the thumb to the tip of the little finger when both are extended; now 9 inches.

stone from the Middle English *ston*, used many years ago as a unit of weight and still used by the British; 14 pounds.

sum from the Latin *summus*, highest.

ton from the Middle English *tonne*, thought to be the weight of 32 bushels of wheat.

volume from the Latin *volvere*, to roll.

yard from the Anglo-Saxon *gyrd*, the length from the end of the nose to the tip of the hand; also thought to be the length of an Anglo-Saxon king's girdle.

zero an Italian word from the Arabic *sifa*, empty, a cipher.

NOTES

1. Information about Cuisenaire rods may be obtained from Cuisenaire Company of America, Inc., 12 Church Street, New Rochelle, New York 10805.

2. J. R. Clark, C. W. Junge, and C. H. Clark, *Let's Count* (New York: Harcourt Brace Jovanovich 1962), p. T15.

3. An excellent treatment of the importance of language in mathematics may be found in R. B. Kane, M. Byrne, and M. Hater, *Helping Children Read Mathematics* (New York: American Book Company, 1974), 150 pp.

4. An excellent source for ideas on an extension of this activity can be found in *Arithmetic Teacher*, Vol. 18, No. 2, 1971, p. 77.

5. Available through Creative Publications, P.O. Box 10328, Palo Alto, California 94303.

6. For greater details on historical numeration systems, see F. Cajori, *A History of Mathematical Notations* (La Salle, Ill.: The Open Court Publishing Company, 1928), Vol. I.

7. See F. J. Mueller, *Arithmetic: Its Structure and Concepts* (Englewood Cliffs, N.J.: Prentice-Hall, Inc., 1965), pp. 193–195.

8. For an excellent teacher resource, see G. James and R. C. James, *Mathematics Dictionary*, 3rd ed. (New York: Van Nostrand Reinhold Company, 1968).

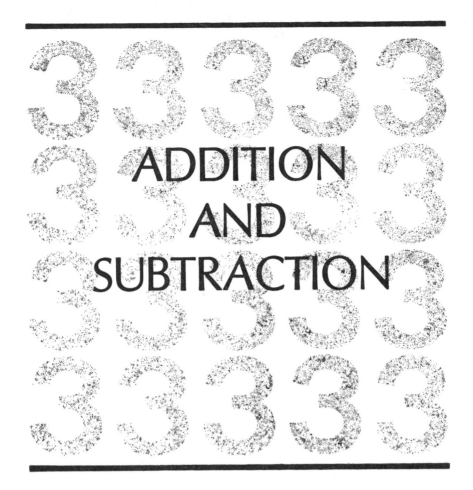

ADDITION AND SUBTRACTION

RATIONALE

The basic operation of addition and the defined operation of subtraction must be learned by children. Further, it is desirable that children learn to provide an automatic response when confronted with basic addition and subtraction sentences. The principal function served by the automatic response is to enable the child to compute correctly and efficiently. This remains important even in today's world of the hand-held calculator. It is clearly more efficient to think the sum 9 for 5 + 4 than to locate a calculator and then press two or three buttons.

   Unfortunately, before and during the process of learning the basic facts and later when dealing with the algorithm, children are often "rewarded" by interminable sets of computational exercises. As a consequence, their mathematics becomes little more than manipulation of numerals and increasingly unpleasant. Despite the need for meaningful practice, we must recognize that long, repetitive, and laborious assignments do not appreciably aid learning. Teachers today realize that the child who can correctly solve four exercises such as $N + 8 < 13$, $N + 3 < 9$, $N + 6 < 14$, and $N + 7 < 12$ is not likely to gain much by completing 20 additional similar exercises. In fact, the same may be said for those who do not understand. What is desirable is for children to experience multiple embodiment when learning the fundamental operations and the number facts associated with them. For children to enjoy mathematics and gain confidence in their ability to succeed in mathematics, they must associate amounts with numerals and models with operations.

From the activities in this chapter, the children will learn:

1. To express the basic operation of addition as the union of disjoint sets.
2. To identify basic sums.
3. To recognize the commutative and associative principles for the operation of addition.
4. To understand and use the algorithm for addition.
5. To define the operation of subtraction as the separation of sets.
6. To demonstrate competence in determining all *one*-digit differences for the numbers 1 to 18.
7. To understand and use the subtraction algorithm.
8. To categorize the defined operation of subtraction as the inverse of addition.

ADDITION

 83 ❀

When teaching the concept of addition as the union of disjoint sets:

A   Organize children into small groups of 4 to 6. Give each group of children 2 sheets of paper of differing color, a box of small objects (tile chips, buttons, beans, plastic counters, bottle caps, etc.), and some pieces of cord of sufficient length to encircle both pieces of paper. The children are then directed to place a set of objects on each sheet, circle the display as appropriate, and announce what has been done. Pupils must tell the cardinal number of each set and the result of their union. Emphasis must be placed on the result of combining, for example, a set of four objects with a set of two objects. The new number named as the result of the union is six, another name for 4 plus 2.

B The children may work independently on the concept of addition as the union of sets. Provide individual children with a string loop or straight wire that has been strung with small spools or beads. The child considers a given

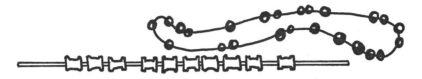

cardinal number, for example, 9, and then identifies all the pairs of subsets that he can form whose sum equals nine. He can record the results as 1 + 8, 2 + 7, 3 + 6, and so forth.

C Provide pairs of children with small felt boards and some felt cutout figures, numerals, geometric shapes, and strips. Utilizing a larger, demonstration felt board, place a set of objects and ask children to identify the number of objects. Divide the board with a felt strip, place another set of objects in the empty region, and have the children identify the number of objects in the second set. Label each set with a felt numeral and obtain the number of objects in the entire set. After the result of the action has been identified as an addition number story, have the children make their own addition stories, labeling the action at each step.

D Use rod materials as developed for Activity 5. Ask each child to select one rod, e.g., black, then make all the patterns of other rods that show the same length (purple and light green; white, red, and purple; etc.). Now, have a child remove the right-hand rod of his pattern, placing it out of sight. Then see who can replace rods correctly by picking up the right one with no fumbling. Follow by removing the left-hand rod. Then follow the same procedure, beginning with a different rod.
Variation Assign numbers to the rods. Then duplicate the papers, showing number patterns with the variable at the right or left. The players are to fill in missing numerals, such as 7 = (4 + 2) + □ or 7 = □ + (2 + 1). The players may check, using rods whenever necessary.

E Duplicate papers showing a series of two sets containing a variety of numbers of members (pictures or geometric figures). Beside each pair, write *N* = _____. The pupils are to write a numeral indicating the number of the union of each pair of sets.
Variation Duplicate papers showing Venn diagrams for nonintersecting sets. Provide pupils with flat beans, corn, or other small objects that will not roll.

Write an ordered pair, such as (3, 4), on the chalkboard. Suggest that children place appropriate numbers of objects in each indicated set and record the number of the union of sets ($N = 7$).

❀ 84 ❀

To demonstrate the relative values of numbers and combinations of numbers, make a simple balancing scale by bending a common wire clothes hanger so as to lower the fulcrum. Tape a clothespin to each end. A paper cup may be attached to each clothespin (or taped directly to each end of the hanger). Cuisenaire rods or similar materials can be weighed to show that combinations of certain kinds will balance; e.g., two light green and one light red will balance one brown. A similar scale can be made from a piece of wire twisted into a loop at the center and turned up $1\frac{1}{2}$ cm at each end. Attach a string to the center loop, or hang the device on a nail. Attach cups or clothespins to the turned-up part.

❀ 85 ❀

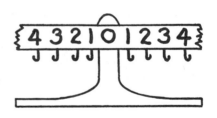

On a long, narrow board, mark off points at equal intervals. Mark the center zero and number in each direction. Place cup hooks at each mark. Balance carefully. Use heavy washers of equal weight or clothespins to show equations such as $4 + 3 = 7$, $5 + 2 = 3 + 4$, $6 + 2 = 4 + 2 + 2$.

Variation Pan balances of any type are useful in this and other mathematics/science activities.

❀ 86 ❀ MAKE A SUM

Purpose To provide practice with addition facts.
Level Primary.
Number of players Two.

Materials needed Two decks of cards, each deck of a different color, containing the numerals 0 to 9. Several dice.

Procedure Each player takes a colored deck, shuffles the cards, and places the deck face down in front of him. A die is rolled to determine who goes first. Each player turns one card face up. Play is started when the first player rolls two or three dice (depending on level) and determines the sum reached. If the sum of the two colored cards is the dice sum, he takes those two cards. If he does not roll the desired sum, the cards remain face up and the dice are rolled and summed by the second player. The game continues until all cards are used and the player with the most cards wins the game.

❀ 87 ❀

To provide practice on basic facts, prepare some cards for the pocket chart, each with the picture of a sailor. Make other pieces of "hats" with slits so they can be set on the heads of sailors.

Write number facts on the hats and answers on the sailors.

Variation A pocket chart (as in Activity 51) which is useful in teaching regrouping and renaming is made by fastening three transparent plastic boxes to a board. Label the one on the right "ones," the next "tens," and the last "hundreds." Short pieces of doweling make convenient markers for accumulating and bundling with a rubber band, or exchanging 10 in one box for one in the next box to the left to illustrate carrying. The process can be reversed in the case of borrowing.

❀ 88 ❀ SAME AS

Purpose To provide experience in finding relationships.

Level K to 2.

Number of players 2 or more.

Materials needed A set of rod material (see Activity 5) for each player.

Procedure Players spread the rods before them. The leader asks the pupils to find as many combinations of rods as they can to match a given rod or combination of rods, e.g., orange rod, blue and yellow rods, or two dark green rods. When nearly all have finished, call time and ask what discoveries have been made. The children can then be asked to record their findings in their mathematics notebooks or the teacher can record their oral reports. Repeat the play with some other standard.

Variation Ask players to join, end to end, two, three, four, or more rods. Then see who can find the fewest rods to match the length of the first series.

✻ 89 ✻ MORE

Purpose To provide practice in addition facts.
Level 2 to 4.
Number of players 2 to 4.
Materials needed Four or five sets of cards numbered 0 to 9.
Procedure Shuffle the cards and place them face down at the center of the table. Each player, in turn, draws two cards and gives the sum of the numbers named, according to the agreed operation. If a player miscalculates, his cards are put back on the bottom of the pile. At the end of each round, the player whose answer is the largest number collects the cards of the other players. The player with the most cards at the end of play is the winner.

✻ 90 ✻ CIRCLE ADDITION

Purpose To provide practice in cumulative addition.

Procedure Six players, A, B, C, D, E, and F, sit around a table with a numbered disk that spins. The disk is spun five times and each player's score for each spin is determined by the numbers on the disk. The person with the highest cumulative score wins. If the arrows land on the lines, the players spin again.

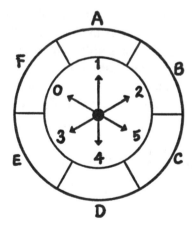

✻ 91 ✻

A motivating device can be had by making a pair of dice with a digit on each face. Use wooden or plastic foam cubes or make from construction paper creased and taped. Pupils may roll the dice and add the numbers named on the top faces.

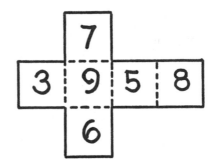

❀ 92 ❀ CHALKBOARD TIGHTROPE

Purpose To provide practice in addition facts.
Level 1 to 3.
Number of players 1 or more.
Materials needed Chalk and chalkboard.
Procedure With chalk, preferably colored, draw a picture of a tightrope.

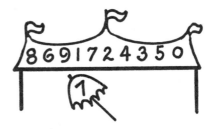

Write numerals over the rope and another numeral on the picture of an umbrella which the "acrobat" will use to help him keep his balance. Each player tries to "walk the tightrope" by adding the number named on the umbrella to those named on the tightrope, or by multiplying the numbers named on the umbrella and the rope. By substituting appropriate numerals on the tightrope, practice may be had in other operations.

❀ 93 ❀

It is sometimes appropriate to give special attention to troublesome facts. Jigsaw-puzzle-type cards can be used to help children learn troublesome facts. Cut each card differently so that only the correct-answer part will fit.

Another method of motivating attention to the troublesome facts is to place a drawing on the chalkboard of a swinging footbridge. On the "bridge" write especially troublesome combinations for certain children. Pupils take turns "crossing the bridge" and coming

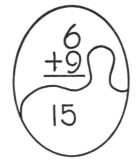

back again by naming answers. For those who succeed, draw a smiling face at one end of the bridge; for those who fail, draw an unhappy face on the rough water below. Emphasize the safe crossings, not the failures.

❀ 94 ❀ EQUAL

Purpose To provide practice in addition facts.
Level 1 to 2.
Number of players 4 or more.
Materials needed Numerals (on cards) for addends on which the players need practice.
Procedure Distribute one card to each player with instructions to stand in a circle and hold the card right side up in front where all can see. Say, "Five and Three, where is your equal?" The children holding the five and three cards go to Eight and say, "Here is our equal; five plus three equals eight." Equals stand together. After a time, players should exchange cards. For subtraction, say "Six minus four; who is your equal now?" The children holding the six and four cards go to stand beside Two and say, "Here is my equal; six minus four equals two."

❀ 95 ❀

A device for individual study of basic facts can be had by making a fat fish with a wheel on the back so that one addend or factor is constant and is written on the mouth, one shows through the eye opening, and the correct answer (on the wheel) is under a fin. Pupils may practice giving answers to facts. When in doubt, they can check by looking under the fin.

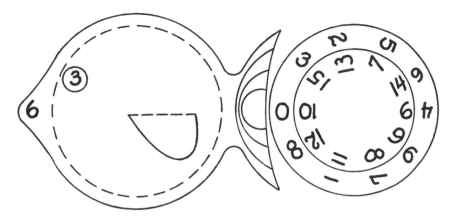

❀ 96 ❀

Addition facts naming the same number can be assembled and organized
for reference or practice by writing the
facts on one side of a card and the
number named on the other. Children
should make this device for their own
use. Sorting the cards is facilitated if a
corner is cut from each card. These
may be called basic sum cards and the
level of difficulty may be varied.

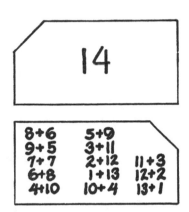

❀ 97 ❀

Draw on the chalkboard a route of any sort that is of interest to children, for
example, the way out of a cave, the path through the woods, or the route to
the beach. Write numerals along the "route." Pupils are to "find their way"
by adding each number to the one before it.

❀ 98 ❀

To provide practice in computation or basic facts, display a series of problems
on cards placed vertically on the left side of a pocket chart. Place an-

swer cards at random on the right. The
pupils must place the correct answer in
the pocket below the problem.

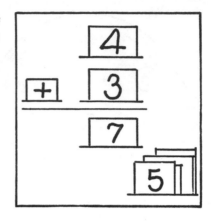

❀ 99 ❀

To provide practice in troublesome facts, duplicate papers containing a
picture of a pumpkin and 8 to 10 leaves. On the pumpkin write a numeral,
e.g., 14. The pupils may write on each leaf an appropriate combination, such
as 8 + 6. Pictures may be varied by using a vase and replicas of the state
flower, a Valentine box and hearts, or other seasonal or local interest items.

For individual practice on basic
facts that a particular child finds difficult, make several folders by creasing
cards so that, folded, they can be
stapled near the crease of each. Write
facts that are difficult for a certain

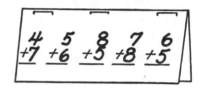

child to learn on the top, or cover, page; write the answers on the undersheet.

❀ 100 ❀ SPIN A SUM

Purpose To provide oral reinforcement with addition facts.
Level 3 to 4.
Number of players 1 to 10.
Materials needed Dial and spinner.
Procedure The players take turns
flipping the spinner. Orally each adds
the number pointed to on the dial to
each of the numbers on the ends of

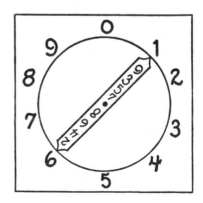

the spinner, as in the diagram: 1 + 9, 1 + 3, 1 + 5, 1 + 7; 6 + 2, 6 + 4, 6 + 6, 6 + 8. One point is scored for each player who makes no mistakes.

❀ 101 ❀ UP THE HILL

Purpose To provide practice in addition facts.
Level 1 to 4.
Number of players 1 or more.
Materials needed Drawing of a hill on a chart or the chalkboard. Write the numerals 1 to 9 in random order on the slope. On a picture of a sled, write a numeral.
Procedure The players take turns "pulling the sled up the hill" by giving sums of the number named on the sled and those on the slope. Change the sled numeral as needed. Products may be given, or, if you write minuends or dividends on the slope, the pupils may give differences and quotients.

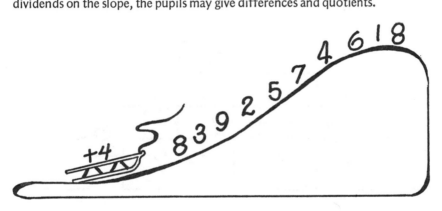

❀ 102 ❀ EQUATION HOPSCOTCH

Purpose To acquire skill with mental addition.
Level 2 to 5.
Number of players 2 teams of 1 to 5 pupils each.
Materials needed Hopscotch design on the floor or playground (may be made on wrapping paper and taped to the floor with masking tape).
Procedure The first player on one

team hops on squares of his choice, calling out the numbers as he lands on the numerals, and inserting signs to make an equation, e.g., "One plus twelve minus five equals eight." If he does this correctly, his team gets one score. Play alternates between the teams.

❀ 103 ❀ SHOW A NUMBER

Purpose   To provide practice in addition facts.
Level   3 to 4.
Number of players   2 to 6.
Materials needed   Two sets of 10 cards, each with a numeral from 0 to 9, for each player.
Procedure   The dealer announces, "Make 17 (or any other number less than 19)," then deals five cards to each player, and arranges the next 10 cards in the pattern shown. Beginning at the dealer's left, each player, in turn, lays

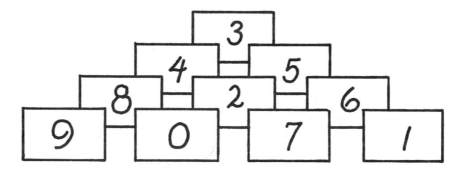

down in front of him all the combinations he can make of any two numbers that equal the number called. He may use any cards in his hand and any cards, from the pattern on the table, that have two or more "free" corners (e.g., 3, 9, 0, 7, and 1 in the illustration). When all players have had a turn, scores are recorded by giving one point for each combination showing. The game ends when each player has been the dealer once. The highest total score wins.

❀ 104 ❀ MATHMOUNTAINS

Purpose   To provide practice in mental arithmetic.
Level   2 to 4.

Number of players   2 teams of 4 players each.

Materials needed   Chalk and chalkboard or pencil and paper.

Procedure   On the board or on a sheet of paper, write three columns of numerals with 15 numerals between 1 and 25 in each column (repetitions allowed), the greatest number of these being in the 8 to 10 range. A sample listing is shown.

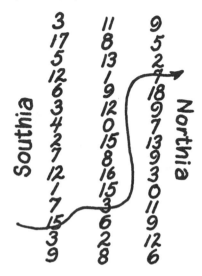

The two teams may be named Southians and Northians, living on opposite sides of the "Mathmountains," represented by the 3 by 15 array of numerals. Starting with the first member of the Southians, and alternating between teams, each team member tries to successfully cross the Mathmountains. This is done by threading out a path of three numbers, one from each column, whose sum is 25. (Numbers and sum can be altered to suit the class and level.) As a player succeeds in crossing he marks his route and thus makes those numbers inaccessible to following players (see the sample route marked in the diagram). The team that succeeds in getting the greater number of its members across is declared the winner.

✿ 105 ✿ ODD OR EVEN?

Level   1 to 3.

Number of players   2.

Materials needed   A deck of 40 cards each marked with a numeral from 0 to 9. An addition or multiplication table.

Procedure   Shuffle cards and divide into two piles to be placed face up in front of the players. The first player names the sum of the first two cards and states whether it is odd or even. If he is correct, he may keep the cards; if not, the cards are placed in a pile to one side. Play then goes to the next player. In case of disagreement, the players refer to a table. When all cards in the two piles are used, the discard pile is shuffled and divided into two piles and play continues. At the end of the game, the player with the most cards is declared the winner. (May be played also for practice on multiplication facts.)

❀ 106 ❀ FACT RUMMY

Purpose   To provide practice with addition facts.
Level   1 to 2.
Number of players   2 to 4.
Materials needed   A set of 90 cards, two each of the addition facts with sums of 10 or less.

Sums of 10 or less

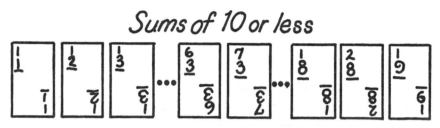

Procedure   Shuffle the cards and deal five to each player. Lay the balance of the cards in a pile face down; turn up the top card. The player to the left of the dealer begins by laying down "books" of three or more cards containing facts with the same sum, e.g., $\frac{3}{2}, \frac{4}{1}, \frac{1}{4}$. He may draw one card from the blind deck or take the turned-up card. If he (on this turn or a later one) finds another fact having the same sum, he may add it to his book. When through playing, he discards one card face up. Play then goes to his left and continues as above except that should there be more than one card in the discard pile, a player may take one, part, or all of them (he must take every one above the one he wants; e.g., he cannot choose the second card down without also taking the top one). Play ends when one person has no more cards. The player with the most cards in his books wins.

❀ 107 ❀ TOTAL OUT

Purpose   To provide practice in addition.
Level   3 to 4.
Number of players   2 to 4.
Materials needed   Four sets of cards, on each of which is a numeral from 1 to 13 (total of 52 cards).
Procedure   Shuffle the cards and deal five to each player. Place the balance of the cards face down on the table. The dealer announces the total to be

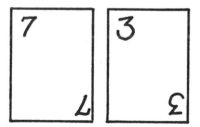

found, any number from 20 to 30. The player to the left of the dealer begins by drawing a card from the top of the blind deck and checking to see if he has numbers that will total the selected amount. If he has, he lays them in front of him in a "book." When he is through, whether or not he found a book, he discards one card to the bottom of the blind deck, except that he need not discard if all his cards make a book. When one player has no cards, he says, "Out." Scores for each player total the value of his books minus the sum in his hand; the one who goes out gets an additional amount equal to the value of one book.

❀ 108 ❀ MAGIC NUMBER

Purpose   To provide practice in addition facts.
Level   2 to 5.
Number of players   2 to 6.
Materials needed   Forty playing cards—four sets of 10 cards, each with a numeral from 0 to 9 on it.
Procedure   The dealer announces whether the game will be addition or multiplication and what the "magic number" will be (for addition any number from 0 to 18, for multiplication any product of two numbers 0 to 9). Deal all the cards face down. The first player turns up one of his cards. The next does the same. This continues until one player recognizes that two of the exposed cards yield the sum or product agreed upon; he must say the "magic number" before anyone else does. He may then collect all the exposed sum or product cards, after which play continues as before. Should a player call "magic number" at the wrong time, he must give each player one of his cards. Play ends when one player is without cards. The winner is the one with the most cards.

❀ 109 ❀

Two rulers may be used as a device for adding numbers; e.g., to add 4 and 3, find 4 on one ruler and place the zero point of the second ruler there; then find 3 on the second ruler; it will be opposite 7 on the first ruler. Of course, in this exercise and above, the inverse operation of subtraction also can be shown. One reads the devices differently, just as one reads an addition table differently to find subtraction answers. The rulers shown indicate that $7 - 3 = 4$, just as they show that $4 + 3 = 7$.

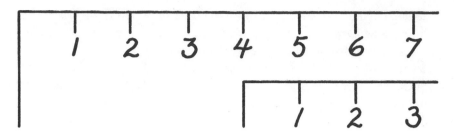

❀ 110 ❀

To provide a challenge as well as to encourage practice in adding, arrange the numerals 1 to 9 in a magic square. Each row, column, and diagonal must add up to the same total.

6	1	8
7	5	3
2	9	4

Solution:

Children will use a trial-and-error procedure, but for interested readers, the diagram shows one way of making a 3 × 3 magic square; in it r, s, and t are whole numbers, $2s \neq t$ and $r > s + t$.

$r - t$	$r - s + t$	$r + s$
$r + s + t$	r	$r - s - t$
$r - s$	$r + s - t$	$r + t$

❀ 111 ❀

Shown here are procedures for constructing magic squares which may be of interest to some pupils.

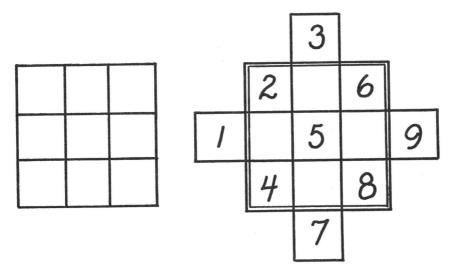

A For a 3 X 3 magic square, first make a grid. Then add a square, or cell, on each side. Now number the cells in a diagonal pattern as shown in the illustration. It wiH be seen that some cells are blank. Fill these by moving the numerals in the outside cells to empty cells as far removed as possible but in the same column or row; e.g., move 1 to the cell between 5 and 9. Pupils should experiment to see if the numbering of cells could begin with some number other than 1, e.g.,

2	7	6
9	5	1
4	3	8

6, 7, 8 . . . , or instead of proceeding by ones, if the numbering could be by twos, fives, or some other consistent order.

B To make a 16-cell magic square, fill a grid of 16 cells with the numerals from 1 to 16 in the usual sequence. Note that the sum of the diagonals is 34. Therefore, all rows and columns must also total 34. This can be accomplished in one of two ways. Leave the numerals in the four corners and the

1	2	3	4
5	6	7	8
9	10	11	12
13	14	15	16

four numerals at the center, but exchange the positions of the others at the greatest distance possible; e.g., 2 and 15 change places.

Another procedure is to leave in position those that you just moved. Instead, the corner numerals are exchanged diagonally and the positions of the four center numerals are exchanged, also diagonally.

1	15	14	4
12	6	7	9
8	10	11	5
13	3	2	16

16	2	3	13
5	11	10	8
9	7	6	12
4	14	15	1

C , Make a 16-cell grid and number from the upper left corner as shown. Begin with any number of your choice. Next exchange the opposite corner numerals, i.e., 3 and 18, 6 and 15; then do the same with the four inner numerals, i.e., 8 and 13, 9 and 12. Do you now have a magic square? Could you have started numbering at any other point in the grid, i.e., at the upper right cell, and proceeded downward?

3	4	5	6
7	8	9	10
11	12	13	14
15	16	17	18

D   The numbers shown on the diagonal of the illustration add to 30. So should the other diagonal, as well as each row and column. Find the missing numbers. (Top row: 12, 7; middle row: 6, 14; bottom row: 13, 8)

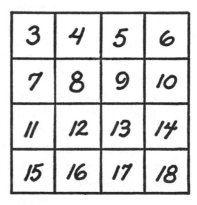

11		
	10	
		9

❀ 112 ❀

Magic circles also are fun. The three
numbers on each straight line will be
found to have the same sum. Pupils
might like to try making other simple
magic circles of this sort, as in the
variation below.

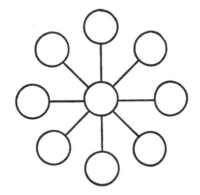

Variation   Make a magic circle by filling in each ◯ with a different
numeral, using each numeral 1 through
9 exactly once.

❀ 113 ❀ PATTERNS IN ADDITION

An addition matrix is helpful to children when making observations and
discoveries about the number pattern.

1. Count by ones from either the
   top or the left side.
2. Count by rows of numbers diagonally.
3. Count by twos diagonally.
4. Note the diagonal (perpendicular to the one in 3, above), all
   2s, all 3s, all 4s, etc.
5. Do you find other patterns?

+	0	1	2	3	4	5
0	0	1	2	3	4	5
1	1	2	3	4	5	6
2	2	3	4	5	6	7
3	3	4	5	6	7	8
4	4	5	6	7	8	9
5	5	6	7	8	9	10

❀ 114 ❀

Number sequence and pattern can be combined to afford children an interesting challenge in problem-solving drill setting. Independent activity work sheets can be designed to utilize the activities that follow. The work sheets can be consumable or students may be given bingo-type tiles with single digits and simply arrange the tiles as called for by the problem.

A Place each of the numerals 1, 2, 3, 4, 5 in one of the circles so that no two consecutive numerals are connected.

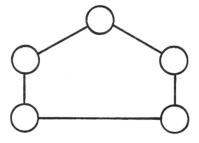

B Place the numerals 1, 2, 3, 4, and 5 in the circles of the "T" so that the sum of the three numbers in each direction is the same. How many different ways can you do it? Record them.

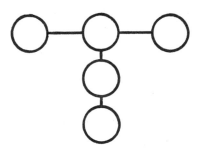

C Now try these using the same number of numerals as circles.

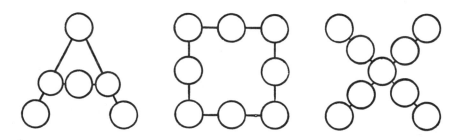

D Use the numerals 1 to 8 so that no two adjacent circles contain successive numerals.

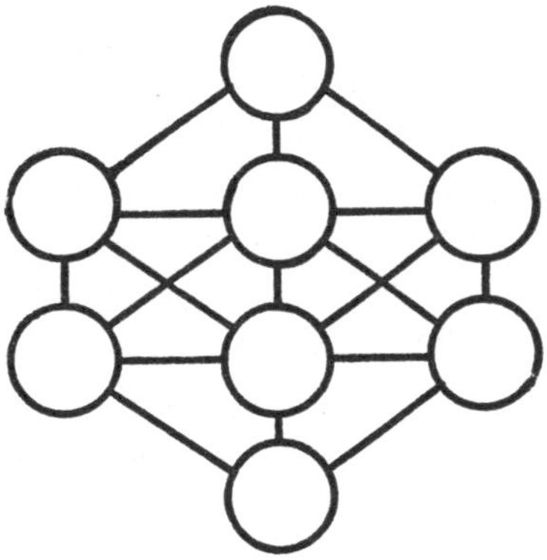

❀ 115 ❀ BOWL SCORE

Level Intermediate.

Number of players 1 or more.

Materials needed A pencil. A bowling score sheet. A pair of dice. A score card.

Procedure The players write their names on the score sheet to determine

BOWL SCORE CARD

Sum of two dice		Result
2		Gutter
3		2 pins
4		4 pins
5		6 pins
6		8 pins
7		10 (Strike)
8		9 pins
9		7 pins
10		5 pins
11		3 pins
12		1 pin

the order of play. The game is carried out in regular bowling fashion except that dice are substituted for a bowling ball. Each player rolls the dice twice in turn and refers to the Bowl Score card after each roll to determine the number of pins. Scoring is as follows: If a strike is made, mark an "X" in the first of the two boxes in the upper right corner of the player's frame. After a strike the next player rolls. If a strike is not made, enter the number of pins in the first of the two boxes in the player's frame. Roll the dice again. If the sum of the pins gained on the second throw and those of the first throw totals 10 or more, a spare is made. The player indicates this in the frame by drawing a diagonal line segment from the lower left corner to the upper right corner of the second box in the frame.   After the second ball of the frame, the next player rolls. If the sum is less than 10, the sum is added to the player's score in the previous frame.

The score for a frame in which a spare is made is computed by adding to 10 the number of pins for the first ball of the next frame. In the tenth frame you get an extra roll if a spare is made. The score for the frame is then computed by adding the pins gained in the frame to the score shown in the previous frame. The score for a frame in which a strike is made is computed by adding to 10 the total score for the next two rolls (10 pins if a spare is made in the subsequent frame). Note that three strikes in a row, sometimes called a "turkey," results in 30 for the first of the three frames. (If a strike is made in the tenth frame, you are allowed two more rolls.)

❀ 116 ❀ IF LETTERS WERE MONEY

An enjoyable pencil-and-paper (or mental arithmetic) experience can be obtained as follows. Display a chart on the bulletin board or the chalkboard which assigns a dollar value to each letter of the alphabet. Children will use addition to make a variety of interesting computations, based on:

A = $1	H = $8	O = $15	U = $21
B = $2	I = $9	P = $16	V = $22
C = $3	J = $10	Q = $17	W = $23
D = $4	K = $11	R = $18	X = $24
E = $5	L = $12	S = $19	Y = $25
F = $6	M = $13	T = $20	Z = $26
G = $7	N = $14		

Example: B   I   L   L   W   A   L   T   O   N
$2 + 9 + 12 + 12 + 23 + 1 + 12 + 20 + 15 + 14 = $70

Children may compute:

1. Their names   5. Their sisters' names
2. The school name   6. The most expensive three-
                           letter word
3. The teacher's name   7. $100 words
                           ($50 words, etc.)
4. The principal's name 8. Least expensive words

Variation Change chart values of letters.

❁ 117 ❁ DOUBLE-COLUMN ADDITION

To add numbers named by two-digit numerals, add the ones and tens alternately.

    42   42 + 7, 49 + 20, 69 + 3, 72 + 50,
    27   122 + 8, 130 + 90, 220
    53
   +98
   ───
   220

Add sums of series, such as 1 to 9. A quick way to find the sum of numbers 1 to 9 is by adding the tens and five. (4 X 10) + 5 = 1 + 2 + 3 + 4 + 5 + 6 + 7 + 8 + 9. Try a similar procedure for finding the sum of numbers 1 to 19 or 1 to 29.

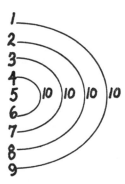

❁ 118 ❁ SCRATCH ADDITION

Purpose To show how addition computations were done many years ago. Four hundred years ago a popular method of performing addition was the scratch method, in which computations were made from left to right.

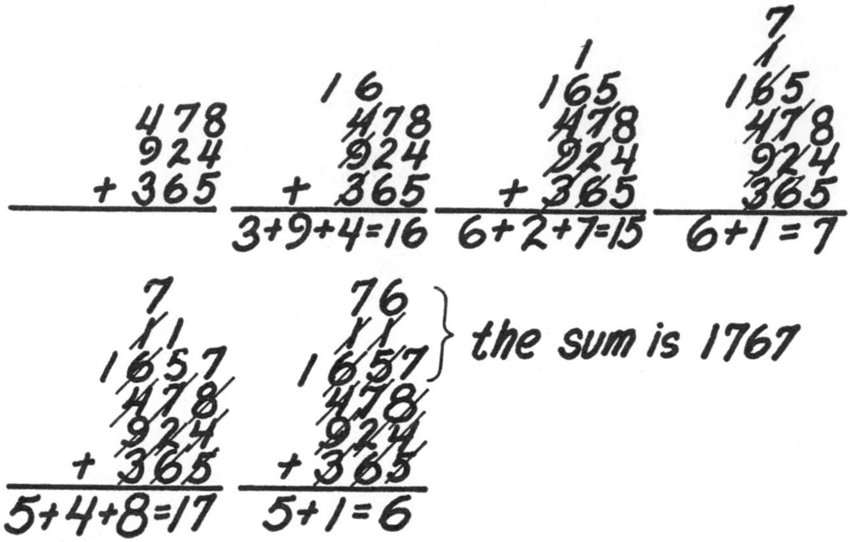

$$
\begin{array}{r}
478 \\
924 \\
+\ 365 \\
\hline
\end{array}
\qquad
\begin{array}{r}
^{1\ 6} \\
478 \\
924 \\
+\ 365 \\
\hline
\end{array}
\quad 3+9+4=16
\qquad
\begin{array}{r}
^{1} \\
^{1\ 6\ 5} \\
478 \\
924 \\
+\ 365 \\
\hline
\end{array}
\quad 6+2+7=15
\qquad
\begin{array}{r}
^{7} \\
^{1} \\
^{1\ 6\ 5} \\
478 \\
924 \\
365 \\
\hline
\end{array}
\quad 6+1=7
$$

$$
\begin{array}{r}
^{7} \\
^{1\ 1} \\
1\ 6\ 5\ 7 \\
478 \\
924 \\
+\ 365 \\
\hline
\end{array}
\quad 5+4+8=17
\qquad
\begin{array}{r}
^{7\ 6} \\
^{1\ 1} \\
1\ 6\ 5\ 7 \\
478 \\
924 \\
+\ 365 \\
\hline
\end{array}
\left.\vphantom{\begin{array}{c}a\\a\\a\\a\\a\end{array}}\right\}\ \text{the sum is }1767
\quad 5+1=6
$$

�֍ 119 ✷ CRYPTORITHMS

Purpose To challenge fast learners and to stimulate versatility in attack on problems.

REPLACE LETTERS WITH DIGITS.	SOLUTIONS

(a)
```
  CROSS
+ ROADS
------
 DANGER
```
(a)
```
  96233
+ 62513
-------
 158746
```

(b)
```
 FORTY
   TEN
+  TEN
-----
 SIXTY
```
(b)
```
 29786
   850
+  850
-----
 31486
```

(c)
```
  SEND
+ MORE
-----
 MONEY
```
(c)
```
  9567
+ 1085
-----
 10652
```

SUBTRACTION

 120 ❀

For general materials useful in teaching the concept of subtraction as the separation of sets, turn to the various descriptions in Activity 83. The following procedures involve some adaptations of those materials and processes:

A With the material illustrated in Activity 83(B), have children work independently to separate the spools or beads into subsets. As an example, when a child forms the subsets 3 and 4 from the set of seven, he should record the related subtraction facts, $7 - 3 = 4$ and $7 - 4 = 3$.

B Individual felt boards, as described in Activity 83(C), are appropriate for teaching the concept of subtraction as set separation. Place a model set of objects on the demonstration felt board and identify its cardinal number. Separate the set of objects with a felt strip and have the children identify the number of objects in each subset. As a result of the action, write two subtraction number stories. Using small individual felt boards, have the children make their own subtraction stories and record the results as related subtraction facts.

C Domino cards may be used successfully to reinforce the basic ideas of subtraction. They work equally well in drill for mastery and have the added advantage of the absence of numerical symbols. Discarded manila folders are sufficiently durable and they contain a natural crease for effective utilization

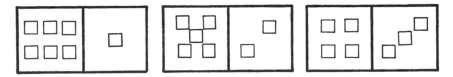

(bending forward and backward). Cut a large piece for each domino and use a felt marker to establish numerical patterns on each domino. (It is also easy to glue chips for the patterns.) As an example, the three illustrative dominos portray the subsets of seven needed to teach six of the subtraction facts associated with 7. They may be used vertically or horizontally and turned once from either position. (They show equally well the addition facts whose sums are 7.)

D As children listen to or sing a holiday song such as "The Twelve Days of Christmas," suggest they assume that one gift will be given each day beginning with December 25. Then on what date will the donor run out of partridges? (Since 12 partridges were given, the last would be sent on January 5.) Follow with 22 turtle doves. And so on. Will there be enough gifts to last a whole year?

E The circle strips and chips described in Activity 52 can be used to help children visualize the different pairs of disjoint subsets in a strip of a given value. Ten strips are made, each portraying the sets 1 through 10. To illustrate the possible combinations of disjoint subsets for any strip, the strip is opened to show all chips or holes. After children identify the cardinal number of a strip, for example,

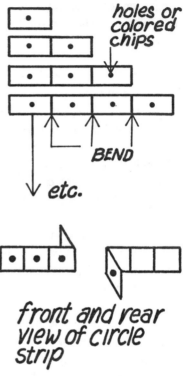

one, two, or three of the sections containing chips may be folded back. Children then record the number of chips they see remaining as well as the number of chips "on the other side" (folded-back portion).

❈ 121 ❈ SUBTRACTION BINGO

Level Variable.

Number of players Not more than 5.

Materials needed A set of subtraction flash cards. Teacher-made bingo cards. Some markers.

Procedure A "caller" shuffles the flash cards as each player takes a bingo card and covers the "free" space. The game proceeds with regular bingo rules. When the caller draws a flash card and announces the subtraction question, each player looks for the difference on his bingo card. If his card contains the number, he covers it and all like it with a marker. The first player to obtain five markers in a row (vertically, diagonally, or horizontally) is declared the winner. The winner's card should be verified for accuracy. **Variation** More difficult differences may be placed on the bingo card, depending upon the level of the students. Also, examples that require both sums and differences may be included in the set of flash cards.

B	I	N	G	O
11	9	6	7	4
4	2	1	8	7
O	3	free	5	12
6	12	7	10	O
9	1	5	11	8

❀ 122 ❀ HOW MANY

Purpose To acquire skill with subtraction facts.
Level Variable.
Number of players Small groups of 2 to 4 children.
Materials needed A piece of butcher paper. Some marking pens. Some dice.
Procedure Two or three dice may be rolled (depending on level) whose sum determines the number to be placed in the middle of each piece of butcher paper. The children then use marking pens to write as many subtraction equations as possible that have a difference the same as the number recorded in the center of the paper.
Variation Use the same procedure but permit two operations or all four operations.

❀ 123 ❀ BOTTOM OUT

Purpose To acquire mastery of subtraction facts.
Level Primary.
Number of players 2 or more.
Materials needed A set of cards containing the subtraction combinations (i.e., $8 - 3$, $9 - 2$, etc.). A die. A piece of paper.
Procedure A die is rolled to determine first player. Play begins with the shuffled stack of subtraction combinations face down on the table between

the players. The first player turns a card up and records the answer. The next player does the same. The player who has obtained the smallest difference wins the pair of cards. For example, if player *A* turns 8 − 3 and correctly records 5 while player *B* turns 9 − 2 and records 7, player *A* would receive both cards. The winner is the player who has the most cards after all have been turned. Any player improperly recording a difference automatically loses the card.

❀ 124 ❀ BEAN GUESS

Purpose To provide practice in subtraction facts.
Level K to 2.
Number of players 2 or more.
Materials needed A supply of beans.
Procedure Divide group into teams of 2. Distribute a given number of beans to players, e.g., 10. One member of each pair places his hands behind him and divides the beans so that some are in each hand. Keeping one fist closed, he opens the other for his opponent to see and so to tell (or guess) how many are in the closed hand. If he is correct, he gets one of the beans (otherwise none) and then has his turn as above. His opponent should note that the total in this case is one more than when play began. After play has proceeded so that there has been some shifting of beans from one to another, beans should be counted before each turn. At the end of play, children count to see who has the most beans. Watch out for loose beans!

❀ 125 ❀ RELATIVES

Purpose To provide practice in subtraction-facts families.
Level 1 to 3.
Number of players 3 or more.
Materials needed Subtraction flash cards. A set of answer cards with the numerals 0 to 9 on them, one numeral per card.
Procedure Players form a semicircle. Distribute a flash card to each. The first player holds up a flash card and selects another player to get the answer card from the display in the chalk tray or on a table. The player then asks, "Who are my relatives?" All children who have "relative" cards hold up their flash cards. Check for lost relatives!

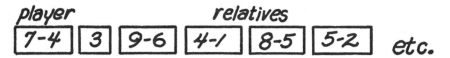

player   relatives

7-4   3   9-6   4-1   8-5   5-2   etc.

❀ 126 ❀ GOING TO THE CITY

Purpose To provide practice with subtraction facts.
Level 1 to 2.
Number of players 3 to 10.
Materials needed Flash cards of combinations on which the players needs practice. Chairs, one for each child.
Procedure Arrange the chairs to form a "train." Each child goes to the teacher's desk for a "ticket" (flash card) and then takes a seat on the train. A child who is selected to be conductor collects the tickets; as each is collected, the passenger must tell the answer. If he cannot, he must take his ticket home and wait for the next train.

❀ 127 ❀ DETECTIVE AT WORK

Purpose To provide practice in addition and recognizing relative size of whole numbers.
Level 2 to 6.
Procedure Provide each student with work sheets with 3 numerals written in each of the 3 boxes as shown. Select problems of appropriate level.

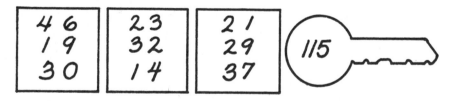

Students are to sum the largest (or smallest) numerals in each of the 3 boxes. Their total should equal the key number.

❀ 128 ❀ SUBTRACTION CARDS

Purpose To provide practice in subtraction facts.
Level 1 to 2.

Number of players 2.

Materials needed Two sets of cards, each with numerals 0 to 18, one numeral per card.

Procedure Shuffle the cards and divide them between the players, placing each stack face down. Each player turns up a card. The pupil whose card names the larger number must give the difference. This will be his score. Continue play until one player reaches 50 or all cards are turned up. The player with the highest score is declared the winner.

❋ 129 ❋ PIN DOWN THE FACT

This activity can be in the form of a bulletin board, or it may be used as a puzzle activity at a mathematics table. Make the shapes from oaktag as shown. There are three basic shapes: triangles, rectangles, and squares. For each corresponding pair of shapes, one contains a subtraction combination and the other contains the difference. Used as a bulletin board, children pin the appropriate difference on the combination. As a table puzzle children simply lay the correct difference on the combination. The difference may be given on the back of the combination pieces.

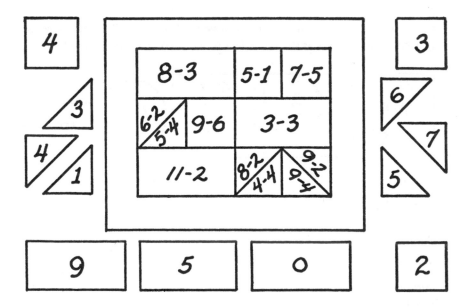

❈ 130 ❈ SUBTRACTION DASH

Level Variable.

Number of players 2.

Materials needed A number line to 100. Chalk and chalkboard. A pair of dice.

Procedure The object is to get to 100 first. Roll a die to determine the player who goes first. Each player in turn rolls the dice and obtains the difference. This difference is the amount by which the player moves forward on the number line. If the number line is permanently attached at the bottom of the chalkboard, children need only place their initials at the appropriate place to indicate their progress along the line.

Variations If a player rolls a double (e.g., pair of threes) he must sum the double and go back that amount. Rolling a seven provides an extra turn.

❈ 131 ❈

Assign the pupils several equations and suggest that they draw sketches to illustrate possible steps of the solution. Do not expect all the children to solve a given problem in the same way.

Example

$$4 + \square = 9$$

$$\square < 9$$

$$\square = 5$$

❀ 132 ❀

Oral drill provides challenging reinforcement in automatic mastery of basic facts. With minor adjustment, the separate activities that follow are equally appropriate for addition and other basic operations. Make the children familiar with the rules of several such games. Then they can engage in the activity independent of teacher direction. One good circumstance for realization is during those frequent times when a lull occurs in the focus of classroom activity, i.e., transferring from one study area to another, getting ready for recess, waiting to go to music, and so forth.

A *Estimating differences.* A "starter" begins by recording secretly two numbers smaller than 10. He then gives the difference between them. Other pupils take turns guessing the recorded pair of numbers.

B *Serial subtraction.* A series of numbers is displayed on a chart, chalkboard, or bulletin board. The displayed numbers would look like as shown.

$$\boxed{11 \quad 7 \quad 9 \quad 5 \quad 12 \quad 8} \quad \boxed{10 \quad 8 \quad 7 \quad 6 \quad 14 \quad 9}$$

Pairs of children represent teams, and on signal a given constant is subtracted from each number. For example, if the constant were 4, the pupil on the left would respond 7, 3, 5, 1, 8, 4, and the pupil on the right would respond 6, 4, 3, 2, 10, 5. The winner scores a point for his team, and two new children are called upon. Constants can be changed as well as the series of numbers.

❀ 133 ❀

Pattern and sequence may be seen in a problem-solving drill format for subtraction. Utilize the suggestions for preparation found in Activity 114.

A Place the numerals 1 to 6 around the circumference in a manner that the difference between neighboring numbers will never be greater than 2.

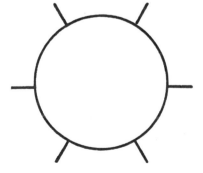

B Try it with 7 numerals and a circle. What happens? Can you do it?

C Place the numerals 1 to 7 in the circles so that for any three in a row, the sum of the end numbers minus the middle is always the same. Will it work with the numerals 11 to 17? 121 to 127?

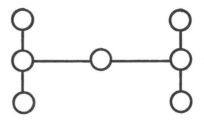

D Ask children to make up some subtraction puzzles using whatever series of numbers and whatever pattern they can design.

❀ **134** ❀

As with addition it is instructive and interesting for children to observe patterns in working with subtraction. In the examples shown an arbitrary number is chosen from which to start the serial subtraction process. A constant (any number) is also selected. Children should be given sheets showing an empty grid where they may record their work. In the example on the left the starting point is 63 and the constant is 9. On the right the key number is 85 and the constant is 7.

pattern	tens digit	unit digit
63	6	3
54	5	4
45	4	5
•	•	•
•	•	•
•	•	•
•	•	•

pattern	tens digit	unit digit
85	8	5
78	7	8
71	7	1
64	6	4
•	•	•
•	•	•
•	•	•

❋ 135 ❋

Another form of problem-solving practice in subtraction (adaptable to other operations and combined operations) is found in supplying children with sheets that contain several grids in which selected cells are blank. The task is to fill in the missing numbers in some orderly, logical manner. In the example shown, a subtraction grid, the first row is differences, the second row is minuends, and the bottom row contains subtrahends. The children should simply be encouraged to begin. Grids can be constructed for combined operations, so answers may vary.

5	10	8		42	21	
8		12	9	49		24
3	5		4			

❋ 136 ❋

A helpful activity to assist the children in grasping the social uses of subtraction is to discuss with them examples of situations in which each type is used. With their help, list many for each.

Examples

Type 1. Finding what part of a group is left.

Joe had 28 cents and spent 12 cents. How much did he have left?

Type 2. Comparing two groups.

Tom had 18 marbles. Jim had 14. Tom had how many marbles more than Jim?

Type 3. Finding how many more are needed.

Ann had 18 cents. How much more would she need to buy a pen that costs 25 cents?

Type 4. Finding an unknown number when the sum and one addend are known.

Sue has 27 stamps, 16 of which are foreign. How many stamps are domestic?

Social uses of subtraction and other operations can be illustrated also through role playing using real or play money and equipment. Pretend to operate a gas station, a department store, or a grocery store.

137

Computer subtraction is effective when additional mastery of the regrouping principle in two-digit subtraction is desirable. (See Activity 66 for the illustration of a simple "computer.") Begin by having children put various numbers less than 1000 "in" the computer. They should record their actions by showing how many beans they used: hundreds, tens, and ones. Leave a number such as 44 "in." Move another computer directly beneath the first one. Place a number such as 16 in it. Ask children to solve the example, 44 − 16, and tell about the trade that was necessary.

138 SUBTRACTION BY COMPENSATION

To subtract numbers that are not multiples of 10, either add or subtract from both minuend and subtrahend so as to leave a multiple of 10: $\begin{array}{r} 48 \\ -22 \end{array}$ may be changed to $\begin{array}{r} 46 \\ -20 \end{array}$ or $\begin{array}{r} 57 \\ -38 \end{array}$ may be changed to $\begin{array}{r} 59 \\ -40 \end{array}$.

139 ESTIMATION WITH SUBTRACTION

Level   4 to 6.
Number of players   2 or more.
Materials needed   20 to 30 cards, each with a large numeral written with a black crayon or felt pen. Numbers selected should depend on practice needed.
Procedure   Shuffle cards. Place five or more cards in the chalk tray in view of all players. Then write a three-digit numeral on the chalkboard. Each player gets one turn at estimating the difference between the sum of the five numbers named by the cards in the tray and the number named on the chalkboard. Each player's estimate is recorded after his name. The player who has the nearest estimate wins. The cards may then be returned to the pack, shuffled, and the game repeated. The activity may be varied by seeking estimates for more than one number.

❀ 140 ❀ NINETY NINE

Purpose   To acquire mental agility with subtraction.
Level   3 to 6.
Number of players,   3 or more.
Materials needed   A deck of ordinary playing cards. A die.
Procedure   Shuffle a full deck and deal 3 cards to each player. The rest are put face down in the middle: the face cards are each 10 and the ace can be 11 or 1. Numerical cards count as their face value, but the 3s and 9s are used as subtractive cards. (They may be played any time.) The first player puts down a card face up in the middle, then draws a replacement card from the pile and puts it in his hand. The second player adds a card from his hand to the middle and calls out the total. Players always take a replacement card, so there are always 3 cards in hand. Play continues as *all* cards add into the total *except* for the 3s and 9s. Players are eliminated from the game when they cannot play without exceeding 99. The winner is the first player to reach exactly 99 or the only remaining player.

CONCURRENT PRACTICE

❀ 141 ❀

Verse can form a challenge in an introduction to practice for mastery in addition and subtraction.

RAYMOND'S RACCOON

> Raymond's raccoon went up a tree,
> Which was sixty feet and three,
> Every day she climbed eleven,
> Every night she came down seven.
> Tell me, if she did not drop,
> When her paws would reach the top.

(She moved up 4 feet per day. In 13 days the raccoon climbed 13 X 4, or 52 feet. Then on the fourteenth day her paws reached the top, since 52 + 11 = 63.)

❀ 142 ❀

To stimulate the learning of addition and subtraction facts, place cutouts of seasonal items, e.g., pumpkins for autumn, on the bulletin board. As each child demonstrates his knowledge of a set of basic facts, print his name on one of the pictures.

❀ 143 ❀ MATCHING

Purpose To provide practice with troublesome addition and subtraction facts.
Level 1 to 3.
Number of players 4 or more.
Materials needed Depending on the time of the year, make paper pumpkins, apples, Christmas cards, Valentines, Easter eggs, or the like. Cut each in two in an irregular manner. On one part write an arithmetic combination and on the second part write the answer. Use whatever facts the children need to practice.
Procedure Divide the players groups into two and distribute the parts that contain combinations to half of the players and the parts that contain answers to the other half. Each player must find who has a part to match his own. When all players have found partners, ask each one who has a combination to say what it is and his partner to give the answer. Redistribute materials and repeat.
Variation For one or two players, place all the materials on a table and let the children find the matching parts.

❀ 144 ❀

Learning addition and subtraction facts at home or at school can be stimulated if, using heavy construction paper, one makes several sets of two disks, one smaller than the other. On the smaller disk, write the basic facts on one side with the answers on the other side, back to back. Cut a window in the larger circle in a way such as to show one basic fact at a time. Use a paper fastener to hold the circles together.

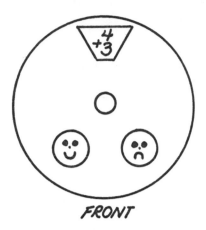

❀ 145 ❀

For practice on addition and/or subtraction, prepare a device of tagboard on which equations are indicated, showing only some numerals or operation signs. Make slits where items are missing and prepare tagboard cards marked with numerals or operation signs. Pupils insert the cards in the appropriate slits.

$$\_ + \_ - 3 = 9$$
$$8 - \_ + 5 = 10$$
$$6 \_ 5 - 4 = 7$$

❀ 146 ❀

To keep arithmetic facts or other items before children, enlist their help in cutting out colored cardboard or plastic geometric figures. On each, print a troublesome fact or word. Suspend these by nylon thread from slim pieces of reed (or a plastic drinking straw or wire) of different lengths. Each pair should balance but not with the fulcrum at the midpoint. Balance the lowest one first. Hang from the ceiling.

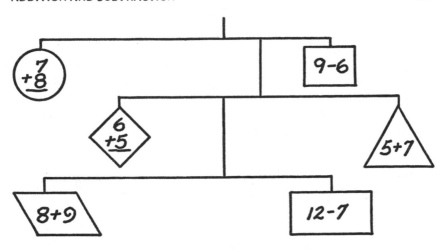

❀ 147 ❀

To keep troublesome addition and subtraction facts before children, cut large (10 to 30 cm tall) numerals from colored paper; on them write basic facts, the answers to which are the number named. Mount on the bulletin board. Change the numerals each week.

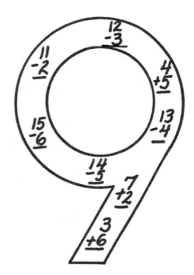

❀ 148 ❀ FAMILY TRAIN

Purpose To provide simultaneous practice with addition and subtraction facts.
Level 1 to 2.
Number of players 2 to 10.
Materials needed Chalk and chalkboard.
Procedure Divide the children into two groups. The first player in each

group goes to the chalkboard and draws a train engine; on it he writes a numeral, an engine numeral determined by the teacher or a leader, e.g., 8. The second player then comes up to draw a coach on which he writes a combination that names the number selected for the engine, e.g., 6 + 2. Continue until a member of the group thinks that all combinations have been shown; he then draws a caboose. The team whose train shows all combinations for the engine number wins.

✿ 149 ✿ BARREL OF FACTS

Purpose   To provide practice in addition and subtraction facts.
Level   1 to 3.
Number of players   1 or more.
Materials needed   An outline of a barrel on the chalkboard.
Procedure   Write a numeral at the top of the barrel. Players take turns writing facts, the answers to which are the selected number. If competition is desired, draw the outlines of two barrels and have the teams see which can record the most facts to "fill the barrel."

✿ 150 ✿ CIRCUS BALLOONS

Purpose   To simultaneously present addition and subtraction facts.
Level   1 to 3.
Number of players   1 or more.
Materials needed   Pictures of balloons on the chalkboard. Write a combination on each.
Procedure   Players take turns trying to "pop the balloons" by giving answers to combinations. The leader or the children may clap hands to indicate the pop of the balloon.

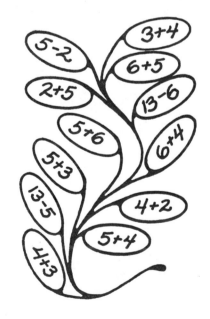

Variation Similar games can be played by varying the pictures, e.g., show a flower garden with combinations on each flower; players will "pick the flowers."

❀ 151 ❀ TRIMMING THE CHRISTMAS TREE

Level   1 to 3.

Number of players   3 or more.

Materials needed   A Christmas tree, which may be real or drawn on the chalkboard. Fancy cards with questions or combinations on them; each should have a string loop attached for fastening to the tree or a bit of masking tape if a chalkboard tree is used.

Procedure   Place cards face down. Each player in turn takes a card and, if he can give the correct answer (sum, difference, quotient, or product), he may place it on the tree; if he cannot give the answer, the card is placed under others.

Variation   Write combinations on papers shaped like pumpkin seeds, placing these in a pumpkin (real or artificial). The children take turns reaching into the container and pulling out a "seed." If they can give the answers to the facts shown, they may keep the seeds; otherwise, they must return them to the pumpkin. Pupils may record combinations they do not know for "pumpkin-seed homework." This game can be adapted further to fit in with individual, local, or seasonal interests, such as hearts in a Valentine box, eggs in an Easter basket, rabbits in a pen, cars in a used car lot, or animals in a barnyard.

❀ 152 ❀ JACK AND THE BEANSTALK

Level   1 to 3.

Number of players   1 or more.

Materials needed   Picture of a beanstalk with combinations written on the leaves.

Procedure   Players pretend to be Jack and try to "climb the beanstalk" by naming the answers to combinations.

❀ 153 ❀ ROCKET TO THE MOON

Level 2 to 4.

Number of players 2 to 6.

Materials needed Addition and subtraction flash cards. Flannel board with cutouts of the moon and of two rockets.

Procedure The teacher or leader shows a flash card to the first player on one team. If he answers correctly, his team's rocket advances one space toward the moon. Play alternates from one team to the other.

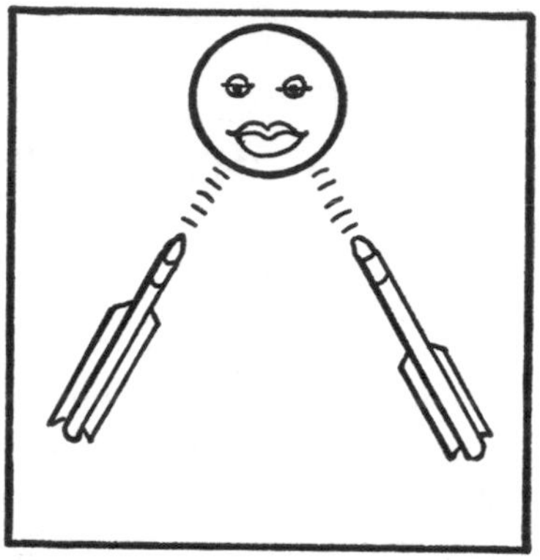

❀ 154 ❀ COMBINATION RELAY

Purpose To provide practice on addition or subtraction facts, and on adding or subtracting a seen number to an unseen number.

Level 2 to 4.

Number of players 2 teams.

Materials needed Two sets of cards with the numerals 1 to 9 on the cards, one numeral on each card.

Procedure Select two teams and distribute the cards so that opposite players have the same numerals. Designate a scorekeeper. When the teacher or leader calls a number, the first player on each team adds it to the number named on his card (or each may subtract, multiply, or divide the two numbers). The one who first gives the correct answer gets a point. After each player has had a turn (or when time for this activity is up), calculate team scores by totaling points earned.

❀ 155 ❀ OUR HOUSE

Purpose To provide simultaneous practice with addition and subtraction facts.

Level 1 to 3.

Number of players 1 or more.
Materials needed Chalk and chalk-board.
Procedure Draw a picture of a house on the chalkboard. Ask a child if he can show all the "relatives" of 4 + 3. He writes the addition and subtraction combinations on the house to show who lives there. If he is correct, he may choose the next player. (Multipli-cation- and division-related facts may be substituted for addition and sub-traction.)

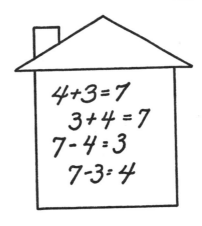

Variation Draw a picture of a house and yard. Write a numeral, e.g., 8, on the house. Say, "On a warm sunny day all the family of eight were in the yard enjoying the sunshine. Who can show me their names?" Call on a volunteer to write the basic facts "in the yard." Ask other players if any members of the family are still indoors. When all are accounted for, erase the facts, write a different numeral on the house, and proceed as before. Basic facts may be written either vertically or horizontally, e.g., $\frac{3}{+5}$ or 3 + 5.

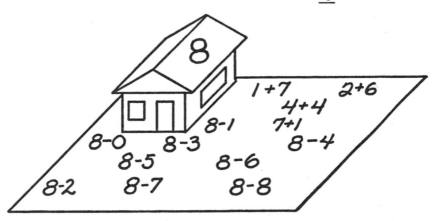

❀ 156 ❀ FALLING THROUGH THE ICE

Level 1 to 3.
Number of players 2 or more.
Materials needed Flash cards of arithmetic facts.
Procedure Players sit in a semicircle "around the frozen lake." Leader

shows flash cards and calls on individuals at random. Anyone who fails to answer correctly "falls through the ice." He may get out again if he can answer correctly after someone else has fallen in.

❋ 157 ❋ WHAT NUMBER AM I?

Level   2 to 4.
Number of players   2 or more.
Materials needed   None.
Procedure   The teacher or leader describes a number by using addition and subtraction; e.g., "If you take me away from eight, I leave three, or if you add me to three, I make eight." The player naming the correct answer then becomes leader.

❋ 158 ❋ POSTMAN

Level   1 to 3.
Number of players   1 to 4.
Materials needed   Post office mail boxes. Instead of names, write the numerals that name the sum, difference, product, or quotient of two numbers on the mail boxes. "Letters" have addition, subtraction, multiplication, or division combinations on them.
Procedure   Players take turns "sorting the mail" by placing the "letters" in the correct boxes.
Variation   Vary the game by having any type of matching desired.

❋ 159 ❋ ADD A TAIL

Level   1 to 2.
Number of players   2 or more.
Materials needed   Flash cards. Chalk and chalkboard.
Procedure   Divide the group into two or more teams. Present a flash card to the first member of each team. The first to answer correctly wins the
round. For him, draw a part of a simple picture of a mouse. Continue in this

manner until the drawing of one mouse is completed (draw the tail last). The first team to get a tail drawn is the winner.

✿ 160 ✿ WOLF AND SHEEP

Level   1 to 4.
Number of players   3 or more.
Materials needed   None.
Procedure   Players are sheep and form a circle with one person in the center who is the wolf. He calls a sheep by name and gives a combination. The sheep must answer correctly or join the wolf. In the latter case, he may get back to the circle by giving the answer to the next combination before the sheep called on can do so or by giving the correct answer if a wrong one was accepted by the wolf.
Variation   The wolf may ask a question to be answered by the sheep or name a term that must be explained or defined by the sheep.

✿ 161 ✿ KANGAROO JUMP

Purpose   To learn to use the number line in adding and subtracting whole numbers.
Level   1 to 2.
Number of players   An arithmetic group.
Materials needed   Chalk and chalkboard.
Procedure   Draw a picture of a number line on the chalkboard. Nearby place a picture of a kangaroo (or grasshopper or frog). Call on a child to come to the board and show how the kangaroo jumps along the number line. "He starts at zero and jumps two spaces to the right, then four more, then three more. Now where is the kangaroo?" Vary the game as desired; e.g., for subtraction the kangaroo might take seven jumps to the right and then four jumps to the left; for counting by twos or multiplying, the jumps may be all of a given length.
Variation   If desired, the kangaroo might jump from the right of zero to the left of zero into the land of negative numbers.

✿ 162 ✿ COMBINATION DRAW

Purpose   To provide practice in addition and subtraction facts.
Level   1 to 2.

Number of players 2 to 6.

Materials needed A deck of flash cards containing the addition and subtraction combinations on which the players need practice.

Procedure Place cards face down at the center of the table. Each player, in turn, draws a card and gives the answer to the combination on it. If he is correct, he may keep the card; if not, he places it face up on the table. The next player may give the answer to the face-up card, keep it, and draw a card. If there is more than one card face up, the player who can give the answer to each may keep it as well as draw from the deck. At the end of play, the one with the most cards is declared winner.

❈ 163 ❈ CIRCLE SCOTCH

Purpose To provide practice in addition and subtraction and in number patterns.

Level 4 to 6.

Procedure Provide students with circle scotch puzzles as shown. The challenge is to find the numbers that should go in the circles without writing the intermediate values.

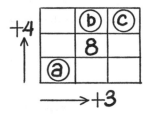
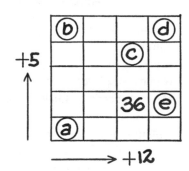

❈ 164 ❈ EQUATIONS

Level 2 to 6.

Number of players 2 to 6.

Materials needed 50 cards, on each of which one numeral appears—five each of numerals 0 to 9. Six cards with equal signs, six with plus signs, and six with minus signs.

Procedure Place equal, plus, and minus sign cards in the middle of the table, face up. Deal three numeral cards to each player; place the balance of the cards face down in the center of the table. Play begins to the dealer's left. Each player, in turn, draws a numeral card and tries to make an equation, selecting signs as needed, such as $5 + 2 = 4 + 3$ or $2 + 3 = 7 - 2$. If he cannot do so, he discards one numeral card face up, and play goes to the next player, who may draw from the blind deck or take the card that is face up. When one person makes an equation, he is declared the winner and the game begins again with a different dealer. (Multiplication and division signs may be substituted for plus and minus or all four used.)

❀ 165 ❀ FACT RELAY

Purpose To provide practice in addition and subtraction facts.
Level 1 to 4.
Number of players 4 or more.
Materials needed Duplicated papers containing as many rows of arithmetic facts as there are players on each team. Select facts on which children need practice: addition, subtraction, multiplication, or division.
Procedure Divide the group into two or more teams, with team members sitting near each other. Distribute the papers face down to the first players on each team. At a signal the first players turn the papers over and write answers to the first row of facts. Then they pass papers to the second players, who do the second row; and so on. Check the answers and record the number correct on each paper. The team finishing first gets an additional 10 points, second place gets 8 points, third place gets 6 points, and fourth place gets 4 points.

❀ 166 ❀ ERASER HAT

Level 2 to 4.
Number of players 2 or 3 teams.
Materials needed A chalkboard eraser for each team. Chalk and chalkboards.
Procedure Divide the group or class into two or three teams. The first player on each team goes to the front chalkboard and places an eraser on his head. The teacher or leader calls a number, at which the players hurry to the back of the room, being careful not to lose the erasers balanced on their heads. A second number is called as pupils near the rear of the room. If there is a rear chalkboard, the children write down both numerals; otherwise, they touch the back wall and hurry to the starting place, where they write the sum of or difference between the two numbers. The first player with the correct

answer gets a point. When all the players have had a turn, the scores are calculated by counting points.

❀ 167 ❀ BEAT THE TIME

Purpose   To practice addition and subtraction.
Level   2 to 4.
Number of players   1 or more.
Materials needed   Duplicated papers showing the numerals 1 to 100 in random order and with space for writing another numeral under each one shown. A sandglass or kitchen timer. A set of cards for each player on which directions are given, such as: Add 4, Add 7, or Subtract 6.
Procedure   Distribute the papers. The leader (or one player) draws a card and shows it to all players. He then sets the timer for a given number of minutes, 3 to 10, and places it in full view. All players proceed to follow the direction given, e.g., add four to each number named on their papers, to see how many computations can be done in the time allotted. If the same direction is followed for a second attempt, pupils can work against their own scores.

❀ 168 ❀ TRAVELING

Purpose   To provide oral practice with addition and subtraction facts.
Level   1 to 4.
Number of players   4 or more.
Materials needed   Flash cards of combinations that need practice. (Game can be played orally with no materials.)
Procedure   One child is selected to "take a trip." He begins by standing beside a seated child. Both look at a flash card and try to be first to give the answer. If the seated player wins, he exchanges place with the traveler and stands beside the next player. The object is to see who can travel the farthest.

❀ 169 ❀ NICKNAME

Purpose   To provide mental practice with addition and subtraction facts.
Level   2 to 4.
Number of players   2 to 10.
Materials needed   None.

Procedure One child who is "It" selects a number from 1 to 20 and tells it to the group; he also thinks of a fact for which his number is the answer. Other players try to guess what "nickname" the child had in mind; they may give addition or subtraction facts; e.g., "Is it seven plus four?" The child who correctly guesses the nickname then becomes "It," and play proceeds. This game may be adapted to work with multiplication and division facts.

 170

To provide practice in solving equations, fill in the missing numerals.

To provide practice in adding and subtracting, an array such as the following can be duplicated with signs or numerals omitted; or, as on the right, with some of each left out.

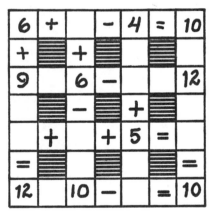

Making a number puzzle such as this one can be quite a trial-and-error chore. Try setting a pattern to be followed in both directions. In the above, note that the answers to the horizontal series are 10, 12, and 12; the answers to the vertical series are 12, 10, and 12 (the first two are reversed). Now note that the totals are reached by using the same combinations except that the commutative principle has been applied to the first pair in corresponding series. Horizontal: $6 + 8 - 4 = 10$, $9 + 6 - 3 = 12$, $3 + 4 + 5 = 12$; vertical: $6 + 9 - 3 = 12$, $8 + 6 - 4 = 10$, $4 + 3 + 5 = 12$.

❀ 171 ❀

Cross number puzzles may be used to provide practice in adding and subtracting:

Across

1. 9 + 9   5. 9 + 7
3. 7 − 6   7. 8 − 2
4. 7 + 8   8. 5 + 7

Down

1. 8 − 7   5. 8 + 8
2. 13 − 5   6. 12 − 6
3. 9 + 6   8. 3 − 2
4. 1 + 0   9. 5 − 3

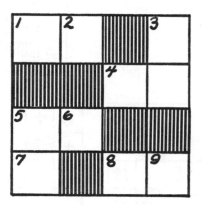

Solution:

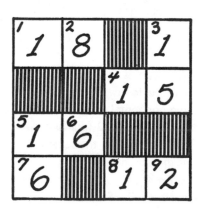

Across

a. 5 + 6	j. 9 + 5
c. 6 + 7	k. 7 + 9
e. 17 − 9	l. 12 − 5
f. 7 + 8	m. 8 + 6
g. 9 − 8	n. 7 − 6
h. 5 + 9	o. 6 + 6
i. 8 + 8	p. 5 + 8

Down

a. 9 + 9	i. 7 + 9
b. 8 − 7	j. 9 + 8
c. 8 + 7	k. 7 + 7
d. 12 − 9	m. 5 + 7
f. 7 + 7	n. 8 + 5
g. 9 + 7	o. 6 − 5
h. 6 + 8	p. 9 − 8

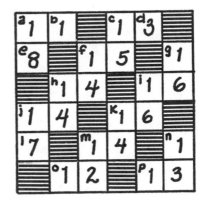

Across

a. 126 − 84	n. 2111 − 757
c. 1144 − 381	o. 494 − 489
f. 680 − 299	p. 165 − 76
h. 230 − 192	q. 523 −127
i. 475 − 467	s. 1034 − 248
j. 1915 − 146	u. 1040 − 986
m. 1095 − 253	

Down

a. 987 − 549	l. 7375 − 1132
b. 490 − 462	n. 407 − 209
c. 873 − 866	o. 915 − 351
d. 767 − 128	p. 468 − 381
e. 529 − 491	r. 118 − 23
g. 7977 − 6794	t. 55 − 49
k. 1614 −869	

4
MULTIPLICATION AND DIVISION OF WHOLE NUMBERS

RATIONALE

Multiple embodiment of concepts and processes is important to children as they learn the fundamental operations and basic facts associated with addition and subtraction, and it is absolutely essential for the operations of multiplication and division. This is true for several reasons. First, each of the latter operations is related to one of the former in a unique way. That is, the operations of addition and subtraction form one functional model for interpreting multiplication and division, respectively. Second, and equally important, multiplication and division may be generated by models that are related to, but not intuitively dependent upon, addition and subtraction. In fact, these independent models focus almost exclusively upon the inverse relationships of multiplication and division. Finally, the defined operation of division has always appeared more difficult for children. Whether this is so

119

because of the "unnatural" form of the algorithm or because division requires reliance on each of the other operations has never been fully determined. It is clear that open experiences and directed practice which transcend the usual workbook and textbook activities are essential for student competence in multiplication and division.

From experience with the activities in this chapter the children will learn:

1. An effective model for rationalizing the operation of multiplication.
2. Automatic response for the products associated with basic multiplication facts.
3. To recognize the associative and commutative properties for multiplication and distributive properties for multiplication over addition and multiplication over subtraction.
4. To use algorithms which make computation with multiplication efficient.
5. To recognize division as a process that seeks a missing factor.
6. To use subtraction for solving a quantitative division situation.
7. Automatic response for the basic division facts.
8. Algorithms that make division computation more efficient.
9. To correctly employ all four basic operations within a single mathematical expression.
10. Competence and confidence in mental calculations.

MULTIPLICATION

 172 ✿

The following activities are appropriate for establishing arrays as a model for the operation of multiplication.[1]

A   Provide individual children with sufficient counters (bottle caps, beans, plastic disks or chips, checkers, rods, etc.) so that they may be arranged on their desks in small row—column arrangements. The materials of each child should be uniform, i.e., all beans, all rods, all bottle caps, etc. The arrangements that children form should be spaced uniformly, and the teacher may use a hundreds board for demonstration purposes. Have children count the number of objects in their arrangement (array). An accompanying discussion should generate appropriate multiplication sentences.

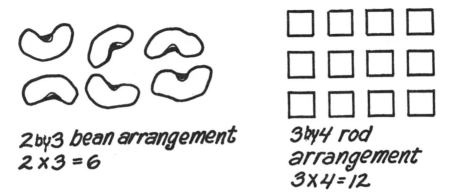

2 by 3 bean arrangement
2 x 3 = 6

3 by 4 rod
arrangement
3 X 4 = 12

B Provide the children with sufficient counters, as above. Give each child several pieces of cord. Ask the children to make any rectangular display they choose on their desktop. Then have the children place the cord so as to make either a row or column arrangement, as shown. The results of the action should be observed, recorded, and discussed.

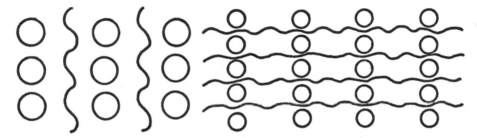

C To develop understanding of the operation of multiplication as well as the basic facts, provide pupils with large graph paper, preferably with 2-cm or 3-cm squares. From these the children may cut rectangles to illustrate multiplication facts. The rectangles may then be arranged in table sequence. Cubes of wood or other material may be used in a similar manner.
Variation Have the children fold (crease) paper (graph or scrap) for the same result.

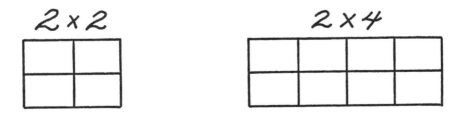

2 x 2   *2 x 4*

D The instructional objectives of the previous activities may also be accomplished by simply providing the children with felt-tip pens (occasionally there will be a need for two colors) and blank sheets of paper. Proceed with activities as described in (A) and (B). Encourage children to make unique arrays.

E Working with a 10 X 10 piece of graph paper or a blank hundreds board and some oaktag cover sheets, help the children rationalize the operation of multiplication. Learn about the properties of multiplication and drill on the basic facts.

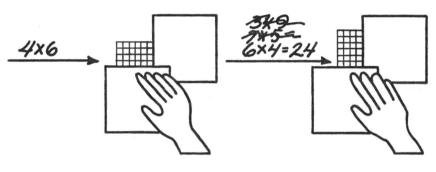

❋ **173** ❋

The commutative nature of multiplication can be discovered by students equipped with geoboards and rubber bands. Ask individual students to place

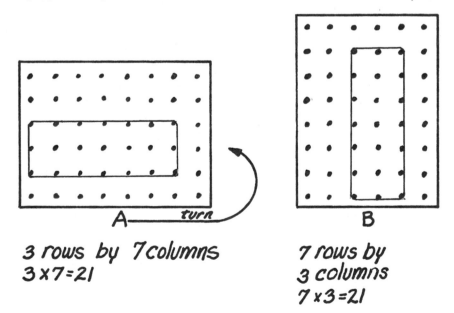

3 rows by 7 columns
3 x 7 = 21

7 rows by
3 columns
7 x 3 = 21

rubber bands around one of the following arrangements of nails or pegs (4 rows by 6 columns, 3 rows by 7 columns, 5 rows by 2 columns, and so forth). Each student may count and record the number of boundary pegs and the pegs (nails) inside the rubber band as well as the multiplication sentence, i.e., $4 \times 6 = 24$, $7 \times 3 = 21$, $5 \times 2 = 10$, and so forth.

Next have the children rotate their geoboards one quarter-turn and record the "new" number of pegs enclosed as well as the new multiplication sentence. The discussion should focus on the number of nails in each case and observable changes.

Variation Provide colored rubber bands for superimposing loops around uniform sets of pegs within the array boundary. For example, each column of three in Activity 172(A) will provide a useful reinforcement of the multiplication model as repeated addition.

❀ 174 ❀ FEED THE DUCKS

Purpose   To provide practice on multiplication facts.
Level   2 to 6.
Number of players   2 to 6.
Materials needed   A chart or chalkboard drawing of ducks and slices of bread, on each of which is shown a combination pupils must practice.
Procedure   Players take turns seeing if they can "feed the ducks" by giving answers to all combinations.
Variation   Make a chart with pictures of ducks with combinations written on them. Make a slot or pocket under each in which cards in the shape of

slices of bread can be placed. On the cards should be numerals that name answers to the combinations. These cards may be in a bag and may be "fed to the ducks" when the children can correctly match cards to ducks.

❀ 175 ❀ MULTO SCOTCH

Level   3 to 5.
Number of players   2 or more.
Materials needed   A nine-square (as illustrated) or hopscotch pattern on a

floor or playground. (May be made on a large sheet of wrapping paper taped to the floor.)

4	7	3
9	6	8
2	0	5

Procedure Divide the group into two or more teams. The first player on one team starts at one corner of the pattern and hops on each square; as he does so, he gives the product of the number of the square and a pre-selected number, e.g., 5. If he makes no mistakes, he scores a point. Then the first player of the next team begins at a different corner and proceeds as did the first player. When all players have had a turn, scores are totaled; the team with the largest total score is the winner. The game may be varied by choosing a different multiplier after each of the four corners has been used for starting.

Variations Sums or differences may be asked for instead of products. For indoor use, players might work their way through the pattern drawn on the chalkboard by pointing to each square instead of hopping.

❁ 176 ❁ FACTOR-PAIR RELAY

Purpose To provide practice with multiplication as ordered pairs of factors.
Level Variable, 3 to 6.
Number of players 2 teams.
Materials needed Chalk and chalkboard.
Procedure Small teams of not more than 5 players per team line up in a row. The teacher writes a numeral on the chalkboard, e.g., 24. The team begins writing factor pairs of this number on the board. After each player takes a turn recording one factor pair, he passes the chalk to a teammate and hurries to the end of the line. A factor pair scores a point for the team, and when no more pairs can be thought of, play is ended and the winning team determined. Any pair may appear on a team's list only once and only on that team's list. Wrong pairs or repeated pairs do not count. It adds to the excitement if the children cannot consult during the game. A sample round for 24 might look like this:

TEAM X	TEAM Y
(4, 7) (error)	(4, 6)
(1, 24)	(2, 12)
(8, 3)	(3, 8)
(2, 12)	(6, 4)
Total 2	Total 4 (the winner)

❁ 177 ❁ PRODUCT RACE

Purpose   To provide practice with multiplication.
Level   3 to 5.
Number of players   2 or more.
Materials needed   Chalk and chalkboard.
Procedure   Divide the group into two teams. Write numerals from 0 to 9 in random order at two places on the chalkboard:

> 3 8 0 2 9 1 6 4 7 5   3 8 0 2 9 1 6 4 7 5

When all are ready, the leader calls, "Multiply by seven," and the first player from each team goes to the chalkboard and records the products of 7 and each number indicated at his place. The first player finished with all answers correct scores a point for his team. A different multiplier should be selected for the next pair of players. At the end of play, the team with the most points is the winner.

❁ 178 ❁ CIRCLE ONCE

Purpose   To provide practice on multiplication facts.
Level   2 to 4.
Number of players   2 to 4.
Materials needed   A circular playing board with numerals 0 through 9 arranged at random around the circle. Two or three sets of cards with the numerals 0 through 9 on them, one numeral per card.
Procedure   Place the board at the center of the table. Shuffle the cards and place them face down on the table. The players take turns drawing a card and attempting to give the sum or product of the number drawn and each number named on the board. If correctly done, the card may be kept. If incorrectly done, the card must be placed under the deck. At the end of play, the winner is the one with the most cards.

❀ 179 ❀ NAME THE SQUARES

Purpose   To provide practice on multiplication facts.
Level   3 to 4.
Number of players   1 to 6.
Materials needed   A pointer. A chalkboard table as shown in the accompanying illustration.

X	1	2	3	4	5	6	7	8	9
6									
7									
8									

Procedure   The teacher or leader points at random to a square; the first player gives the product of the number named above and the one named at the left. Each player gets three turns. The leader controls the time allowed for an answer by silently counting to five. A point is given each player for each correct answer within the time limit.

Name the Squares may be played without competition for points. The leader may simply point to squares at random and players take turns giving the products.

❀ 180 ❀ FACTOR CLAP

Purpose   To provide practice in multiplying.
Level   3 to 5.
Number of players   2 or more.
Materials needed   None.
Procedure   Players alternate counting. When one comes to a predetermined number, such as 6, he claps his hand instead of saying the word. Thereafter, clapping must be done on every number of which 6 is a factor, or if the numeral has a 6 in it, e.g., 16.

181 ❀

Prepare a key code such as the one shown and some message to be decoded. This is an excellent activity for focusing on more difficult facts. Have children prepare some original key, codes, and design messages for their friends to solve.

CODE:

A	B	C	D	E	F	G	H	I	J	K	L	m
18	25	49	6	40	14	9	30	35	22	4	8	21

N	O	P	Q	R	S	T	U	V	W	X	Y	Z
27	10	24	28	12	63	15	36	32	16	42	20	46

A SECRET MESSAGE FOR YOU TO DECODE:

4 x4	5 x8	2 x4	7 x7	5 x2	3 x7	8 x5	5 x3	2 x5	4 x3	5 x2	5 x2	7 x3	5 x4
16													
W													

5 x3	5 x6	5 x7	9 x7	7 x5	7 x9	3 x5	6 x5	5 x8	7 x2	2 x5	6 x6	2 x6	3 x5	5 x6

3 x3	2 x6	3 x6	3 x2	5 x8

(The message: Welcome to Room Y, or 20. This is the fourth grade.)

❀ 182 ❀ PASS RED

Purpose   To provide practice on multiplication facts.
Level   2 to 4.
Number of players   2 to 6.
Materials needed   Red and blue cards of playing-card size. On the red ones record arithmetic facts and reverses: e.g., on one red card show 2 X 7; on another show 7 X 2. On the blue cards show the answers. A deck is 52 cards.
Procedure   Shuffle cards and deal seven cards to each player. Place the remaining cards face down at the center of the table. The first player draws a card from the deck and looks for a set of cards having a fact, its reverse, and the answer. If he has such a set, he lays it on the table before him; if not, he discards a card face down and play proceeds to the next player. The winner is the first player to lay down all his cards or the one who has the most "books" at the end of the play period.

❀ 183 ❀ COMBINATION RUMMY

Purpose   To provide practice on multiplication facts.
Level   2 to 6.
Number of players   2 to 6.
Materials needed   A deck of 51 cards with a numeral on each which is either a factor or a product (for addition, use addends and sums); 34 cards should be used for factors and 17 should name products. Select those on which pupils need the most practice.
Procedure   Shuffle the cards. Each player draws a card; the one with the largest number becomes the dealer. Deal five cards to each player. Place the balance of the deck face down on the table; turn up one card. The player to the left of the dealer begins. He may draw either the card face up on the table or one from the "blind" deck. He looks to see if he has two factors and a product, e.g., 3, 6, and 18. If so, he has a "book" which he may lay on the table before him. When he has played, he discards one card face up. Subsequent players may take all of the cards in the discard pile, only the top card from the discard pile, or one from the blind deck. When a player has no more cards, he says, "Rummy!" The score is obtained by totaling the cards in "books" held and subtracting the total of the cards still unplayed.

✽ 184 ✽ GUZINTA

Purpose   To provide practice in multiplying and adding.
Level   3 to 6.
Number of players   2 to 6.
Materials needed   A "board" (tagboard or similar) squared off into 10 X 10, or 100, squares. A collection of 100 small square cards, each with a one-digit numeral on it; there should be 10 cards for each of the 10 numerals 0 to 9.
Procedure   The game is played in a manner similar to Scrabble, the object here being to form sums that are multiples of 3. Each player is given five cards to start with, and the remaining cards should be placed face down. After each play the number of cards held by the player is brought back up to five by taking the necessary number of cards from the stack. Play proceeds in turn among the pupils with a play consisting of putting down one, two, or three cards onto the board in a line horizontally or vertically so that the sum of the numbers on the cards is a multiple of 3. A student may use one or more cards already on the board to form his line of two or more cards. Should more than one line of two or more cards be formed at a play (e.g., a line horizontally as well as a line vertically), then every such line of cards must have a sum that is a multiple of 3. A line may not exceed five cards in length. A play may be made in only one direction (horizontally or vertically) and the cards making up a line must be on adjacent squares. Each play scores the total of all lines made in that play. Here is an example of a sequence of plays:

First play:	3, 1, 8
Score:	12
Second play:	5, ③, 4
Score:	12
Third play:	⑧, 6, 4
Score:	18
Fourth play:	④, 5, ⑥
Score:	21
Fifth play:	9, 2, 1
Score	42

(A circle around a numeral means that it was already on the board.)

The game may be continued as long as there are cards to draw from or until a predesignated total score is reached. Each student should keep his own score; but appoint one pupil to serve as master scorekeeper, to keep a running total of everyone's score and to check the score on each play. Vary by using multiples other than 3

❀ 185 ❀ SOLITAIRE THRÉE

Purpose   To provide practice in multiplying and adding.
Level   3 to 6.
Number of players   1.
Materials needed   Same as for Guzinta (Activity 184).
Procedure   This is a solitaire version of the Guzinta game, in which the student is in competition with himself, seeking to improve his score on successive games. The player uses only a 5 X 5 section of the playing board. He draws 25 cards at random from the set of 100 cards and tries to play as many cards as possible into the 25 squares, observing the rules of the Guzinta game. Basically, that means that every time two or more cards are adjacent to one another on the board either in a horizontal or vertical line they must add up to a multiple of 3 or other designated number. His score becomes the number of cards played. On successive games he tries to improve on previous scores. A perfect game would occur, of course, if all 25 cards were played.
Variation   Require that sums be a multiple of any designated number.

❀ 186 ❀ MULTIFACTO

Purpose   To provide practice in recognizing multiples and factors.
Level   5 to 8.
Number of players   2 to 6.
Materials needed   A playing board marked off into 8 X 8 squares, each square being about 5 cm by 5 cm. A set of 100 cards, each about 4 cm by 4 cm and having on its face a numeral at each of its four sides. The numbers named on the top and left sides are 12 or greater and, in general, composite numbers, while the right and bottom-side numerals are single-digit numerals.

Procedure Deal each player 10 cards. The players play in turn. A play consists of placing one card on the board adjacent to at least one previously played card (except that the first play may be made anywhere on the board), so that the numbers on any two adjoining edges are such that one is a multiple of the other (and hence one a factor of the other). The object is to win by being the first to play out all cards. When a player is unable to make a play with the cards he has, he draws from the reserve card stack (those not dealt out originally) until he can make a play. If no cards remain in the reserve stack and a play cannot be made, the turn is passed.

For a play that joins one edge, a score of 1 is earned. When two sets of edges are joined on one play, the player scores 3. When three sets of edges are joined (a play into an open "hole"), the score is 10. The game ends when a player is out of cards; he receives a bonus of 20 on his score. Each player then must subtract from his accumulated score 2 points for each card he holds. The player with the highest score is declared the winner.

The diagram shows a sequence of play (the circled letter on each card indicates the order in which the cards are played).

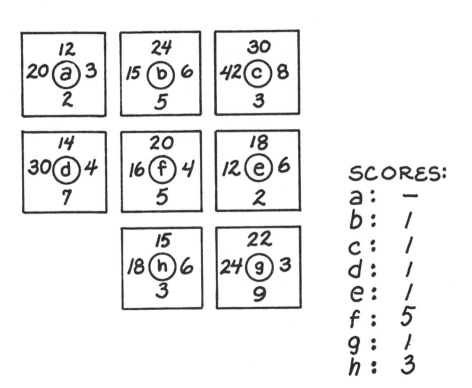

SCORES:

a: —
b: 1
c: 1
d: 1
e: 1
f: 5
g: 1
h: 3

❀ 187 ❀ FINGER MULTIPLYING

Now we describe (and enjoy) a historical multiplying procedure in which one needs to know only the facts to 5. Once common, finger multiplying is fun to use if one forgets the products of pairs of numbers between 5 and 10, e.g., 6 X 8. Think: eight is three more than five and six is one more than five. Bend down three fingers on the left hand and one finger on the right hand. The number of fingers bent down (3 + 1) tells the tens' digit (4). The product of the number of unbent fingers on each hand (2 X 4) tells the ones' digit (8). 6 X 8 = 48.

Variations First give numbers to the fingers of each hand beginning with "6" for the thumb. To multiply 8 X 7, place the "8" finger of one hand against the "7" finger of the other hand, holding the hands with thumbs up. Bend down the fingers below the "8" and "7" fingers. Count the pointed fingers (the two touching and those above them) for the tens' digit and multiply the number of bent fingers on one hand by the number of bent fingers on the other hand for the ones' digit.

$$3 + 2 = 5$$
$$2 \times 3 = 6$$
$$8 \times 7 = 56$$

Another variety of hand multiplication is used to show the multiplication facts involving 9 as one factor. In this instance, number the fingers of both hands from one to ten (one to five on one hand and six to ten on the other). To show 3 X 9, bend down finger "3"; the two fingers on one side of the bent finger tell the tens and those on the other (seven) tell the ones.

❀ 188 ❀ MULTIPLYING BY FACTORS

Any set of its factors may be substituted for a multiplier, e.g., 27 X 342:

342	342	342	Factors of
X27	X3	X3	27 are
2394	1026	1026	(3, 9) and
684	X9	X3	(3, 3, 3)
9234	9234	3078	
		X3	
		9234	

36 X 481:

481	481	481	Factors of
X36	X2	X4	36 are
2886	962	1924	(2, 2, 3, 3) and
1443	X 2	X9	(4, 9)
17316	1924	17316	
	X3		
	5772		
	X3		
	17316		

❀ 189 ❀   MULTIPLYING WITHOUT CARRYING

Care must be taken to ensure that place value is kept intact. Pupils who have difficulty in this matter may find it helpful to use the straight edge of a card or ruler. Note that in the multiplication example, the addition to achieve the final product is not done from the "front end," although it could be.

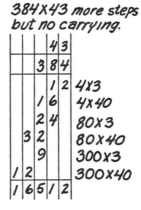

384 X 43 more steps but no carrying.

❀ 190 ❀

For children who get bored with arithmetic but who still need practice on basic facts, suggest some "front-end" adding and multiplying. Have a care for place value!

ADDITION	MULTIPLICATION
4682	967
7349	X87
+6754	72
17	48
16	56
17	63
15	42
18785	49
	84129

❀ 191 ❀ HALVING AND DOUBLING

Next we shall enjoy an unusual method of multiplying in which one only needs to know how to multiply and to divide by 2 (also to provide some historical appreciation of arithmetic).
A multiplication procedure employing halving and doubling was once common. To multiply 42 × 294, write the two numerals and successively divide 42 by 2 and multiply 294 by 2 (ignore the remainders). Cross out both numerals if the halved one is even (42, 10, 2). Add the remaining numbers on the right; 42 × 294 = 12,348.

```
4 2 - - - - - 2 9 4
2 1         5 8 8
1 0 - - - 1 1 7 6
5           2 3 5 2
2 - - - - 4 7 0 4
1           9 4 0 8
          1 2,3 4 8
```

Written in base 2, 42 would be 101010 or (1 × 32) + (0 × 16) + (1 × 8) + (0 × 4) + (1 × 2) + (0 × 1). Note that 32 × 294 = 9408; 8 × 294 = 2352; 2 × 294 = 588; and that 32 + 8 + 2 = 42. The crossed-out numerals were the ones in which zeros occurred in the rewriting of 42. The doubling was done on an abacus as 294 + 294 = 588; 588 + 588 = 1176; and so on.

Variation You can also double both columns, beginning on the left with 1 and proceeding until there are numbers in the left column that will total exactly 42. Note that in doubling beginning with 1 we will write the binary numeration place values.

```
1 - - - - - 2 9 4
2           5 8 8
4 - - - 1 1 7 6
8           2 3 5 2
1 6 - - - 4 7 0 4
3 2         9 4 0 7
4 2       1 2,3 4 8
```

❀ 192 ❀ LATTICE MULTIPLYING

In 1478 a book printed in Treviso, Italy, showed a method of multiplying called the Gelosia (lattice) method. Here is how one would use this method to multiply 486 by 739. Note that in the upper right square is the product of 6 and 7, 42. To its left is the product of 8 and 7, 56. Others are

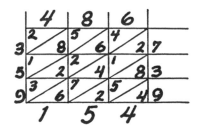

done in a similar manner. The final product is found by adding numbers along diagonals starting with the lower right square, "carrying" to the next diagonal where necessary. The product of 486 and 739 is 359,154.

❀ 193 ❀

Late in the sixteenth century a Scotchman, John Napier, improved on the lattice method by inventing strips (originally made of bone or ivory and therefore known as Napier's bones) on which products from a multiplication array were shown. The strips could be arranged so as to make multiplication easy. The array shown indicates how Napier marked his strips. On the right are shown three strips (and multipliers) for multiplying 374 by some other number, let us say 89. The products of 9 and 3, 7, and 4 are 27, 63, and 36, as shown to the left of 9 as $\frac{2}{7}\frac{6}{3}\frac{3}{6}$. Adding diagonally as in the lattice method, we have that $9 \times 374 = 3366$. Similarly, 8×374 is seen to be 2992.

These products should be recorded as

$$\begin{array}{r} 3366 \\ 2992 \\ \hline 33286 \end{array}$$

and added in the usual way.

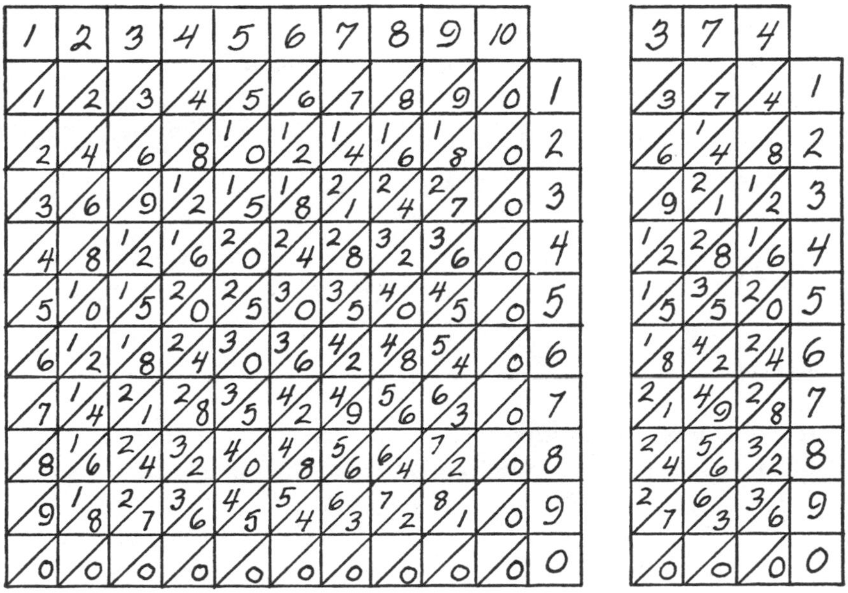

❀ 194 ❀ LIGHTNING OR CROSS MULTIPLICATION

This method also appeared in the arithmetic printed in Treviso, Italy, in 1478; it was one of three methods shown. It also was one of the eight methods appearing in Pacioli's *Suma,* 1494. Earlier (c. 900) it appeared in an Arab manuscript with the vacant places filled by zeros. Computation is done mentally. The diagrams show how it works with the example 39 X 43.

Step 1
9 X 3 = 27
Write 7 ones and carry the 2 tens.

$$\begin{array}{r} 4\,3 \\ \underline{X\,3\,9}_1 \\ 7 \end{array}$$

Step 2
9 X 4 tens = 36 tens
3 tens X 3 = 9 tens
36 + 9 + 2 = 47 tens
Write the 7 in the tens' place and carry the 4 hundreds.

$$\begin{array}{r} 4\,3 \\ \underline{X\,3\,9} \\ 7\,7 \end{array}$$

Step 3
3 tens X 4 tens = 12 hundreds
12 + 4 = 16 hundreds
Write the 16 hundreds.

$$\begin{array}{r} 4\,3 \\ \underline{X\,3\,9} \\ 7\,7 \end{array}$$

Multiply as usual for a check.

For the problem 482 X 36, the diagram would look like this:

begin here

Can you write out the steps for this one?

❀ 195 ❀

To multiply two numbers equidistant from a multiple of 10, such as 52 and 48, where each is two removed from 50, square 50, and subtract the square of 2 (difference between 50 and both 48 and 52):

$$52 \times 48 = (50 \times 50) - (2 \times 2) = 2500 - 4 = 2496$$
$$17 \times 23 = (20 \times 20) - (3 \times 3) = 400 - 9 = 391$$

❀ 196 ❀ SUPPLEMENTS AND MULTIPLICATION

A supplement of a number is the difference between it and the next lower power of 10; e.g., the supplement of 103 is 3 because 103 − 100 = 3. The supplement of 17 is 7 because 17 − 10 = 7. To multiply two numbers, each of which is a little more than the same power of 10, e.g., 103 and 106, add the supplement of one number to the other (103 + 6 or 106 + 3), then annex the product of the supplements (prefix a zero if the product is less than 10): 103 + 6 = 109_ and 3 × 6 = 18; therefore, the product is 10,918. Similarly, 16 × 17: 16 + 7 = 23_ and 6 × 7 = 42; therefore, the product is 272 (note that the 3 of 23 and the 4 of 42 are added).

$$103 \times 106 = (100 + 3) \times (100 + 6) = 10,000 + 600 + 300 + 18$$
$$= 10,000 + 900 + 18 = 10,900 + 18 = 10,918$$

Notice that 900 is the sum of the two supplements multiplied by 100; therefore, the 109 equals either original number plus the other supplement: 103 + 6 = 106 + 3. The 18 is the product of the supplements.

❀ 197 ❀ COMPLEMENTS AND MULTIPLICATION

A complement of a number is the difference between it and the next higher power of 10, e.g., the complement of 8 is 2 because 10 − 8 = 2. The complement of 45 is 55 because 100 − 45 = 55. To multiply two numbers each of which is a little less than the same power of 10, e.g., 93 and 95, subtract the complement of one from the other (such as 95 − 7 or 93 − 5), then annex the product of the complements (prefix a zero if the product is less than 10): 95 − 7 = 88_ and 7 × 5 = 35; therefore, the product is 8835. Similarly, 992 × 994: 994 − 8 = 986_ and 8 × 6 = 48; therefore, the product is 986,048.

$$93 \times 95 = (100 - 7) \times (100 - 5) = 10,000 - 500 - 700 + 35$$
$$= 10,000 - 1200 + 35 = (10,000 - 1200) + 35 = 8800 + 35 = 8835$$

The 88 equals 100 minus the two complements, which is the same as either number minus the other number's complement.

❀ 198 ❀ MULTIPLYING BY 11

To multiply a two-digit number by 11, add the digits of the number being multiplied, and rewrite with their sum as the middle digit, e.g., 27 × 11 = 297. If the sum of the digits is itself a two-digit number, write the ones'-place digit between the two digits and carry the tens digit to the hundreds' place; e.g., 86 × 11 = 946 because 8 + 6 = 14. Note that 27 × 11 = 27 × (10 + 1) = 270 + 27 = 297 and that when multiplying a number by 10, each digit is moved one place to the left, as in the algorithm.

```
     27
    X11
     27
    270
    297
```

❀ 199 ❀

When boys and girls have achieved all the learning that can reasonably be wrung from checking computations by various manipulations of base 10 numeration, they may find both pleasure and utility in checking by using a finite number system: A widely used check on the accuracy of computations, especially multiplication, known as "casting out nines," may be of interest and value to children. This procedure consists of noting the excess of nines (the remainder when a number is divided by 9) in the factors, multiplying these, and comparing with the excess of nines in the product, as in this example:

```
  386  (nines excess = 8)       8
  X68  (nines excess = 5)      X5
 3088                          40   excess of
 2316                               nines = 4
26248  (nines excess = 4) 4 ←────────┘
```

Since the excess of nines in the product of 8 and 5 is the same as the excess of nines in the computed product, the computation is considered to be correct. Note that this check will not detect an error that is due to a reversal of digits. For example, if the product of the computation shown above had been written as 62248, the excess of nines still would have been four.

A quick way to find the excess of nines is to add the digits of a number, "dropping off" the nines as one proceeds, e.g., in the case of 386, 8 + 3 = 11; dropping 9 from 11 leaves 2; 2 + 6 = 8; the excess of nines in 386 is 8.

Another way to find the excess of nines quickly is to add the digits of a number and if their sum is greater than nine, add the digits of that sum: e.g., for 386, 3 + 8 + 6 = 17 and 1 + 7 = 8; the excess of nines in 386 is eight. Although it is possible to check a computation by casting out any number, one should note that a large number, such as 9 or 11, is more likely to indicate accuracy than is a small number, such as 2 or 3. For example, when casting out twos, the excess of an even number is always zero and of an odd number is always 1; this provides some check on the ones place but no more. Since our numeration system has a base of 10, a checking number near 10 is most likely to detect errors. To understand the principle of casting out nines, one needs to understand some aspects of modular arithmetic. Note that the excess of nines in 10 is 1; also that 10 is one in mod 9. The digits of a numeral tell us how many there are of each power of 10, and since each 10 would be recorded as one in mod 9, adding the digits of a numeral tells us how the number would be recorded in mod 9. Multiplying the mod 9 numbers of a computation and comparing with the answer (also in mod 9) provides a check on a computation done in base-10 numeration representing numbers from an infinite set.

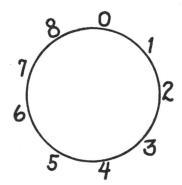

10 base 10 = 1 mod 9
20 base 10 = 2 mod 9
100 base 10 = 1 mod 9
400 base 10 = 4 mod 9
23 base 10 = 5 mod 9
92 base 10 = 2 mod 9

❀ 200 ❀ CRYPTOBETS

Now we shall discuss a way in which to challenge fast learners and give them practice in using alternative approaches to problem solving if one approach does not lead to a solution. Replace the letters with digits.

Solution:

(a)

ABC	125
×ABC	×125
DBC	625
BCE	250
ABC	125
ACDBC	15625

(b)
```
      DEF                        105
     XDEF                       X105
      FGF                        525
     DEFE                       1050
    DDEGF                      11025
```

(c)   Now try this:
```
            8                          80809
   XXX/XXXXXXX              124/10020316
         XXX                         992
        XXXX                        1003
         XXX                         992
        XXXX                        1116
        XXXX                        1116
```

Any digit may replace a given X. The procedure for solving is mainly one of trial and error.

DIVISION

❀ **201** ❀

An amusing rhyme can be used to help children enjoy division.

GUZINTA

In school I have an awful time to learn 'rithmetic.
That's one thing that gets my goat, and teacher thinks I'm sick;
She makes me learn guzinta, 'though I declare I won't;
There are some things I can understand—but other things I don't.

One guzinta two, and two guzinta four.
Ma guzinta Pa's pants when he guzinta snore!
Pa guzinta trouble and then guzinta fight,
But Ma comes out with a rolling pin 'n Pa guzouta sight!

Guzinta should be easy work for kids as smart as me.
Why, I know in an automobile the gear guzinta three;
And when I've finished my lessons, you'll have a chance to see
How much bread and jam guzinta a hungry kid like me!

One guzinta three, and three guzinta six.
Oh, shux, nuthin' ever stuck to me, not even six times six.
Sister Sue guzinta her room and makes herself look swell.
But what guzinta fixin' her, I promised not to tell!

Two guzinta four, and four guzinta eight.
Pa guzinta his club and stays our awful late;
Ma guzinta hysterics and then guzinta bed,
But what guzinta Pa, I can't get through my head!

Five guzinta ten, and ten guzinta twenty.
And when I don't know my 'rithmetic, teacher guzinta plenty!
But five what guzinta ten what, I never can see—
'N that's why no 'rithmetic ever guzinta me!

Author Unknown

 202 ❀

Identifying equal subgroups provides a foundation for rationalizing the operation of division while providing practice on basic division facts. Duplicate a supply of sheets such as the one shown. The illustrative sheet has been divided into four sections, each containing various arrangements of 12 objects. Starting with the upper left section, children are asked to circle as many groups of two as they can find and write the corresponding division fact they have demonstrated. The procedure would be repeated for each section, using

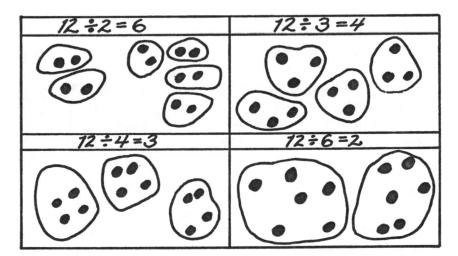

3, 4, and 6, respectively. This activity can be adjusted to paper that has been creased or to actual objects for children to group using short pieces of string to encircle subgroups. An overhead projector can be used by the teacher to guide the activity.

❀ 203 ❀

Array arrangements as used in multiplication are effective as a model for
the operation of division. Provide children with a given (known) number of
counters. Ask them to arrange the
counters in rows and count the number of objects in each row. An arrangement for 15 might look as shown.
Squared paper and felt-tip pens will

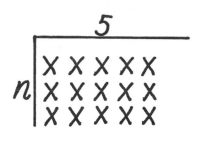

serve equally well. Have the children color sets of 5 squares each inside a
predetermined boundary, e.g., 25 squares. In the case of uneven division,
attention should be directed to the number of colored squares, and the
number of uncolored squares within the boundary suggests the numerous
ways to record and read the results.

❀ 204 ❀

To help children understand the relations of division to sets and subsets as
well as to repeated subtraction, duplicate papers on which dots show the
dividend. Pupils are to circle sets, each
with as many dots as the divisor indicates. Counting the sets, they get the
quotient and the remainder.

    Preparation for understanding divi-
sion by partition may be facilitated by
showing equal subsets of a given number on a strip of paper which is then
folded in alternating directions to
separate the subsets. The illustration
on p. 142 shows that there are two
subsets of four each in a set of 8; three
subsets in a set of 12; ten subsets in a
set of 40.

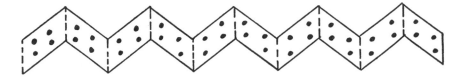

❀ 205 ❀

Charts can be made to illustrate difficult concepts and remain displayed for reference purposes. Using concrete materials, manipulation and demonstrations should precede the introduction of a chart. The boxes illustrate the two division situations—measurement and partition.[2]

> **DIVISION BY MEASUREMENT**
>
> How many marbles at 3 cents each can Peter buy for 12 pennies?
>
> $$\frac{4}{3\overline{)12}}$$
>
> We know how many in each set, but we do not know how many sets.

> **DIVISION BY PARTITION**
>
> How many of Lee's 12 pennies can he give to each of his three friends if he gives each the same number?
>
> $$\frac{4}{3\overline{)12}}$$
>
> We know how many sets, but we do not know how many in each set.

❀ 206 ❀ THROW A FACT

Purpose   To provide practice on division facts.
Level   1 to 6.

Number of players 1 or more.

Materials needed A design on the floor (or on paper taped to the floor), consisting of nine squares, in each of which is a numeral appropriate to the practice needed. Numbered bean bags.

Procedure Players stand behind a mark and throw a bean bag onto the squares. If practice is needed in division facts, each player must give the quotient of his two numbers—the one named on the bean bag and the one named in the square on which the bag lands. The standing distance from the squares should be regulated according to the developmental levels of players. Note that fractional numbers may be substituted for whole numbers. Sums or differences may be given instead of quotients. Scores may be kept if desired. If there is only one player, he may try to beat his best score. The number of throws per player should be agreed on before the game begins.

9	14	16
10	15	12
8	32	18

❀ 207 ❀ COMBINATION TENNIS

Purpose To provide practice on division facts.

Level 2 to 4.

Number of players 2 to 10.

Materials needed Two sets of flash cards.

Procedure Divide the group into two teams, to be stationed at either side of a table on which are two sets of flash cards. Select an umpire and a scorekeeper (one may be the teacher). The first player on team A holds up a flash card. If the first player on team B gives the correct answer without hesitation (as judged by the umpire), A's serve is broken and he must go to the back of his row and his adversary becomes server. Should the first B player hesitate too long or give the wrong answer, he must go to the end of

his line; the A player has made a point and continues to serve. At the end of play, the team with most points is declared to be the winner.

❀ 208 ❀

Problem-solving patterns provide excellent motivation during study of division facts for mastery. Reproduction of simple patterns for individual completion by children is effective. Have the children make some original "box" patterns for their friends to solve. Complete the chart.

5		6			8	4			2
5	7		9	8			5	6	
25	56	36	63	32	48	20	45	24	16

What's the rule? Supply the missing number.

8	64
	24
	48
	32
	56

9	81
	36
	27
	72
	45

7	49
	42
	63
	35
	49

❀ 209 ❀ GOLD BRICK

Purpose To provide practice on division facts and different names for numbers.
Level 3 to 5.
Number of players 2 to 6.
Materials needed A deck of 52 cards consisting of five sets of division facts, nine each with quotients of 5, 6, 7, 8, and 9, e.g., $10 \div 2$, $1X = 5$, $25 \div 5$, $3X = 15$, $20 \div 4$, $\frac{30}{6}$, $45 \div 9$, $8X = 40$, $50 \div 10$. Seven cards have "gold bricks" on them. (If you do not have gold paint, a rectangle can be drawn and "gold" written on it.)
Procedure Shuffle the cards and deal five to each player. Place the balance of the cards face down in the center of the table. The first player chooses one

of his cards, gives the answer, and lays it down at the center of the table. The next player must place a card with the same quotient on the first card played. If he cannot, he must play a gold brick and change the suit. Should a player be unable either to follow suit or to play a gold brick, he must draw from the center deck until he can play. The first person to dispose of all his cards is the winner.

❀ 210 ❀ FACTORS RACE

Purpose   To provide practice in selecting factors.
Level   4 to 6.
Number of players   2 or more.
Materials needed   None.
Procedure   Form two teams, which line up facing the teacher or leader. The teacher or leader calls a number and the first players on each team compete to see who can first name a pair of factors of that number (excluding 1); e.g., if 28 is called, seven and four are possible factors; if 18 is called, either two and nine or three and six are acceptable. The leader may attempt to trick the players by calling a prime number, such as 29. A point is scored by the team from which the first correct pair of factors is heard. The team with the most points at the end of play is the winner.

❀ 211 ❀

Provide small groups of children with 40 cm by 40 cm pieces of butcher paper. Have them write all the division facts they can about a number, e.g., 8. **Variation** Have them write any closed number fact naming 8 (i.e., 16 − 8, 2 X 4, 3 X 4 − 4, and so forth).

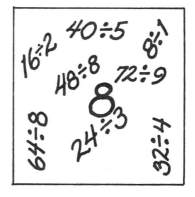

❀ 212 ❀ FACTOR FISH

Purpose   To provide mental practice in seeking the missing factor.
Level   Intermediate.

Number of players   2 to 4.

Materials needed   20 product cards (81, 72, 64, 63, 54, 49, 48, 45, 42, 40, 36, 35, 32, 28, 27, 24, 21, 36) and 40 factor cards (8 nines, 8 eights, 8 sevens, 6 sixes, 3 fives, 4 fours, and 3 threes).

Procedure   A card is drawn from the product deck to determine the dealer and the first player; high card wins. The product cards are shuffled and placed in the center of a table with one turned up. Each player is dealt seven factor cards and the remainder form a "draw" pile. Players make "books" with two factors and the turned-up product card. Books are made by having factor pairs in the hand or asking for and receiving a card from a fellow player. A player may make only one book per turn, and as long as the factor cards last, players replace any cards used, keeping seven in the hand at all times. The play moves when a player cannot make a book, and when no players can make a book, a new product card is turned. The winner is the player with the most books after all cards are turned.

✿ 213 ✿ ALL THE WAY HOME

Purpose   To provide practice in division with remainders.

Level   Variable.

Number of players   2 or 3.

Materials needed   A playing "board." An identifying marker for each player. 24 small cards containing the numerals 2 through 9 (three of each). Some scratch paper.

31	59	48	53	21
36	42	26	54	62
15	56	home	17	14
74	19	44	20	47
89	24	113	49	start 16

Procedure Markers are placed at "start" for each player and play is begun when the first player turns over the top card of the deck of 24 cards. He determines a quotient by dividing the number under his marker by the number named on the card. When there is a remainder, he moves his marker as many spaces as the remainder indicates. If there is no remainder, his marker does not move. Play proceeds in turn. Players check each other's work. The first player to reach home wins.

❈ 214 ❈

A small teacher-directed group may practice activities such as the following for short, concentrated periods of time. Such sessions are more attractive for children of similar abilities when they are in a "gentle" competitive setting. Provide each student with duplicated pages containing a division ladder similar to the one in the example. Distribute the pages to the students face down. On signal all students begin work (up the ladder). When finished, they signal the teacher, who records their time. When all are finished, the correct quotients are given. For incorrect responses, the students add 10 seconds to their time. The student with the shortest time wins.

Variation Have several duplicated sheets of division examples of varying difficulty. Let the students keep charts of their times and repeat the same "ladder" several days hence, thereby showing each child his degree of improvement.

```
777 ÷ 21
462 ÷ 8
375 ÷ 25
97 ÷ 3
86 ÷ 12
23 ÷ 2
99 ÷ 11
36 ÷ 9
16 ÷ 4
10 ÷ 5
```

❈ 215 ❈ TIC-TAC MULTIPLY

Purpose To provide practice in dividing and recognizing prime and composite numbers.

Level 3 to 5.

Number of players 2.

Materials needed Paper and pencil or chalkboard and chalk.

Procedure Players take turns filling places with composite numbers. The first one to find three in a row, horizontally, vertically, or diagonally, which are divisible by a single prime number, wins.

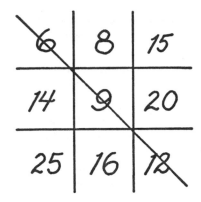

❊ 216 ❊ TWO WORDS

Purpose To provide practice in recognizing perfect squares and multiples of selected numbers.

Level 3 to 6.

Number of players 2 or more.

Materials needed None.

Procedure Select two words, mathematical or otherwise, e.g., "plus" and "minus." Designate some ordering of the pupils in the room, and decide on some number, preferably in the range 3 through 9. Suppose, for example, that seven is chosen. The players, in turn, are then to say the number names in order. The exceptions are that when the number is a perfect square (1, 4, 9, 16, etc.), the pupil is to say "plus" instead of the number word; and when the number is a multiple of seven (7, 14, 21, etc.), the pupil is to say "minus" instead of the number word. Example: plus (since 1 is a square), two, three, plus (since 4 is a square), five, six, minus, eight, etc. Play proceeds until the first "plus–minus" number is reached, which will be the square of the number chosen (49 in the case of 7). Whenever a mistake is made by a player, the sequence is ended and a new start made with the next pupil. The one who finally completes the sequence with "plus–minus" may be declared the winner.

❊ 217 ❊

There are tests of divisibility to help children deal efficiently with certain kinds of problems (e.g., can 463/9 be changed to lower terms?) and to add some insights regarding number relationships. (Memorizing the rules of divisibility by certain numbers, such as six and eight, may be of doubtful value.) The tests are as follows:

a. A whole number is divisible by 2 if its ones' digit is divisible by 2.

b. A whole number is divisible by 3 if the sum of its digits is divisible by 3.

c. A whole number is divisible by 4 if the number named by its tens' and ones' digits is divisible by 4, or if the ones' digit plus two times the tens' digit is divisible by 4.

d. A whole number is divisible by 5 if its ones' digit is divisible by 5.

e. A whole number is divisible by 6 if it is divisible by 2 and by 3.

f. A whole number is divisible by 8 if the number named by its hundreds', tens', and ones' digits is divisible by 8, or if they are all zero.

g. A number is divisible by 9 if the sum of its digits is divisible by 9.

h. Any number is divisible by the product of two or more of its prime divisors; e.g., a number divisible by both 2 and 3 is also divisible by 2 × 3, or 6. A number divisible by a composite number is also divisible by the prime factors of the latter; e.g., a number divisible by 6 is also divisible by 2 and 3.[3]

❀ 218 ❀ GALLEY METHOD OF DIVIDING

Purpose To provide practice in performing division of numbers, insight regarding the process, and historical appreciation.

The galley method of dividing is an adaption of a Hindu procedure. It was used in Europe from the twelfth to the seventeenth centuries. To divide 10215 by 37, proceed as follows:

1. Write the divisor under the dividend. Determine the first quotient figure by mentally dividing 102 by 37; write 2 to the right:

$$10215$$
$$37 \qquad 2$$

2. 2 × 3 = 6; cross out 3 of 37. 10 − 6 = 4; cross out 10 and write 4 above it. 2 × 7 = 14; cross out 7 of 37; cross out 42 and write 28 (42 − 14 = 28):

$$
\begin{array}{l}
2 \\
\cancel{4}8 \\
\cancel{10}\cancel{2}15 \quad 2 \\
\cancel{3}\cancel{7}
\end{array}
$$

3. Rewrite the divisor one place to the right. Determine the second quotient figure by mentally dividing 281 by 37; write 7. 7 × 3 = 21;

cross out 3. 28 − 21 = 7; cross out 28 and write 7. 7 X 7 = 49; cross out
7. 71 − 49 = 22; cross out 71 and write 22:

$$
\begin{matrix}
& 2 & \\
& 2\!\!\!/7 & \\
& 4\!\!\!/8\!\!\!/2 & \quad 27 \\
& 1\!\!\!/0\!\!\!/2\!\!\!/15 & \\
& 3\!\!\!/77 & \\
& 3\!\!\!/ & \\
\end{matrix}
$$

4. Rewrite the divisor one place to the right. Determine the third quotient
   figure by mentally dividing 225 by 37; write 6. 6 X 3 = 18; cross out 3.
   22 − 18 = 4; cross out 22 and write 4. 6 X 7 = 42; cross out 7. 45 − 42
   = 3; cross out 45. The remainder is 3.

$$
\begin{matrix}
& 2\!\!\!/ & \\
& 2\!\!\!/7\!\!\!/4 & \\
& 4\!\!\!/8\!\!\!/2\!\!\!/3 & \quad 276\ r3 \\
& 1\!\!\!/0\!\!\!/2\!\!\!/1\!\!\!/5 & \\
& 3\!\!\!/7\!\!\!/77 & \\
& 3\!\!\!/3\!\!\!/ & \\
\end{matrix}
$$

❊ 219 ❊

Utilizing a shortened form of the division algorithm provides excellent practice for reinforcement of the defined operation of division while providing
the opportunity for mental practice of all the operations necessary to complete division. The process illustrated below is still in use in some South
American countries.

Our Method

$$
\begin{array}{r}
1 \\
24\overline{)432} \\
\end{array}
$$
(a)   Estimate the quotient figure and record.

$$
\begin{array}{r}
1 \\
24\overline{)432} \\
\underline{24} \\
192 \\
\end{array}
$$
(b)   Do the appropriate multiplication (10 X 24),
record the product, subtract, and record
the difference.

$$
\begin{array}{r}
18 \\
24\overline{)432} \\
\underline{24} \\
192 \\
192 \\
\end{array}
$$
(c)   Determine the final quotient figure, complete
the multiplication, and record.

The Short Method

432|24   (a)   Estimate the first quotient figure and set (record) as shown.
   |1

432| 24   (b)   Do the appropriate multiplication (10 X 20) and mentally
192| 1   find the difference between the product and dividend
                through additive subtraction. Record the difference.

432|24   (c)   Determine the second quotient figure and proceed as in (b).
192|18   The division is complete since it was even. In uneven divi-
                sion, the remainder is set as a partial dividend, smaller than
                the divisor.

Such an algorithm may be utilized as a setting for reintroduction to the study of division in grade five or six. Initially, children may simply be presented with an example of the new algorithm to see if they can "figure it out." Subsequently, it may be utilized in computation exercises and "last-year's method" can be used as a check. The teacher-directed discussion should focus on advantages and disadvantages.

❀ 220 ❀

Some children may enjoy demonstrating their ability to divide by 9 by working backward: e.g., 660 ÷ 9. First, determine the remainder through the "casting-out-nines" procedure[4] (6 + 6 + 0 = 12 and 1 + 2 = 3). Subtract the remainder from the dividend. The quotient digit in the units' place must be a number that is a multiple of nine ending in seven: 27, or 3 X 9, is such a number. The quotient digit in the tens' place must be a multiple of nine ending in three: 63, or 7 X 9, is such a number.

Variation A method that works but may be difficult to explain is as follows (see the illustration on p. 153): First determine the remainder by "casting out nines"; 7 + 3 + 2 = 12; 1 + 2 = 3. Write the remainder over the digits'

$$9\overline{)660}$$

$$\begin{array}{r} r3 \\ 9\overline{)660} \\ -3 \\ \hline 657 \end{array}$$

$$\begin{array}{r} 3\ r3 \\ 9\overline{)660} \\ -3 \\ \hline 657 \\ -27 \\ \hline 630 \end{array}$$

$$\begin{array}{r} 73\ r3 \\ 9\overline{)660} \\ -3 \\ \hline 657 \\ -27 \\ \hline 630 \\ \underline{63} \end{array}$$

place of the dividend. Subtract the units' number from the remainder $(3 - 2)$ and write the answer over the tens' place. Subtract the tens' number from the number just recorded $(1 - 3$; if this cannot be done, add 10 to the first: $11 - 3)$ and write the answer over the hundreds' place. Subtract as before $(8 - 7$, but remembering that 1 was borrowed, we have $7 - 7)$.

$$
\begin{array}{ll}
\text{(a)} \quad 9\overline{)732} & \text{(c)} \quad \overset{1\ r3}{9\overline{)732}} \\[2ex]
\text{(b)} \quad \overset{r3}{9\overline{)732}} & \text{(d)} \quad \overset{81\ r3}{9\overline{)732}}
\end{array}
$$

❀ 221 ❀

Mod 11 (excess of 11s) can be used to check computations. The principle is the same as that of casting out nines, but the procedures differ.

A

$$
\begin{array}{r}
247 \\
97\overline{)23959} \\
194 \\
\hline
455 \\
388 \\
\hline
679 \\
679 \\
\hline
\end{array}
$$

247 ÷ 11 leaves remainder of 5
97 ÷ 11 leaves remainder of 9
23959 ÷ 11 leaves remainder of 1
45 ÷ 11 leaves remainder of 1
(the "excesses" match)

$$
\begin{array}{r}
5 \\
\times 9 \\
\hline
45 \\
\end{array}
$$

B   Method of even places from odd places[5]:

$$
\begin{array}{r}
247 \\
97\overline{)23959} \\
194 \\
\hline
455 \\
388 \\
\hline
679 \\
679 \\
\hline
\end{array}
$$

4 from $(2 + 7) = 5$
9 from $(7 + 11) = 9$
$(3 + 5)$ from $(2 + 9 + 9) = 12$
1 from $2 = 1$
4 from $5 = 1$
(the "excesses" match)

$$
\begin{array}{r}
5 \\
\times 9 \\
\hline
45 \\
\end{array}
$$

The reason that method (a) works is that multiples of 11, less than 100, repeat a digit, as 22, 99, 66, etc. Therefore, to cast out elevens from a number, such as 23, one may shorten the procedure of subtracting $23 - 22$ to

$$
\begin{array}{r}
247 \\
-22 \\
\hline
27 \\
-22 \\
\hline
5 \\
\end{array}
$$

3 − 2. In the case of 247, one first subtracts 22 from 24 to remove the elevens, then 22 from 27; this is done quickly by first subtracting 4 − 2 = 2, then 7 − 2 = 5. Method (b) simply accumulates (by adding) numbers so as to permit the subtraction to be done in one operation; the procedure makes use of the principle of compensation. (In 247, instead of 4 − 2 followed by 7 − 2, one adds 2 + 7 and then subtracts 4.)

MULTIPLE OPERATIONS

X	1	2	3	4	5
1					
2					
3					
4					
5					

❀ 222 ❀

To help children rationalize a multiplication or division matrix, mark the inside of a box lid as illustrated. Cut squares of paper slightly smaller than the squares on the outline.

On each, arrange dots to show sets equivalent in number to the products required:

Keep in an envelope. On other squares mark numerals:

Store in another envelope.
    Children are to place the small papers on the appropriate outline squares, first using the sets of dots and then numerals.

❀ 223 ❀ PRODUCT BINGO

Purpose   To provide practice on multiplication facts and division facts.
Level   2 to 4.
Number of players   2 or more.

4	12	16
15	14	9
21	25	24

$8 \times 2 = \square$

$12 \div 3 = \square$

Materials needed   A bingo-type card for each player. Make cards and arrange products in a different order on each card, selecting nine of the following: 4, 6, 8, 9, 10, 12, 14, 15, 16, 18, 20, 21, 24, 25. On smaller cards write multiplication facts (or the corresponding division facts) on one side and products on the other. Twelve beans or other markers for each player.

Procedure   Select a caller to read equations. Other players place beans on products found on their cards. The first player to get three beans in a row (horizontal, vertical, or diagonal) calls "Bingo!" The caller reads answers as a check. Write the name of the winner on the chalkboard with colored chalk.

 224 ❀

Cross number puzzles are an excellent format for combined practice in multiplication and division.

A   To provide practice on multiplication and division facts

Across

a. 4 X 4	j. 6 X 9
b. 5 X 9	k. 8 X 5
e. 24 ÷ 6	l. 30 ÷ 5
f. 7 X 5	n. 36 ÷ 9
g. 25 ÷ 5	o. 9 X 6
h. 7 X 8	p. 6 X 8
i. 4 X 6	

Down

a. 2 X 7	i. 5 X 4
b. 42 ÷ 7	j. 8 X 7
c. 9 X 5	k. 6 X 8
d. 35 ÷ 7	m. 6 X 4
f. 6 X 6	n. 8 X 6
g. 6 X 9	o. 40 ÷ 8
h. 9 X 6	p. 32 ÷ 8

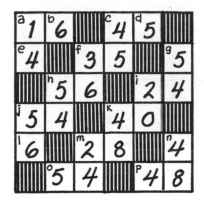

B To provide varied practice

Across

1. 774 ÷ 86
2. 271 X 6
6. 61 X 3
8. 117 ÷ 88
9. 204 ÷ 34
10. 809 X 3

12. 427 X 5
14. 84 ÷ 12
15. 396 ÷ 4
16. 76 X 7
18. 2459 X 3
20. 144 ÷ 16

Down

1. Nine hundred sixteen thousand, two hundred ninety-seven
2. 49 X 27
3. 42 ÷ 7
4. 37 X 6
5. Six hundred ninety-seven thousand, seven hundred twenty-nine
7. 232 ÷ 29
11. 651 X 7
13. 57 + 136

17. 1467 ÷ 489
19. 4704 ÷ 672

C To provide practice in multiplying and dividing

Across

a. 37 X 23
d. 29 X 19
g. 42 X 18
h. 45 X 17

i. 1728 ÷ 27
k. 1710 ÷ 18
l. 1081 ÷ 47
n. 336 ÷ 48

o. 3157 ÷ 77
p. 1440 ÷ 15
q. 1587 ÷ 23
s. 17 X 12

u. 72 X 8
x. 20 X 20
y. 16 X 18

Down

a. 1914 ÷ 22
b. 2090 ÷ 38
c. 83 X 2
d. 2337 ÷ 41
e. 78 X 73
f. 47 X 33
j. 28 X 17
l. 86 X 34
m. 75 X 48
r. 34 X 28
t. 1040 ÷ 26
v. 1794 ÷ 23
w. 3876 ÷ 57

a 8 b 5 c 1 d 5 e 5 f 1
g 7 5 6 h 7 6 5
i 6 j 4 k 9 5
l 2 m 3 n 7 o 4 1
p 9 6 q 6 r 9
s 2 0 t 4 u 5 v 7 w 6
x 4 0 0 y 2 8 8

❀ 225 ❀ FILL THE SQUARES

Purpose To provide practice on mixed facts.
Level 2 to 4.
Number of players 1 or more.
Materials needed Paper and pencil.
Procedure Each player folds his paper until creases show 16 squares (grids may be duplicated beforehand). As directed by the teacher, each child writes numerals across the top and at the left side. When all are ready, the teacher calls out the operation to be performed. The players fill in the squares and the first who has them all right is the winner, or the names of all who have correct papers may be written with colored chalk on the chalkboard. With a stopwatch or a sand clock, a child can record his own time and compete against himself each time he repeats a set.

+	3	4	5	6
3				
4				
5				
6				

−	8	9	10	11
3				
4				
5				
6				

×	2	4	6	8
2				
4				
6				
8				

÷	6	12	16	18
2				
3				
4				
6				

❀ 226 ❀

To provide practice in the four fundamental operations, choose someone's telephone number and write it on the chalkboard. Suggest that pupils find how many fives, or multiples of five (or any other number less than 10), can

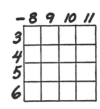

be found by adding and/or subtracting the numbers indicated by the digits. **Example** The phone number 642-3726 could be analyzed as $2 + 3$, $7 - 2$, $6 + 4$, $(7 + 6) - 3$, etc. For more advanced pupils, permit the inclusion of multiplication and division: $(3 \times 7) - 6$, $(4 \times 7) + 2$, $6/2 + 2$, etc.

❀ 227 ❀ CHECKOUT

Purpose To provide mixed practice on facts.
Level   3 to 5.
Number of players   1 or more.
Materials needed   A figure for each player such as the one shown. Use fewer and smaller numbers for beginners.

Procedure   Players fill in blanks. Then add the numbers named in each row and in each column. The sum of the totals for the rows and the sum of the totals for the columns should be equal. Generally, the pleasure of this game comes from finding the key total rather than from competition.

	x4	+6	-9	total
4	16	22	13	51
6	24	30	21	75
5	20	26	17	63
3	12	18	9	39
7	28	34	23	85
total	100	130	83	313

Variation   Alter the numbers and the order of operations.

❀ 228 ❀ EQUATION LINE-UP

Purpose   To provide practice in arithmetic facts and in relations between numbers.
Level   2 to 4.
Number of players   10 or more.
Materials needed   Two sets of numeral cards, 0 to 9, for each player. One each of cards with such operation, relation, and variable signs as required for the practice desired:

$$+, -, \times, \div, >, <, =, \square$$

Procedure   Choose five children to come to the front of the room to hold up cards to form an open sentence, e.g., $4 + \square = 9$. The pupils at their seats hold up the answers from their numeral cards. After five equations have been shown, select five other children to come to the front of the room.

❀ 229 ❀ TRICHOTOMY OF RELATIONS

Purpose   To provide practice on the components of the trichotomy of relations.

Level   2 to 4.

Number of players   1 or more.

Materials needed   Duplicated papers containing many and varied number patterns, depending on the proficiency of the players, for example:

$(3 \times 1) + 1$	$(2 \times 4) + 3$	$(2 \times 2) \times 2$
$(2 \times 3) + 2$	$(3 \times 2) + 3$	$(3 \times 2) \times 1$
$(4 \times 1) + 3$	$(4 \times 2) + 1$	$(4 \times 1) \times 2$
$(5 \times 2) + 2$	$(2 \times 5) + 3$	$(5 + 3) + 2$

A strip of colored paper with the word "Trichotomy" written on it; some rods or other checking device.

Procedure   Distribute the materials to the players. Indicate that at a signal they are to write after each pattern the correct relation sign ($<$, $=$, or $>$) between it and the numeral selected by the leader; e.g., if 7 is the numeral shown, write <7 after $(3 \times 1) + 1$. Record the names as the players finish. The one who has the largest number correct in the least amount of time is the winner and gets to wear the Trichotomy crown. Rods may be used as an aid for those who need it or to check if a disagreement arises.

❀ 230 ❀ SECRET OPERATIONS

Purpose   To provide practice in work with equations, and in mental arithmetic—keeping in mind one operation while experimenting with a second.

Level   2 to 4.

Number of players   2 or more.

Materials needed   Duplicate on papers a number of equations involving two or more operations with the operation signs omitted: e.g., $(7 \circ 4) \circ 5 = 8$ for $(7 - 4) + 5 = 8$; $(9 \circ 2) \circ 8 = 10$ for $(9 \times 2) - 8 = 10$.

Procedure   At a signal players try to "break the code" by inserting correct signs. As each finishes, he stands. Record names in order of completion. Check to see if each is correct. Indicate first, second, and third places after disqualifying those with errors.

❀ **231** ❀

To provide practice in solving equations, duplicate a series of equations that are related such that a given geometric figure represents the same number wherever it is found. Different shapes represent different numbers. The pupil must solve equations in sequence. Example:

$$\square + 5 = 9$$
$$(2 \times \square) + (3 \times \triangle) = 17$$
$$(\triangle + \square) - (\triangle - 2) = 6$$
$$(\square \times \triangle) - (\triangle + \square) = (\triangle \times \triangle) - (\triangle + 1)$$

❀ **232** ❀ **EQUATION SCRABBLE**

Purpose   To provide practice in multiplication and addition and in their inverses.
Level   4 to 6.
Number of players   2 to 6.
Materials needed   A scrabble board or cardboard marked off in squares. 120 small squares of cardboard each with a numeral (0 to 9) or an operation symbol $(+, -, \times, \div)$. (Each player gets one = sign.)
Procedure   Place cardboard squares face down at the center of the playing board. Each player draws one square; the one who draws the card showing the numeral nearest to 1 will begin play. Replace the squares. Each player in turn then draws 10 squares and tries to make an equation, e.g., $2 \times 3 = 6$. If he cannot, he may exchange one of his pieces for one from center supply. The next player proceeds in the same manner. Play ends when one player has used all his squares or when each has had a specified number of turns. Scoring is as follows: Each number in an equation has its face value plus 10 points for an addition equation, 20 for subtraction, 30 for multiplication, and 40 for division.

❀ **233** ❀

A "machine" to show the relation of ordered pairs to basic operations can be made of heavy cardboard with a pointer to indicate the symbol for one of the operations. Ordered pairs may be "fed into the machine" orally or a

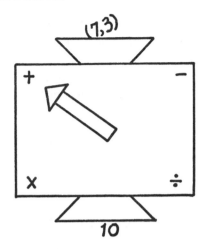

set of cards may be made for the purpose. Children respond, orally or in writing, with the number that "will come out of the machine."

❀ 234 ❀

For practice on fundamentals, duplicate a drawing of a grid filled in with one-digit numerals and with operation signs. Vary the size of the grid and operations according to the ability of the pupils. Children enjoy this different form in which to practice operations.

9	-3	x5	-2	÷7	=
1	+9	x3	+6	÷9	=
8	÷7	x2	-9	÷3	=
2	x8	+4	÷5		
7					

❀ 235 ❀

Oral (mental) practice with combined whole-number operations is interesting and challenging for students. Simply say (or a student may say) "We are going to play follow the leader. See if you can follow me."

A Begin with 14. Add 7. Subtract 5. Add 8. Add 20. Complete by subtracting 6. What is the result? (38)

B Begin with 40. Subtract 7. Subtract 6. Take one half of that number. Add 2. Now double the result. What is your answer? (31)

C Start with $\frac{1}{3}$ of 15. Multiply by 7. Add 7. Subtract 6. Divide by 4. Double that amount. Add 14. Find $\frac{1}{4}$ of that sum. (8)

D Varying exercises such as those given above according to the interest and ability of the group will make this activity adaptable.

❀ 236 ❀ DO YOU MATCH ME?

Purpose   To provide practice on multiplication and division facts, and on the use of parentheses and brackets in the mathematical expression.
Level   2 to 5.
Number of players   6 or more (or 1 or 2—see the variation below).
Materials needed   A set of cards, each containing a numerical expression for some number and each number being named by three different cards. Three cards naming five might be:

$$[12 \div (2+2)] + 2 \qquad (2 \times 2) + (2 \div 2) \qquad (3 \times 7) - (4 \times 4)$$

Procedure   Distribute the cards to the class, one card to each pupil. Should there be one or two pupils over a multiple of 3, designate them as referee(s) for that game. Next game's referees may be chosen from the winning group of the previous game.

At a signal the pupils are to move around the room examining other pupils' cards until each finds the other two students having cards naming the same number as his own card. As each group of three gets so assembled, it should report to the referee for checking of cards and then go to some designated place in the room. The first group to finish and have cards checked is declared the winner of that game. The cards can then be collected, shuffled, and redistributed for another game. After several games the pupil who has been a member of the most winning groups may be designated the individual winner.

Variation   One or two children can play this game by grouping cards that name the same number and then giving these to the teacher for checking.

❀ 237 ❀ OPERATION SUCCESSFUL!

The digit is alive and well. Have the children name each of the digits 1 through 9 using any one or more of the four basic operations to combine exactly four 3s. Example: $2 = (3 \div 3) + (3 \div 3)$ or $8 = (33 \div 3) - 3$. Can you form the same digit but in different ways?

Variation Try with four 4s, etc. Some possible solutions:

$1 = (4 \div 4) \times (4 \div 4)$ $6 = (4 + 4) \div 4 + 4$

$2 = (4 \div 4) + (4 \div 4)$ $7 = 4 + 4 - (4 \div 4)$

$3 = (4 + 4 + 4) \div 4$ $8 = 4 - 4 + 4 + 4$

$4 = (4 - 4) \times 4 + 4$ $9 = 4 + 4 + (4 \div 4)$

$5 = (4 \times 4 + 4) \div 4$

❀ 238 ❀ HOW MANY PEGS?

Purpose To provide an opportunity for geoboard exploration.

Level Variable.

Number of players Pupils in pairs; whole class.

Materials needed A geoboard and some rubber bands for each pair of students.

Procedure Ask the students how many pegs there are on their geoboard. When they respond 16, 25, or 36 (depending on the geoboard), a response probably obtained by counting, ask them to show their answer with rubber bands. Most children will show 4 rows of pegs by 4 columns of pegs or 4 columns of pegs by 4 rows of pegs, as shown. Now ask the students to use

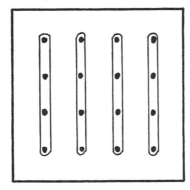 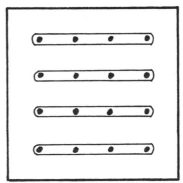

rubber bands to show, without counting, as many ways as they can that there are 16 pegs. They may record the number sentences. Responses will include the six illustrated.

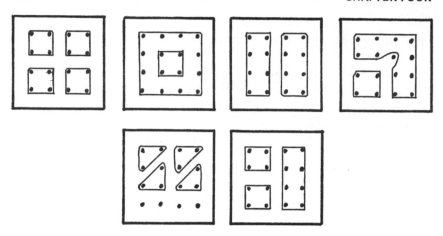

 239

The following are shortcuts only if practiced frequently and long enough to establish proficiency. In this age of computers, learning these procedures for the sake of utility may be a waste of time; but some insight with regard to interesting aspects of numbers and numeration systems may well be outcomes when interested children work their way through the following computation methods.

A The following method helps children use the decimal property of the Hindu–Arabic numeration system to multiply and divide quickly. To multiply by 10, 100, 1000, etc., annex as many zeros to the multiplicand as there are in the multiplier, e.g., 387 X 100 = 38,700. This has the effect of moving the multiplicand as many places to the left of the decimal point as there are tens in the "tens" multiplier.

To divide by a power of 10, move the dividend as many places to the right of the decimal point as there are tens in the divisor; e.g., 387 ÷ 100 = 3.87.

B If one number is divisible by another, the smaller is said to be an aliquot part of the larger, e.g., 25 is an aliquot part of 100 and 25/100 = 1/4. To multiply by 25, one may first multiply by 100 and then divide by 4 (or in reverse order). $25 \times 32 = \frac{32 \times 100}{4} = \frac{3200}{4} = 800$ or $25 \times 32 = (32/4) \times 100 = 8 \times 100 = 800$.

Similarly, 50/100 = 1/2; therefore, 50 × 324 = (324/2) × 100 = 162 × 100 = 16,200.

Also, 125/1000 = 1/8. 125 × 400 = (400/8) × 1000 = 50 × 1000 = 50,000.

$33\frac{1}{3}$ × 339 = (339/3) × 100 = 113 × 100 = 11,300

20 = 1/5 × 100 $16\frac{2}{3}$ = 1/6 × 100

5 = 1/2 × 10 $12\frac{1}{2}$ = 1/3 × 100

To multiply by a two-digit number in which one digit is the aliquot part of the other, as in 24 (2 is an aliquot part of 4), first multiply by the smaller, being careful of place value, and then by the number naming the relationship of the second digit to the first.

24 × 4862:

4862	4862 × 2 = 9724
× 24	4862 × 4 = 9724 × 2 = 19,448
9724	
19448	
116688	

Use the preceding principle in certain division algorithms, e.g., 31,298 − 372. Here the second quotient figure is an aliquot part of the first (4 is an aliquot part of 8). Hence 1488 is 1/2 × 2976.

84	36	
372)31298	461)16596	
2976	1383	6 (in 36) = 2 × 3
1538	2766	2766 = 2 × 1383
1488	2766	
50		

Some divisions can be performed quickly by multiplying, using the principle of aliquot parts. Thus, to divide by 25, multiply by 4 and divide by 100, e.g., 462 ÷ 25 = (462 × 4) ÷ 100 = 1848 ÷ 100 = 18.48. Or, as another example, 235 ÷ $33\frac{1}{3}$ = (235 × 3) ÷ 100 = 705 ÷ 100 = 7.05.

C Changing multipliers. Sometimes it is easier or quicker to multiply by changing the multiplier, e.g., 18 × 55 can be changed to 9 × 110 by halving the 18 and doubling the 55. Similarly, 24 × 121 can be changed quickly to 8 × 363 by taking 1/3 of 24 and multiplying 121 by 3. (The principle of compensation is employed; one factor is multiplied by the same number by which the other factor is divided.)

D To find the sum of a series of numbers the first of which is 1, add the first and last numbers, multiply by the last number, and divide by 2. The sum of the series 1 to 12 is $\dfrac{(1 + 12) \times 12}{2} = \dfrac{13 \times 12}{2} = \dfrac{156}{2} = 78$. Note that by adding the first and last numbers and dividing by 2, one finds the average of the series. The sum of a series is the average times the number of numbers in the series.

E Multiplying by a number almost a power of 10. A number such as 99 is almost 100. When using such a number as a multiplier, first multiply by 100 and then subtract the number, e.g., $99 \times 48 = (100 \times 48) - 48 = 4800 - 48 = 4752$. Similarly, $29 \times 98 = (100 \times 29) - (2 \times 29) = 2900 - 58 = 2842$. Or, if the multiplier is more than 100, add instead of subtract: $103 \times 31 = (100 \times 31) + (3 \times 31) = 3100 + 93 = 3193$.

(Since 9, 99, 999, etc., are each one less than a power of 10, one may first multiply by a power of 10 and then compensate by subtracting one times the number.)

F The average of an odd number of consecutive numbers is the middle number, e.g., the average of 4, 5, 6, 7, and 8 is 6. The average of an even number of consecutive numbers is the average of the two middle numbers; e.g., the average of 4, 5, 6, 7, 8, and 9 is $\dfrac{6 + 7}{2} = \dfrac{13}{2} = 6\frac{1}{2}$.

The average of both kinds of series shown above can be found also by averaging the first and last numbers, e.g., $\dfrac{4 + 8}{2} = \dfrac{12}{2} = 6$ and $\dfrac{4 + 9}{2} = \dfrac{13}{2} = 6\frac{1}{2}$. Note that the rule works with any series in which the interval between numbers is constant; e.g., with 2, 4, 6, 8, and 10, the average is $\dfrac{2 + 10}{2} = \dfrac{12}{2} = 6$; or with 21, 28, 35, and 42, the average is $\dfrac{21 + 42}{2} = \dfrac{63}{2} = 31\frac{1}{2}$.

NOTES

1. The meanings and terms of the operation of multiplication are thoroughly developed in Klaas Kramer, *Teaching Elementary School Mathematics*, 3rd ed. (Boston: Allyn and Bacon, Inc., 1975), pp. 220–225.

2. See C. W. Schminke, N. Maertens, and W. Arnold, *Teaching the Child Mathematics* (Hinsdale, Ill.: The Dryden Press, Inc., 1973), pp. 144–152.

3. For further explanations of divisibility, see a reference such as J. Houston Banks, *Elementary School Mathematics* (Boston: Allyn and Bacon, Inc., 1966), pp. 87–92.

4. One method of "casting out nines" from a multidigit number is to add the numbers represented by the digits; do the same with this sum if it is also a multidigit number, continuing until a single digit is the sum. This will be the number of the remainder if the original number were divided by nine. Example: To cast out nines from 8375, proceed as follows: $8 + 3 + 7 + 5 = 23$; $2 + 3 = 5$. Five is the remainder when 8375 is divided by nine.

5. Successive subtraction commencing with the left-hand digit also works when the principle of "adding eleven" is invoked, e.g., $97 = 9$ from $(7 + 11) = 9$, and so on.

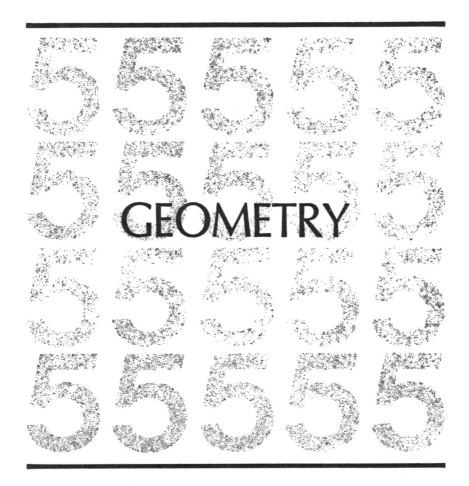

GEOMETRY

RATIONALE

Whatever may be the reason, visits to elementary school classrooms have usually confirmed that geometry receives far less attention than arithmetic in the elementary school mathematics curriculum.[1] This appears to remain true today in spite of the space exploits of the past decade and in spite of a new national awareness relating to distinguishing features and properties in our natural environment. Stated simply, the child's environment is rich with geometric models and the school environment need only capitalize on that by providing an extension of prior experience through activities that sharpen perception while inductively developing ideas about spatial relationships. Initially, we must recognize that pupil involvement and learning are inseparable, the former a necessary condition of the latter. An intuitive study of geometry offers a natural condition to utilize basic dimensions of pupil involvement in the mathematics curriculum. It is, of course, advantageous for

169

teachers and other adults as well as children because the resultant excitement and enthusiasm provides an opportunity for adults to discard old fears and uncertainties associated with classical study of geometry.

Second, in life outside school prior to and all through the elementary school years, children have an abundance of informal experiences containing notions about spatial relationships. They have had experience with simple closed figures, interior and exterior regions, and boundaries as they have played hopscotch or prepared a ring for playing marbles. While making a kite, decorating a Christmas tree, or choosing a site and setting up camp, they have observed symmetry, lines as edges of solids, and points as fixed locations in space. They have consumed milkshakes through straws of identical length, excellent examples of congruent line segments. All children have utilized paper from a packet of uniform size, of which any two sheets provide a most useful model of congruent rectangular regions. The commercially prepared game of Battleship has provided most children a familiarity with a coordinate plane.

Against this background the most important rationale for utilizing the activities of this chapter is neither comforting nor specific. The activities have been arranged in a kind of intuitive, developmental hierarchy from simple, informal experiences through activities that move progressively toward a more highly developed sense of perception and intuitive feeling for spatial relationships. Still the activities defy a strict sorting into disjoint sets of activities designed exclusively for primary children or exclusively for inter-mediate-grade children. Accepting the elusive nature of placement, Activities 240 through 251 are intended principally for the early school years and Activities 252 through 281 for the upper grades. Nonetheless, the thoughtful user will first peruse all activities and initially select those which appear to suit the developmental levels of the children. Once an experience base is developed, grade placement is a less important consideration.

From experience with the activities in this chapter the children will learn:

1. To develop an awareness of shape and form in connection with the environment.
2. To identify basic geometric shapes by characteristics and properties.
3. To recognize, name, and make pictorial representations of common plane figures.
4. To distinguish lines and curves as boundaries for identifying the interior and exterior of plane figures.
5. To use the notion of coincidence, congruent and noncongruent line segments, and space figures.

6. An intuitive understanding of solid shapes by constructing polyhedra and classifying them as they recognize segments as edges of solids.

7. To do geometric constructions with a ruler and compass.

8. To use ordered pairs for locating points in the coordinate plane.

GEOMETRY FOR PRIMARY GRADES

 240

The child's ability to reconstruct spatial notions in any form is dependent upon the development of his perceptual sense about space. Common classroom activities such as the following will contribute to continuous perceptual development.

A To familiarize children with geometric shapes, duplicate papers on which are two rows of shapes, each of two sizes. Pupils may use a crayon to join those that are alike. Follow with instructions such as "color the large triangles blue."

B To stimulate some creativity, outline various shapes of more than one size. Let children cut out shapes and arrange into "pictures" or patterns of their own creation.

C Develop sensitivity to common geometric figures by having children look for familiar shapes about the classroom or on the school grounds. List the items reported.

D To help children learn to follow directions while working with geometry, encourage them to draw large shapes on sheets of paper, or duplicate papers for children; four on a paper may be sufficient. Suggest that pupils "draw a small triangle inside the large circle"; proceed similarly with other shapes.

E For primary-grade children, label some boxes "Triangles," "Squares," "Rectangles," etc. Children may be invited to make or find appropriately shaped objects to be placed in the boxes.

F To interest children in the names of figures, cut a variety of geometric shapes, appropriate to the grade level, from colored paper. Provide labels in one envelope and pins in another so that children may match shape and name. Include one or more shapes not likely to be familiar. If desired, place blank slips in the label envelope for pupils to print the names of shapes and then attach them in the correct places.

G To help children learn about some of the properties of common geometric shapes, provide pupils with strips of stiff paper punched at each end and a handful of paper fasteners. Some of the strips should be the same lengths. Encourage children to make figures of three, four, five, and more sides; then explore the ways in which some shapes can be changed without exchanging strips and what kinds of shapes cannot be changed. Among other things, they should learn that none of the triangles can be changed but that squares and rectangles can be made into parallelograms having no right angles. How could these figures be made rigid?

❀ 241 ❀

Make some oaktag cutouts of geometric shaped regions (triangle, square, rectangle, rhombus, and so forth). Then use a felt-tip pen to design a bulletin board chart display of the same shapes. Place the cutouts in a large paper bag and have the children find (without looking in the bag) a cutout corresponding to one they have designated on the bulletin board.

Variations

1. In small groups give each child a felt-tip pen and have him draw a shape. Collect the shapes and ask each child to pick the shape he drew from the set of drawings of different shapes.
2. From discarded magazines have children cut out examples of various geometric shapes and sort them into piles according to characteristics.
3. Have individual children take an object, for example, a toy truck, and describe or list all the geometric figures they observe within the object.

❀ 242 ❀ DOMINO GEOMETRY

Level Variable
Number of players 2 to 4.
Materials needed A set of geometry dominoes such as the ones in the illustration. Utilizing six different basic geometric shapes, it is necessary to make 28 dominoes.
Procedure All dominoes are placed face down and each player draws 7

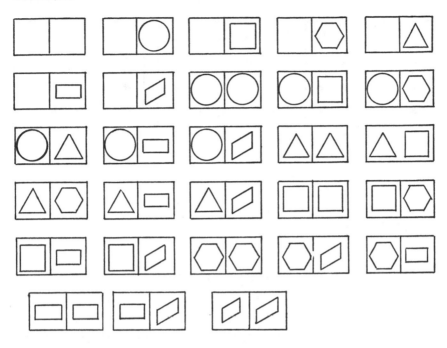

dominoes. A player with a "double" begins play. Each player in turn says the shape names and plays as in a regular domino game. The winner is the player who has played all dominoes, or the player with the smallest number of dominoes when all players must pass.

❀ 243 ❀

Make a geoboard from a piece of plywood or shipboard about 1 or 2 cm thick.[2] Size may vary but a 20-cm or 25-cm square of material is preferable. Make a paper grid of 25 (36 or 49 may be preferable) congruent squares and fit the paper exactly over the board. Drive small finish nails through the paper at each line intersection. Remove the paper and you will have a 6-nail by 6-nail geoboard. If you use a paper grid model of 36 or 49 congruent squares, you will have a 7-nail by 7-nail or 8-nail by 8-nail geoboard. In initial work with geoboards children are given some rubber bands and then should experiment without direction. Let them get the feel of the board while making patterns on their own. The illustration portrays some patterns that will emerge from exploration by young children. After they experiment for 5 or 10 minutes you may direct the free play by providing additional exploratory experiences, such as these.

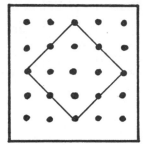 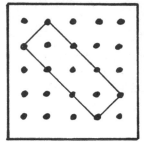 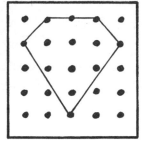

1. Make a stop sign. Make some other road signs.
2. Make the numeral 4. Make some other numerals.
3. Make a four-pointed star.
4. Make some uppercase (capital) letters.
5. Make your name.
6. Make a picture of a chair. A car. A bicycle.
7. Make a picture of your house.

Beyond exploring with geoboards, children need experience with recording results. This may be accomplished simply and inexpensively by providing dot paper. The dot paper can take the form of a sheet of paper completely covered with uniformly spaced dots. For variation it is appropriate to fill other sheets with a series of simulated, 5-peg by 5-peg geoboards.

❀ 244 ❀

The early grades need a simple beginning to topology activities. Suggest that pupils "take their crayons for a walk" by starting at one edge of their papers and making a continuous curve ending at the opposite edge. They may then fill in each region in a contrasting color.

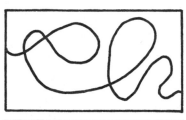

Another kind of simple topological activity can be had by drawing a maze similar to the one illustrated. Children may draw a "short way home" using a red crayon.

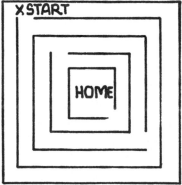

245 ❀

Connecting dots[3] to make triangles in the context of strategy affords an interesting context to reinforce the prerequisite imagery for recognizing geometric shapes. Make some duplicate dot sheets, as shown. This activity may

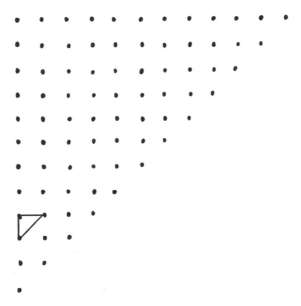

be played in pairs. Each player draws one line. If he completes a triangle, he can draw one more line. On each triangle he completes, he writes his initial. The winner is the player who completes the most triangles.

Variation Make some duplicate dot sheets for the other basic shapes and proceed in the same manner.

❀ 246 ❀

Room decorations designed to help children become familiar with shapes can be had if one cuts, with the children's help, colored cardboard or plastic geometric figures. Have the children suspend these by nylon thread from slim reeds (or plastic drinking straw, or wire) of varying lengths. Each pair should balance but not with the fulcrum at the midpoint. Begin the balancing procedure with the bottom pair. Suspend the mobile from the ceiling.

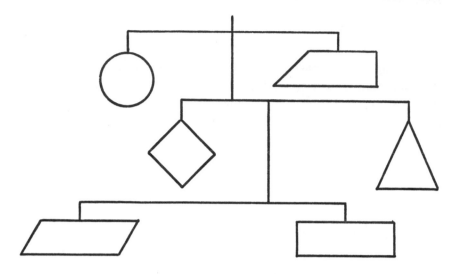

Variations

1. Do the same as above but with the names of the shapes on each item. Effective mobiles can be made using three-dimensional shapes.
2. To keep geometric terms and/or symbols before children, cut (with the pupils' help) colored cardboard or plastic circles, with diagrams and/or symbols of line segments, angles, radii, diameters, chords, etc. Suspend these by nylon thread from slim reeds (or plastic drinking straw, or wire) of different lengths. Each pair should balance but not with the fulcrum at midpoint. Begin the balancing procedure with the bottom pair. Suspend the mobile from the ceiling.

❀ 247 ❀ GEO-GAZE

Level   Variable.
Number of players   Children in pairs.
Materials needed   Some dot paper. A geoboard. Rubber bands. A mirror.
Procedure   Show the children some half-designs on dot paper. Ask each pair to reproduce the half-design on the geoboard as shown. Then ask the children to use a mirror to observe what the completed picture would look like. Complete the design with rubber bands. The children should have noticed that the last design forms the letter A. Now have them use the geoboards and mirrors to discover which letters of the alphabet *cannot* be formed with a geoboard and a mirror.

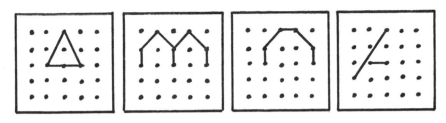

❀ 248 ❀ GEO-CHECK

Level   Variable.
Number of players   2.
Materials needed   A geoboard. Enough rings (in two colors), such as washers, doughnut chips, and the like.
Procedure   Set up the board as in a regular checker game. Play just as you would with checkers, with two exceptions. First, any piece may move forward, sideways, or diagonally any number of spaces when there is an unobstructed path. When the path is blocked, the attacker may remove the opponent's blocking piece and put his piece in its place. Second, there are no kings in this game, thus no backward moves. The object of the game is to capture all or most of the opponent's pieces.

❀ 249 ❀

Geometric figures with variously arranged interior regions present interesting coloring problems. For example, pupils may experiment to see how few colors are required to color each interior region of the following figures without having the same color on any two adjacent areas. Challenge the pupils to draw a figure that requires more than four colors. (None has been found to date.)

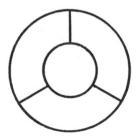 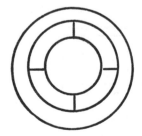 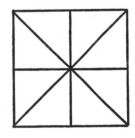

more figures on following page

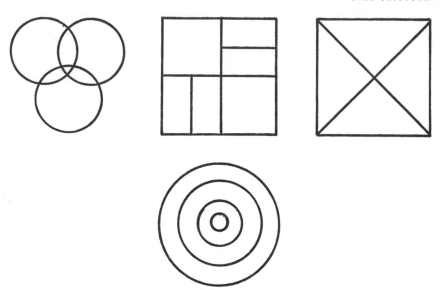

❀ 250 ❀

Congruency, geometric figures of exactly the same size and shape, can be easily explored through informal experiences in sectioning a geoboard. Provide geoboards and rubber bands and have the children explore and record (on dot paper) the different patterns that can be developed by sectioning a geoboard into two congruent parts or four congruent parts. The illustration portrays several patterns that will emerge in each case. There are others.

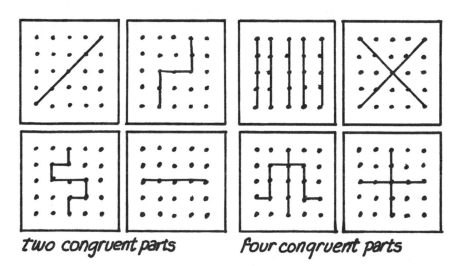

two congruent parts   *four congruent parts*

❀ 251 ❀

To make a tangram divide a large square as shown. Seven pieces form a tangram. The model may be prepared on a ditto master (or by other appropriate processes) for reproduction on a base more substantial than paper. The pieces should be the same color on both sides. Each pupil can store his own tangram in a manila envelope. After a period of initial exploration using "all seven pieces" to form original figures, a variety of teacher-directed activities are possible. Selec-

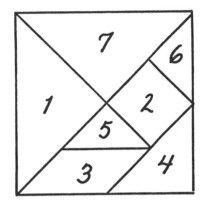

tion of illustrative activities will depend upon the age and experience of the students. Examples follow:

1. Write the names of all the pieces you have. Form a square with all seven pieces. (Provide a pattern.)
2. Make a square from two pieces and write their numerals.
3. Put two △s over one △, so they cover it. Write the ones you used.
4. Place two △s over a square. Which ones did you use?
5. Place a ◻ and two △s over another △. Which ones did you use?
6. Put the pieces back to form the square you started with. (No pattern.)
7. Use the square and two small triangles to make these figures.

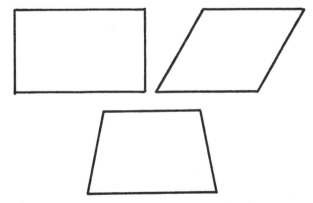

8. Provide the children with a table like the one shown and use it as a continuing challenge. Have them record progress by placing a small drawing of the number pieces used in each instance. Write "Not possible" for the ones that cannot be made. See the filled-in examples.

FIGURE TO BE FORMED

number of pieces	□	△	▭	⬠	▱
1		△ 1			
2		△ 5 6			
3					
4					
5				5 6 / 1 3 7	
6					
7					

GEOMETRY FOR INTERMEDIATE GRADES

❁ 252 ❁

In the intermediate grades, informal geoboard activities may take the form of teacher-directed geoboard problems. Children should record their explorations on dot paper and in some cases (as in 4 below) dot paper should be used before the geoboard.

A Make a square ⌐⌐ with no pegs in the middle (one geoboard square). Make a square enclosing two geoboard squares. Are there any pegs in the middle? Make a square with one peg in the middle ⬚•⬚ . How many geoboard squares were necessary? If you leave 9 pegs in the middle, how many geoboard squares will be used to make a square?

B This triangle  surrounds one geoboard square. Can you find other shapes for triangles that contain a single geoboard square?

C Make the smallest triangle in area that you can. Make the largest triangle that you can. Are you sure they are the smallest and largest? How many geoboard squares in each? Make some triangles for the following numbers of geoboard squares: $2\frac{1}{2}$, 5, and 8.

D If your dot paper has a line segment on it that looks like this,  , make it on your geoboard. Make some longer line segments and shorter ones in both places. Count the pegs and line segments. See how many different-length line segments you can make on your geoboard.

E Use some line segments to make numerals like this:  Make all the numerals that you can. Make all the letters of the alphabet that you can. Use line segments to make some open figures like this:  Count the pegs and segments. Make some closed figures. Make some double closed figures, like this  . Count the pegs and segments.

❊ 253 ❊ SQUARES AND MORE SQUARES

Purpose To provide practice in noting similarities and differences in geometric figures and in visualizing rearrangements.

Level 3 to 6.

Number of players 2.

Materials needed A scissors. A ruler. Paper and pencil.

Procedure Each of two players obtains a square piece of paper by folding the shorter side of a normal sheet onto the longer side and cutting off the excess. He then cuts the square into two odd-shaped pieces, rearranges the two pieces by abutting together two edges of the original square, tracing out the figure on another piece of paper, and cutting out the traced figure. This figure is then given to his opponent, who is challenged to make one straight cut and reassemble the pieces to form a square.

The three examples given in the following diagrams show where cuts would be made to allow rearrangement of pieces into squares. Each player can offer challenges to his opponent until one student gives up or fails to solve the problem in the agreed-upon time.

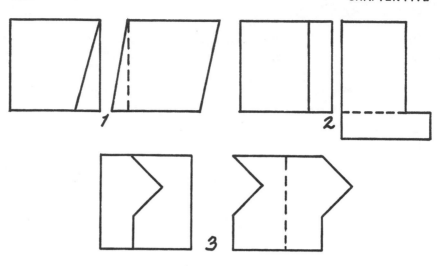

❀ 254 ❀

Puzzles made by cutting squares in various ways challenge boys and girls. Use paper of different colors for each square to distinguish the pieces for each design, in case there is some mixing. Place pieces in envelopes available to pupils who complete their work. Triangles, rectangles, parallelograms, circles, or other shapes also can be cut to make puzzles; draw the desired shape on the envelope.

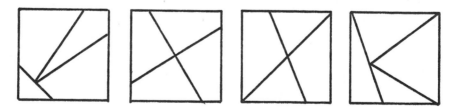

❀ 255 ❀

A task that provides a challenge involves cutting a paper of one shape in such a way that the pieces can be assembled to form another shape. Some

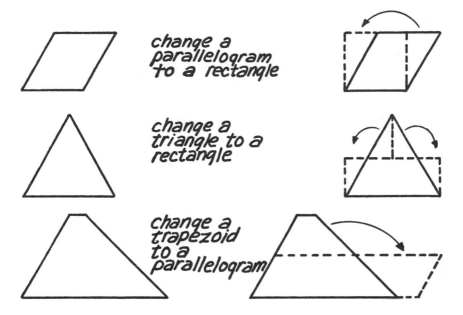

change a
parallelogram
to a rectangle

change a
triangle to a
rectangle

change a
trapezoid
to a
parallelogram

examples are shown. This activity is a good one for developing the notions of
equal area for various shapes.

 256 ❀

To determine the regions in a plane figure, provide each student with a 5 X 5
geoboard and rubber bands.[4] The area surrounded by the outside rubber band
is one region. Place a rubber band at a slight diagonal across the upper region
of the geoboard. The geoboard now has two regions. Now place a second

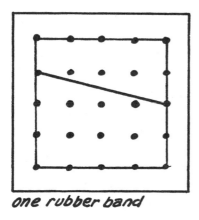

one rubber band

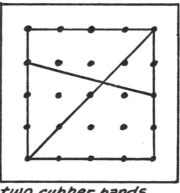

two rubber bands

rubber band on a diagonal from the lower left corner to the upper right corner. How many regions are formed by two rubber bands? Place a third rubber band so that it intersects the first two rubber bands. The three rubber bands now separate the geoboard into seven regions. Place a fourth rubber band on the geoboard so that it intersects each line segment formed by the previous rubber bands. Can you place a fifth rubber band in such a manner that all previous rubber bands are crossed but it does not pass through the intersection of any two other bands? How many regions are formed by the five rubber bands? Have the children construct a table such as this one (and then generalize it):

NUMBER OF LINE SEGMENTS	REGIONS
1	2
2	4
____	____
____	____

Variation   Provide children with a compass, a ruler, and some geometric figures (circle, rectangles). Have them successively divide the interior regions into equal parts.

❀ 257 ❀

How many squares there are within a square poses a challenging question. Students may explore the problem individually or in pairs. Supply some 4 X 4 geoboards and rubber bands of varying color. Begin the exploration by asking students to place rubber bands around as many squares as they can "see" on their geoboard. If most of them identify 9 squares, tell them to keep on looking. Someone will undoubtedly remember to place a rubber band around the 12 pegs (perimeter) of the board. Now 10 squares have been formed. Leave all the rubber bands in place. If pupils cannot go on, ask them to observe the peg dimensions for each of the 9 squares. All will be two pegs by two pegs: ⌐⌐ . Ask the peg dimensions of the tenth square. (The peg dimensions of the perimeter will be 4 X 4.) Now, ask the children to determine whether or not there are any squares within the 4-peg dimension whose peg dimensions are 3 pegs by 3 pegs. How many? (When squares do not overlap completely, they are considered to be different squares.) The total number of squares is 14, or 9 + 1 + 4.

Variation Repeat the activity on a 5 X 5 geoboard, then on a 6 X 6 geoboard. This activity can be extended to rectangles in a square.

❀ 258 ❀ GEO-STRAD

Level Variable.

Number of players 2.

Materials needed A geoboard. Two sets of geoboard circles, each set a different color. (Use loose-leaf reinforcers, painted washers, or doughnut chips.)

Procedure Roll a die to decide who's to be the first player. He gets his choice of colored markers. The first player puts his piece on any geoboard nail. The second player puts his piece on another nail. Keep going. The first player to get four pieces in a line vertically, horizontally, or diagonally is the winner. If all pieces are played with no one winning, collect the pieces and start again.

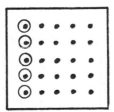 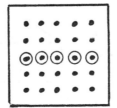 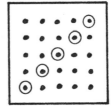

❀ 259 ❀ NAME THE FIGURE

Purpose To provide practice in attaching the most descriptive names to shapes.

Level 3 to 6.

Number of players 2.

Materials needed Two sets of 15 or more geometric figures and one with corresponding names. (Suggestions: square, triangle, circle, rectangle, isosceles triangle, scalene triangle, obtuse angle triangle, acute angle triangle, quadrilateral, pentagon, hexagon, octagon, prism, cone, sphere, pyramid, cylinder.)

Procedure Shuffle the sets separately. Place cards with drawings face down on the table. Deal five vocabulary cards to each player. The first player turns

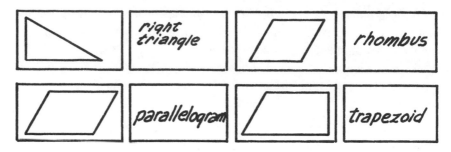

up one figure card. If he has the corresponding name card, he may lay both cards before him. If he cannot match cards, he must draw one card. If he still cannot make a match, the figure card is placed face down at the bottom of the deck from which it came. At the end of the playing time or when one player has no more cards, the figure cards each has matched are counted. The winner is the one with the largest number.

❀ 260 ❀

To encourage children to visualize geometric puzzles, try this activity. If a 3-inch cube is painted on all sides and then cut into twenty-seven 1-inch cubes, how many cubes are found to be painted on three faces? On two faces? On one face? On no face? (The answers are 8, 12, 6, and 1. The 1-inch cubes with three painted surfaces are those cubes located at the eight corners of the large cube. Those with exactly two painted surfaces are all

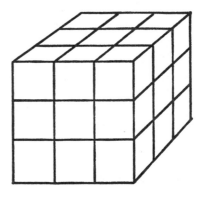

cubes located at the edges of the large cube less those eight with the three painted surfaces. The 1-inch cubes with one painted surface are those located at the center of each side of the large cube, and the unpainted cube is the one located in the center of the large cube.)

❀ 261 ❀

Folding paper squares can enhance spatial perception and discrimination. Have the children cut a paper strip 3 squares long. Ask them to fold along the

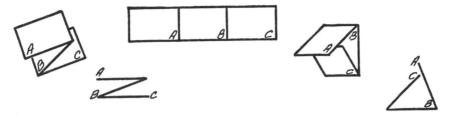

edges as shown in the illustration and record the "cutaway" view. In folding three squares, two distinct (different) models are possible. Models are considered different only when it is not possible to rotate one of them in space so that its structure is the same as the other.

Cut out four-square and five-square strips to determine the different ways they may be folded. Record the various "cutaway" views.

❀ 262 ❀

Paper folding can be used to involve children in an investigation of the properties of triangles. Have children cut triangles of various sizes from paper. Household wax paper is excellent because creases are vivid. Before folding begins, collect some of the triangles of various sizes and shapes, display them, and rotate them, verifying the number of straight edges irrespective of position. Then have each student hold his triangle in a position with point C (vertex) at the top. Fold point C to line segment AB directly below. Now fold point A to meet C and point B to meet C. Children should "discover" that the sum of the measures of the angles of any triangle is a single straight angle, as demonstrated by the positions in the final fold. Other interesting discoveries can be demonstrated through paper folding: that angle bisectors of the three angles of a triangle have a common intersection within the triangle, and that altitudes and medians are concurrent.

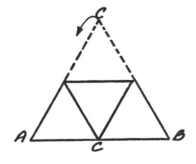
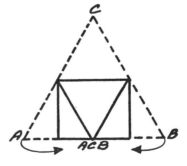

❀ **263** ❀

Surprising and hence interesting to children is the Möbius strip, which is said to have only one side. To make one, cut a 40 cm to 50 cm strip of tagboard about 5 cm wide and form it into a loop; but before gluing, give one end a half twist. One may now place his finger at any point on the surface and move it along to any other point without crossing an edge. Permit the pupils to check this unusual fact for themselves.

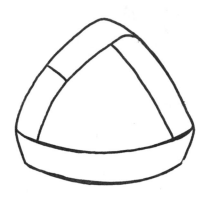

Ask the children what the result would be if they were to cut the Möbius strip in two by cutting along the center, making the strip only one half as wide as it is now. After discussion, let someone cut to verify conclusions reached. If the strip is wide enough, follow with a second cut to make the strip half again as wide. Also try making the first cut one third of the width.

❀ **264** ❀

An interesting way to make a regular pentagon is first to cut a long strip of paper of consistent width. Tie it into a knot and press it flat. The knot part will approximate the form of a regular pentagon.

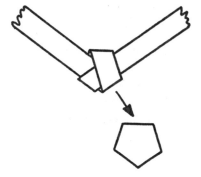

❀ **265** ❀

To maintain interest in terms related to geometry, post 5 to 10 squares (not all of the same size) on the bulletin board, each divided by one device or another into a variety of numbers of parts. Number each square. Each day place at the top or bottom of the board a strip of paper on which a question is written, such as: Which square is marked off into triangles? Which square is largest? Which square is divided into the most parts? And so on. At a corner of the board, place a small pad of paper, a pencil on a string, and an envelope. Instructions might be "Write your answer and your name on a paper. Place it in the envelope."

 266 ❀

Construction of models of polyhedrons provides the opportunity for many useful explorations by children. Provide stock pieces (posterboard is an appropriate material) of various polygons, such as triangles, squares, rectangles, parallelograms, and so forth, and let the children assemble various structures, fastening them with transparent mending tape or rubber bands. A variety of useful activities can precede and follow the construction period.

1. Prior to assembly, classify the polygons with questions such as: (a) Are all pieces regular polygons? (b) Which quadrilaterals are squares? Which are rectangles? (c) Are all squares rectangles?
2. Immediately after assembly, classify the figures that have been constructed as either a model of a polyhedron or not a model. To be a member of the first set, every face must be flat and every surface closed. Children's construction work can probably be further classified as regular and nonregular polyhedra. The set of regular polyhedra would possess the following characteristics: (a) Each surface would be a regular polygon; (b) all surfaces would be congruent, and (c) the same number of edges would form the vertices.
3. A teacher-directed group activity may be used to investigate the properties of polyhedra. Students, in pairs, may count the number of faces, edges, and vertices and record the data in chart form. The teacher may need to supply the name of an unusual polyhedron constructed by children.

POLYHEDRON	FACES	EDGES	VERTICES
TETRAHEDRON	4	6	4
CUBE	6	12	8

Variation Make some models of polyhedra of construction paper held together with masking tape so that the children can take the objects apart to see how to make models of their own. For permanent models, cut the tabs and glue.

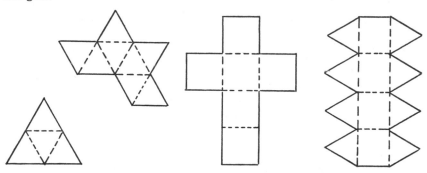

✲ 267 ✲ GEO-LOTTO

Purpose To provide practice in discrimination and spatial perception, involving color, pattern, texture, shape, and so on.

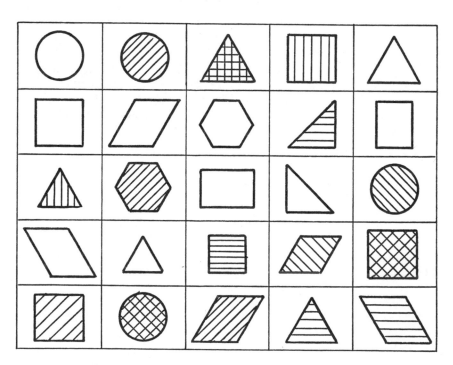

Level   Variable.

Number of players   Groups of 4 to 8.

Materials needed   Some permanent game boards for the players. A set of 25 call cards, each one of which contains a geometric figure exactly like one on the game board. (The call cards should be marked with T for top.)

Procedure   The game is played much as ordinary bingo except that characteristics like size, shape, and color are used instead of numerals. One student is chosen as the game manager. He shuffles the twenty-five cards and play begins when he flashes one for all to see. Players use a disk to cover that region on their board which contains a figure identical in every way to the one that is flashed. The first player to cover five regions in a row vertically, horizontally, or diagonally calls "geo-lot" and is declared the winner after the accuracy of his play has been verified by the game manager.

❀ **268** ❀

Advance conceptual skills related to congruency can be developed and reinforced by an activity such as the following. Provide dittos of the pattern shown. Students are to number the shapes on the first ditto. Letter and then cut out the shapes on the second ditto. Have children match the numbered shapes with the lettered shapes. They must be of the same size and shape. Provide a place to record the matching.

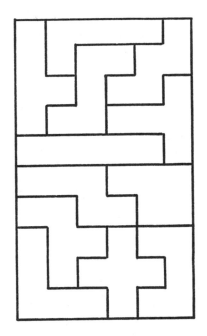

1._____   7._____

2._____   8._____

3._____   9._____

4._____   10._____

5._____   11._____

6._____   12._____

Variation   Each of the 12 figures in the pattern shown is known as a pentomino.[5] Each of the 12 pentominoes constitutes one of the possible arrangements that may be formed with five unit squares. Provide a model from which each student may cut an individual set of pentominoes and use them to explore geometric relationships. A simple beginning would be to arrange the 12 pentominoes to form rectangular figures.

❀ 269 ❀   COORDINATE BINGO

Number of players   4 to 12.
Level   Intermediate.
Materials needed   A geoboard for each player. Five peg markers for each player. A set of 25 cards numbered with coordinates of each peg. The peg in the lower left of the illustration is designated (0, 0), and 24 additional cards are made containing number pairs, each designating a peg coordinate.

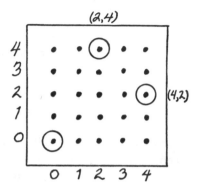

Procedure   Each player is given a unique home row (one of the 12 possibilities on the board for "5 in a row"), the deck of 25 cards is shuffled, and a caller is selected who draws the top card of the deck and reads the coordinate aloud. The players cover the peg with a ring when the given coordinate designates a peg in their home row. The caller continues until the winner completes his home row and calls "Bingo."

Variation   Rather than a home row, designate the formation of a letter of the alphabet as the object. For example, the coordinates (1, 0), (2, 2), (1, 3), (2, 3), (1, 1), (1, 2), and (3, 3) form the letter F.

❀ 270 ❀

A square may be drawn by first making a circle. Crease the paper through the center point of the circle. Now fold the paper again so as to make another crease, at right angles to the first. Join the points where the crease lines intersect the circle.

Variation   Rather than creasing the

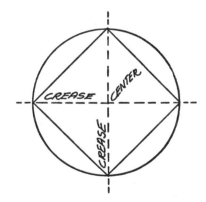

paper by folding, have students mark off six arcs on the circle, each the approximate length of the radius. Use a ruler to construct line segments connecting arc points. Complete a beautiful design by filling in various regions with color.

❀ 271 ❀

Use the ruler and compass to draw an equilateral triangle. First draw the base line of desired length. Then use the compass to make arcs with radii the same length as the base line.

Variation Skills acquired from the above activities may be extended to provide children experience with reproducing angles, bisecting line segments, and constructing a perpendicular.

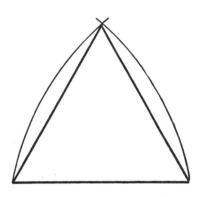

❀ 272 ❀

Pupils may find that making repeating patterns of geometric designs is an interesting activity. Rulers, compasses, stencils, cutouts, and the like will give children a variety of possibilities.

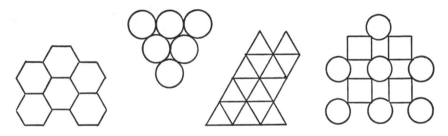

❀ 273 ❀

Designs made with straight lines that leave the impression of curves interest many youngsters at intermediate grades. The one shown is made by marking dots equidistant from each other on each side of an angle, numbering them in opposite orders, and then connecting the dots similarly numbered.

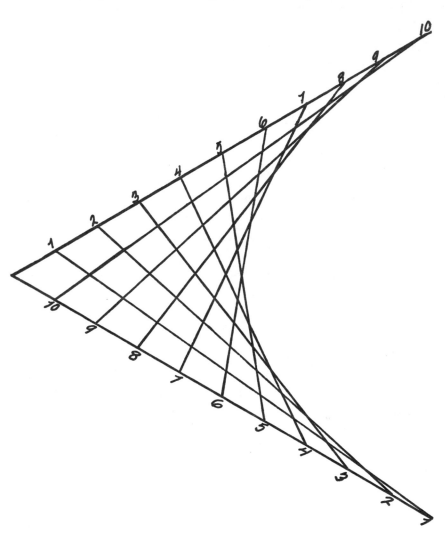

 274 ❀

Considerable motivation for the study of topology can be found in challenging pupils to find ways of tracing the lines in each of the figures shown without lifting the pencil or retracing.

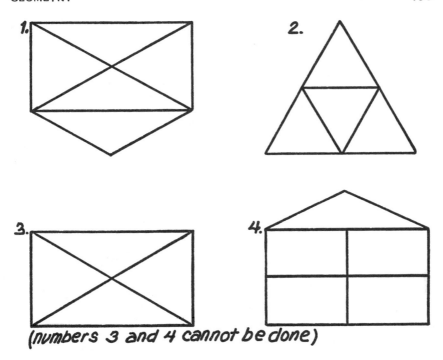

(numbers 3 and 4 cannot be done)

❀ 275 ❀

The mystery of knots used in scarf tricks by magicians will interest many pupils. Begin by making a square knot; then weave one end through both loops as shown by the arrows in the illustration. When the ends are pulled, the knot disappears.

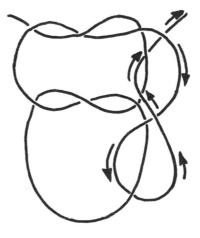

Another knot trick is done by tying two knots loosely in succession on a cord. Work one knot toward and through the other; both knots will remain unchanged.

❀ 276 ❀

To provide an interesting topological puzzle, make nine dots in the form of a square, as shown in the diagram. Draw four line segments so as to connect

Solution

every dot; do not mark any dot more than once, or retrace any line, or lift
the pencil before completing the drawing.

❀ 277 ❀

Boys and girls may be interested in
puzzles that seem impossible at first
glance, as in the following: Dale
wanted to plant 10 trees in a way so as
to make five rows of four trees each.
How did he do it?

Solution

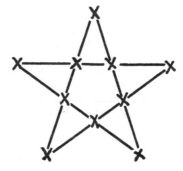

❀ 278 ❀

Many children will be interested in one of the oldest problems of topology,
that of the Königsberg bridges. Seven bridges connected parts of the city with
two island parks, the latter with a bridge between them. The townspeople
became intrigued with the problem of taking a walk that would take them
over each bridge once and only once. Draw a simple map such as that

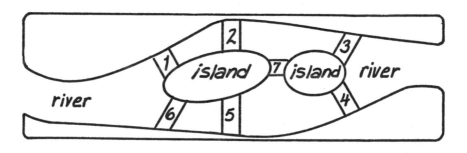

illustrated and challenge pupils to find a path to solve the problem. They may begin their walk at any point. (No matter where they start, they will not make it!)

279

A problem similar to that of the Königsberg bridges is that of a house tour in which one is expected to go through each door once and only once. Start in any room and return to that room. (It cannot be done.)
Variation Challenge pupils to supply electricity, gas, and water to each house without crossing pipes or wires. (This is also impossible.)

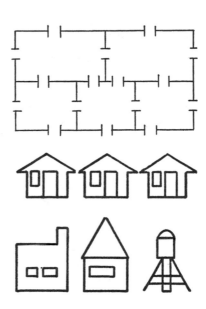

280

Optical illusions provide an interesting diversion for intermediate-grade children. On a stiff rectangular paper draw 10 parallel, evenly spaced line segments of the same length. Cut the paper diagonally in such a way that the cut touches the lower end of the first line segment and the upper end of the last one. Now move the top triangle one space to the right. Count the line segments. Are there still 10?

If you measure the line segments in both parts A and B of the diagram, you will see that those in part A are one-tenth again as long as those in part B. The slightly greater length is hardly visible, but the accumulation accounts for a full line segment.

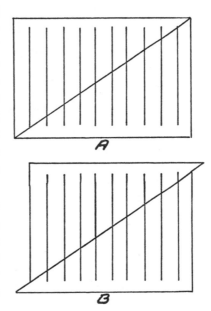

❀ **281** ❀

Many children, and adults, too, will be interested in "The case of the disappearing circle." First make a circle at least 6 inches in diameter on a piece of stiff paper. Next, carefully draw circles equidistant from each other at each of 12 clock positions; proceed so that the inner one at the seven o'clock spot is not quite fully inside the circle. The one at the six o'clock position has a little less of its area inside the circle. Continue in this fashion so that at the one o'clock place the small circle is half in and half out. By the time the seven o'clock position is reached again, the small circle is almost completely outside. Thirteen small circles will have been drawn. Now with a

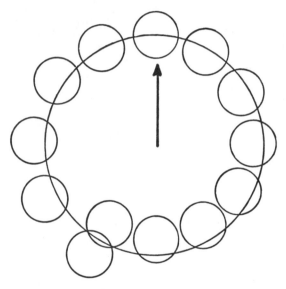

razor blade or a very sharp knife point, cut along the circumference of the large circle. By turning the circle so that the arrow points to the eleven o'clock position, only 12 small circles appear. What has become of the thirteenth?

In the illustration here, the circles have to be placed with great care. Irregular pictures, as of rabbits, might be easier for showing the illusion.

NOTES

1. A superior source of additional information about the role of geometry in elementary school mathematics is M. Brydegaard and James Inskeep, Jr., eds., *Readings in Geometry from the Arithmetic Teacher* (Reston, Va.: National Council of Teachers of Mathematics, 1970).

2. Commercially prepared geoboards are available from Scott Scientific Company, P.O. Box 2121, Fort Collins, Colorado 80521.

3. A humorous story with wide appeal that can be read to children in connection with an activity such as this is: Norton Juster, *The Dot and the Line* (A Romance in Lower Mathematics), (New York: Random House, Inc., 1963).

4. For a variety of supplemental hands-on and developmental laboratory activities in geometry, see Dale G. Jungst *Elementary Mathematics Methods: Laboratory Manual* (Boston: Allyn and Bacon, Inc., 1975).

5. See Martin Gardner, *New Mathematical Diversions from Scientific American* (New York: Simon and Schuster, 1966) for an extension of ideas that use pentominoes.

FRACTIONAL NUMBERS

RATIONALE

Of all the mathematical concepts encountered by elementary school children, those dealing with fractional numbers seem to remain the most bothersome and least understood. Why is this so? First, two numerals are used to name one number. Later the child is confronted with something called equivalent fractions and overwhelmed by their apparent size. Furthermore, all of this seems cumbersome, since the child was dealing orally with fractions ("Give me half your apple!") long before he met fractional notation in the formal setting of school. Admonitions such as "invert and multiply" are given but then followed by a discussion of ratio and proportion. The latter simply requires an understanding of the relationships involved. The fraction $\frac{16}{64}$ yields $\frac{1}{4}$ easily by canceling the 6s, but $\frac{13}{39}$ fails to equal $\frac{1}{9}$ and bewilderment builds when $1 \div \frac{2}{3}$ does not become $1\frac{1}{3}$. Finally, the fractional number in fractional form such as $\frac{2}{5}$ seems unclear and ambiguous to the child because it is used in the physical world to represent several different ideas. Teachers and other adults often have difficulty in helping children interpret and ascribe meaning to fractional numbers; the root of the problem for the child is most often the lack of ample exploration and discovery experiences to determine and internalize fractional relationships. Once children have grasped the fundamental relationships of fractional numbers, computational skills will increase markedly, because all the properties of operations with whole numbers hold for fractional numbers.

From experience with the activities in this chapter the children will learn:

1. The meaning of common fractions as a part of a whole.
2. To recognize that a common fraction may be an expression of relationship between two numbers.
3. A process for generating equivalent fractions.
4. To determine common denominators using equivalent fractions.
5. To perform the four basic operations with fractional numbers.
6. To recognize and use decimal names for fractional numbers.
7. To interpret per cent as part of 100.
8. To distinguish the relationship among fractional, decimal, and per cent numerals.

CONCEPTS OF COMMON FRACTIONS

❀ 282 ❀

A To help children to understand fractions and to develop some skill in estimation, place rice, wheat, small beans, or other small items into similar transparent pillboxes so that each child has a fraction of a full one: $\frac{1}{2}, \frac{1}{3}, \frac{2}{3}, \frac{1}{4},$ $\frac{3}{4}$. A small piece of masking tape on the bottom may give the fraction. Pupils can arrange the boxes in order of increasing or decreasing size of contents. Hold a contest to see who can most nearly guess the number of items in each container.

B Place a series of drawings (geometric shapes or other familiar objects) on cards or on the chalkboard. Have a broken line segment pass through each so

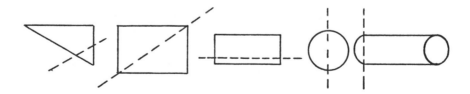

as to cut it into two parts. Ask the children to identify two sets, one set to contain objects not divided in two equal parts. Variations of this activity may be used to demonstrate the meaning of thirds, fourths, and so forth.

 283

Provide pairs of children with a set of counters, such as paper clips, beans, unit rods, plastic disks, and some short pieces of string. Then, as they work in pairs, give children directions such as these:

1. Take 12 counters. Give one half of them to your partner.
2. Sort out 20 counters. Put a string around one fourth of them.
3. Find 7 counters. Can you put a string around one half of them?
4. Find three fourths of 18 counters.

When utilizing introduction activities such as these, it is a good idea to have children record their responses.[1]

 284

To acquaint children with fractional parts of wholes, pin a sign reading "Fraction Cracker Box" at the top of a bulletin board. In random fashion pin up tagboard "crackers" marked in wholes, halves, thirds, fourths, etc., and some in pieces of unequal size. Number each. Below list some questions, such as: Which crackers are marked in fourths? Which crackers are wholes? Which crackers show three unequal parts? Provide a pad of paper, pencil, and an envelope for depositing answers.

285

To provide practice in recognizing fractional parts of a group, duplicate papers on which there are bars divided into variously numbered parts, some of which are shaded. Suggest that pupils mark after each the fraction telling what part is shaded.

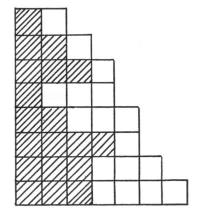

286

Make separate strips of paper of the same length but divided into various fractional markings, as in the example. Pupils may manipulate strips to compare fractions.[2] Appropriate teacher guidance includes such inquiries as: How many sixes (sixths) are there in a whole 1? How many sixes (sixths)

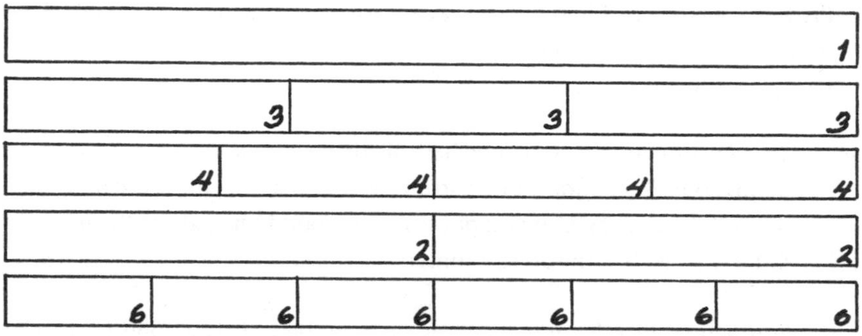

				1
3		3		3
4	4		4	4
		2		2
6	6	6	6	6	6

are needed to make a three (third)? Are three fours (fourths) more or less than five sixes (sixths)? And so on.

287

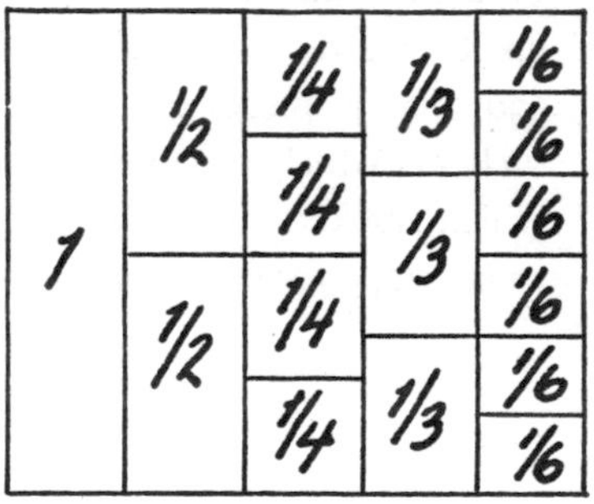

On a rectangular piece of stiff paper, draw stripes, each divided into common fractional parts. If desired, color each stripe using thinned watercolors. Make as many of these fraction equivalence charts as needed. Incorporate into a bulletin board display.

Variation Later, introduce charts of different sizes but with the same fractions involved. The metric influence will suggest the use of fifths and tenths with more frequency than in the past.

1	½	¼	⅓	⅙
				⅙
		¼	⅓	⅙
	½	¼		⅙
		¼	⅓	⅙
				⅙

288

Make a frame from a piece of plywood on which narrow strips of wood are nailed or glued. Now make strips of stiff paper of a size to fit between the wooden strips. Mark each strip into fractional parts and cut the parts so that the children can place them into position on the board and make their own comparisons.

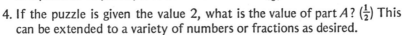

❀ 289 ❀

The Tangram constructed in Activity 251 may be used in a teacher-directed activity that provides a wide variety of pupil involvement with fractional numbers. It is important that children feel free to move puzzle pieces about in any manner as they discover and record relations.

1. Using one or more sets of Tangram pieces, ask children to discover what part $(A + B)$ is of the entire puzzle. $(\frac{1}{2})$ What about part A? $(\frac{1}{4})$ B? $(\frac{1}{4})$ How many small triangles are there in the large triangle? (4)

2. Repeat for parts C and D or F. $(\frac{1}{8}$ and $\frac{1}{16})$

3. A more difficult discovery, perhaps requiring insight into decomposition of pieces, is to ask about E or G. $(\frac{1}{8})$

4. If the puzzle is given the value 2, what is the value of part A? $(\frac{1}{2})$ This can be extended to a variety of numbers or fractions as desired.

5. Addition or subtraction operations can be devised, using, e.g., a "unit" puzzle, where $(E + F) - (G)$ implies that $\frac{3}{16} - \frac{1}{8} = \frac{1}{16}$.

❀ 290 ❀

Geoboards sectioned with rubber bands are useful during early instruction with fractional numbers. For initial work, children should place a rubber band around the perimeter and consider this "largest square they can make" to be one unit. Subsequent teacher-directed developmental activities can include:

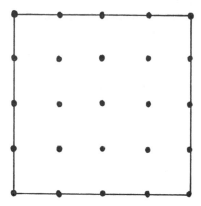

1. Use a rubber band to divide your square into two equal parts. Record the fractional name of each part.

2. Remove your rubber band. Now use the rubber band at least three more times to divide your square into two equal parts. Record each way on dot paper. (Parts 1 and 2 may be repeated for thirds, fourths, fifths, sixths, and so on.)

3. Provide children with duplicated pictures of geoboards already containing fractional parts and shaded areas such as those shown. Accompany the sheet with verbal instructions, such as:

(a) Use your geoboard to make a picture like *B*.

(b) Write the name of the shaded area in *C*.

(c) How large is the shaded area in *F* compared to the shaded area in *E*?

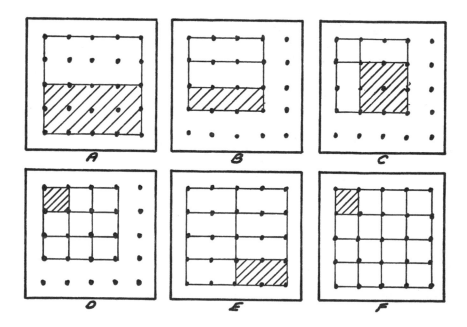

❀ 291 ❀ FRACTION TAG

Purpose To provide practice in addition of fractional numbers.
Level Variable.
Number of players Class divided equally into two teams.
Materials needed A set of cards, each containing a fractional number name, i.e., $\frac{1}{2}$, $\frac{2}{8}$, $\frac{1}{5}$, and so forth.
Procedure All the members of each team are given a card bearing a fractional number name which is kept throughout the game. One player on each team is designated the "tagger," and he begins play by tagging any other child on the opposing team. The tagger must then add his number to that of the child he has tagged and call out the correct sum. The tagged player is now the new tagger and the play continues between each team until all children have been tagged and the team with the most correct sums is declared the winner. Variations are possible involving other operations as well as equivalent fractions. The complexity of the game is controlled through the fraction cards.

❀ 292 ❀

Children need practice in interpreting fractions or geometric figures in which regions are congruent. Draw shapes and shade some of the regions. Suggest that the children indicate the ratio of shaded parts to total or to unshaded parts.

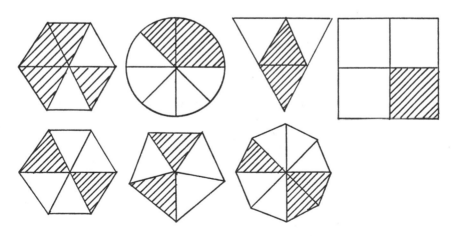

❈ 293 ❈ FRACTION BASKETBALL

Purpose   To become familiar with values of fractions as part of a whole, and ratios.
Level   Variable.
Number of players   Children in teams of 3 to 5 players per team.
Materials needed   Something to toss (crumbled paper or chalkboard eraser). A container.
Procedure   Each team is given a container (basket), which is placed on the floor, table, or chair a specified distance apart. The teams stand in rows behind the containers. Each player is given some objects (three, four, or five) to toss into the container. As each player tosses, he calls out his score, expressing it as a fraction. One basket in four tries would be one fourth, three would be three fourths, and so on. Scores may be kept for each pair of tosses and/or each round of tosses. The team with the highest score wins.[3]

ROUND	1		2		3		RATIO
name	TOSSES		TOSSES		TOSSES		tosses made
	made	taken	made	taken	made	taken	to Total tosses taken
						TEAM TOTAL	

❈ 294 ❈ BALL CONTROL

Sports people generally agree that the team that controls the ball is the team that usually will win the game. It is further agreed that controlling the ball is a matter of controlling the rebounds during a game. From the Sunday (or weekend sport pages) ask the children to use the reported results of two of their favorite basketball teams to compare the relationships between the number of rebounds and the final score. The data can be recorded on a chart such as the one shown. Are sports people correct? Do it for two weekends. Three weekends. Now do you think they are correct?

team	rebounds	score
$\frac{1}{2}$ vs.		
$\frac{1}{2}$ vs.		
$\frac{1}{2}$ vs.		

Variations This activity may be associated with other sports and appropriate charts designed for recording. For example, in baseball, compare errors or bases on balls to the final score. In football, compare first downs or the number of plays run to the final score. And so on.

❀ 295 ❀ HALF A ROD

Purpose To provide practice in using rods to show one half of even whole numbers less than 12. May be used without winners as an activity to discover certain relationships.
Level 1 to 3.
Number of players 1 or more.
Materials needed Rods. Material as in Activity 6.[4]
Procedure Tell the players that, at a signal, they are to show all rods or combinations of rods that measure one half the length of some other rod; e.g., red is one half the length of purple; light green and white are one half the length of brown. Note that some rods, such as black, will have no half-length combinations. The winners are the players with the most correct examples.
Variation Give the rods number values (one for white, two for red, three for light green, etc.) and ask the players to record on paper all whole numbers (or combinations of whole numbers) that equal one half of every even number less than 12 [$\frac{1}{2}$ of 10 = 5 = 4 + 1 = 3 + 2 = 1 + 4 = (2 X 2) + 1, etc.]. The winners are the players with the most correct examples.

❀ 296 ❀ ROD COMPARISON

Purpose To provide practice in recognizing fractional parts of wholes; may be used also as a discovery activity without winners.
Level 1 to 4.
Number of players 1 or a small group.

Materials needed   Rods as in Activity 295. Duplicated papers on which are written such items as:

> White is what fraction of red? _____
> White is what fraction of purple? _____
> White is what fraction of light green? _____
> Red is what fraction of purple? _____
> Red is what fraction of dark green? _____
> Red is what fraction of white? _____
> Etc.

Procedure   Distribute papers face down. Instruct the players that at a given signal they are to turn the papers over and record as many answers as they can before time is called. If a pupil succeeds in finishing all the items before the closing signal, he is to stand. When five pupils have finished, say, "Pencils down." Check the answers using rods when necessary. Winners are those of the first five players to finish who have correct papers. Those who did not complete their work may now do so.

EQUIVALENT FRACTIONS

✿ 297 ✿   FRACTION BINGO

Purpose   To provide practice in naming equivalent fractions.
Level   3 to 6.
Number of players   4 to 6.
Materials needed   A 3 X 3 playing mat or card with 9 calls for each player, containing the notation for frequently used fractions. Some "call" cards, containing different names (or notation) for the fractional numbers on the playing mat. Playing mats and the corresponding "call" cards may be made of any lightweight posterboard. A variety of colors adds interest. Call cards may

contain a visual cue to the meaning of the fraction as a part of a whole, but that is not essential.

Procedure The game is played like bingo. A caller is chosen and holds up a card from the "call pile." Any player with an equivalent fraction covers the corresponding call (or calls) with a disk. The first player to obtain three disks in a row (vertically, horizontally, or diagonally) is the winner.

❋ 298 ❋ DOUBLE TROUBLE

Purpose To provide practice in comparing relative sizes, finding common denominators, and finding equivalent fractions.

Level Intermediate.

Number of players 2 to 6, grouped by ability.

Materials needed Some scratch paper. A pencil for each player. A deck of 66 cards, each containing one of the following fractions:

$$\frac{1}{2}, \frac{1}{3}, \frac{2}{3}, \frac{1}{4}, \frac{2}{4}, \frac{3}{4}, \frac{1}{5}, \frac{2}{5}, \frac{3}{5}, \frac{4}{5}, \frac{1}{6}, \frac{2}{6}, \frac{3}{6},$$

$$\frac{4}{6}, \frac{5}{6}, \frac{1}{7}, \frac{2}{7}, \frac{3}{7}, \frac{4}{7}, \frac{5}{7}, \frac{6}{7}, \frac{1}{8}, \frac{2}{8}, \frac{3}{8}, \frac{4}{8}, \frac{5}{8}$$

$$\frac{6}{8}, \frac{7}{8}, \frac{1}{9}, \frac{2}{9}, \frac{3}{9}, \frac{4}{9}, \frac{5}{9}, \frac{6}{9}, \frac{7}{9}, \frac{8}{9}, \frac{1}{10}, \frac{2}{10}, \frac{3}{10},$$

$$\frac{4}{10}, \frac{5}{10}, \frac{6}{10}, \frac{7}{10}, \frac{8}{10}, \frac{9}{10}, \frac{1}{11}, \frac{2}{11}, \frac{3}{11}, \frac{4}{11}, \frac{5}{11}, \frac{6}{11}, \frac{7}{11},$$

$$\frac{8}{11}, \frac{9}{11}, \frac{10}{11}, \frac{1}{12}, \frac{2}{12}, \frac{3}{12}, \frac{4}{12}, \frac{5}{12}, \frac{6}{12}, \frac{7}{12}, \frac{8}{12}, \frac{9}{12}, \frac{10}{12}, \frac{11}{12}$$

Procedure The cards are shuffled and dealt equally, face down to the players. The cards remain face down, and each player simultaneously "rolls" (reveals) the top card. The player with the fraction of highest value receives all the rolled cards. In the event of a tie (equivalent fractions are rolled) "double trouble" is declared and the opportunity for a bonus arises. Each player involved in "double trouble" removes his next three cards, placing them aside face down, and rolls the fourth card. Now the player with the fraction of highest value takes all the cards, including those that were set aside. Play continues until one player loses all his cards or time is called. The winner is the player with the most cards.

Variation Fraction "go fish" may be played with a deck of fraction cards, where every fraction has exactly one other equivalent fraction in the deck. Children draw cards and discard pairs of equivalent fractions. The winner is the first player to discard all his cards. Children obey the simple rules of the regular "go fish" card game.

❀ 299 ❀

A fraction "builder" is a simple device appropriate for relieving children of the burdensome computations involved in finding fractions equivalent to a given fraction. Provide the children with two pieces (8 X 10) of accurately lined oaktag and instruct them to number and label each strip as shown in the figure. To operate the fraction builder, the denominator strip is placed on top

NUMERATOR		DENOMINATOR	
1		1	
2		2	
3		3	
4		4	
5		5	
6		6	
7		7	
8		8	
9		9	
10		10	
11		11	
12		12	
13		13	
14		14	

of the numerator piece such that all numerals on both pieces may be seen with the two N and D lines touching precisely *and* the numerator and denominator lines of the given fraction for which equivalency is sought also touching precisely. This is accomplished by "dialing" the denominator strip counterclockwise. Several adjustments are usually necessary and children may enjoy using space or computer language in operating their builder. The figure shows a builder properly set for finding a fraction equivalent to $\frac{2}{3}$. Answers are read from left to right wherever lines exactly touch to yield ratios of lengths with integral values. In the figure $\frac{2}{3}$ is equivalent to $\frac{4}{6}$, $\frac{6}{9}$, $\frac{8}{12}$, $\frac{10}{15}$, and

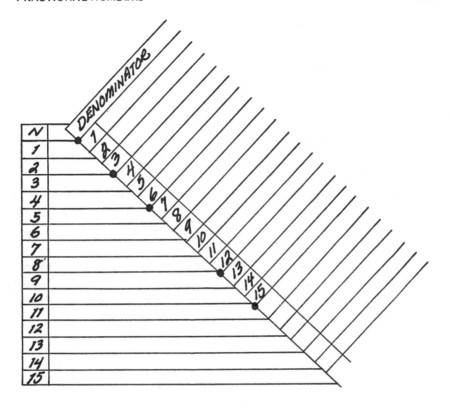

so on. For further exploration and variation, more complex fraction builders may be designed.

❀ 300 ❀ NAME THE FRACTIONAL NUMBER

Purpose To provide practice in naming fractional numbers.
Level 4 to 6.
Number of players 2 or more, with ability a consideration.
Materials needed A set of three 3- by 5-inch cards for each player. On each card write the numeral for a fractional number.
Procedure The teacher, or leader, names a fractional number. The player who has a card naming that number must hold up the card and give another name for the number before the leader can count to five. If he succeeds, he may keep the card; failure means that the card goes to the first player who can give another name for the number. The winner is the pupil accumulating the most cards.

✿ 301 ✿ FRACTIONAL NUMBER NAME RUMMY

Purpose   To provide practice in recognizing other fractional number names.
Level   4 to 6.
Number of players   2 to 4.
Materials needed   A pack of cards each marked with a fractional number name. For each number, there must be three cards, each with a different fractional number name: for example, $\frac{1}{2}, \frac{2}{4}, \frac{6}{12}$, or $\frac{3}{4}, \frac{6}{8}, \frac{9}{12}$. There should be 18 to 20 such sets.
Procedure   Players draw to be dealer; the largest number named indicates the dealer. Five cards are dealt to each player. Place the balance of the deck face down with the top card turned up. The player to the left of the dealer begins. He may take either the turned-up card or the top card from the "blind" deck. If he has the three cards that contain three different number names, he lays them before him. When he has finished, he discards one card face up. Play then proceeds to the left. When one player has no cards, the game ends and the one with the most sets wins. This activity may be adapted to work with decimal and per cent names.

OPERATIONS WITH FRACTIONAL NUMBERS

✿ 302 ✿

To facilitate understanding fractional relationships and to provide a concrete manipulative aid for verifying computations with fractional numbers, a fractional number "machine" provides an ideal and inexpensive opportunity for discovery learning. Each child may develop a "fractional number kit" of his own. The amount of teacher guidance necessary during the construction will depend on the age and experience of the children. The fractional number kit contains 24 pieces. Begin by drawing a 6-inch circle on a piece of 20 cm by 20 cm clear posterboard, and divide the circle into eight equal parts, with line segments as shown in the figure on the left. (Note that labeling began at "three o'clock" and that only the simplest name is used for labeling.) Next, five 15 cm circles are made and cut from durable posterboard, each circle of a different color. When each of the five circles is cut into its respective unit part—halves, quarters, thirds, sixths, and eighths—23 additional pieces are produced.

Although the unit part is identifiable by color, it is a good idea to label the halves, thirds, and fourths on both sides with a felt-tip pen. All the pieces necessary for the kit are now constructed, and all that remains is to complete the labeling of the unit circle. Use the pieces for thirds and sixths to locate the appropriate points for labeling, again labeling the simplest name. The second figure shows how the unit circle should now appear. To do an accurate job, the final marking of the circle will require a protractor graduated in half-degrees. The circle should now be divided into 24 equal parts. To avoid confusion, the 24ths may be named by small whole numbers (numerators). The third figure shows the completed fractional number circle. Uses for the kit range from foundation experiences in comparing relative size and determining other names to performing computations.

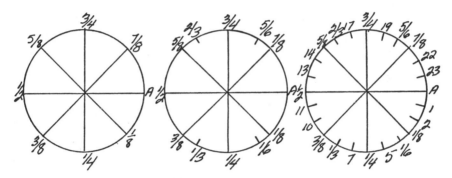

Simply exploring with the fractional pieces by superimposing them on the labeled unit circle will enable children to discover that $\frac{1}{6}$ is half of $\frac{1}{3}$, that $\frac{2}{6}$ and $\frac{1}{3}$ name the same fractional number, that $\frac{1}{3}$ is larger than $\frac{1}{6}$, and so on. Suppose that the task is to add the fractional numbers $\frac{2}{3}$ and $\frac{1}{4}$. The appropriate pieces are selected and placed on the circle, clockwise beginning at the "three o'clock" position. The parts, when correctly selected, will reach the 22 mark, which is $\frac{22}{24}$ or $\frac{11}{12}$. Subtraction may be performed by locating the minuend on the circle and laying the pieces representing the subtrahend in a counterclockwise direction from the radius of the minuend. As an example, consider $\frac{5}{6} - \frac{1}{4}$. Place the $\frac{1}{4}$ piece on the circle in a counterclockwise direction beginning at the $\frac{5}{6}$ radius. The result read from the unit circle will be $\frac{14}{24}$ or $\frac{7}{12}$. **Variation** Rectangular regions are easier to construct and use than circles but do not exhibit the whole unit as naturally. Division can be accomplished by placing the number pieces equal to the divisor on the circle in a clockwise direction until the dividend fractional number is reached. The number of pieces needed to reach the dividend is the quotient. If the problem is to divide $\frac{1}{4}$ by $\frac{1}{8}$ we see that exactly two $\frac{1}{8}$ pieces are needed to reach $\frac{1}{4}$. For children who are beginning the study of fractional numbers, a partial kit may be sufficient. Such a kit would include halves, fourths, and eighths. With a little exploration and imagination it is possible to solve many quantitative situations in each of the basic operations with fractional numbers. Children are highly motivated by reading the answers directly from their fractional number machine.

❀ 303 ❀ WHAT DOES IT?

Purpose   To provide practice In recognizing the relation of a given fractional number to a pair of other fractional numbers.
Level   5 to 6.
Number of players   2 or more (or individuals).
Materials needed   10 cm by 15 cm cards on which there are equations without operation signs. For quick checking, record the operation sign on the reverse side. Some examples of cards are shown.

Procedure   Divide the group into two teams. The players stand in parallel lines. The teacher or leader shows a card and the first players on each team try to be the first to name the operation sign. The winner scores a point for his team. The first players then go to the rear of their respective lines and play proceeds with the second players. The team with the highest score wins. "What Does It?" could be played also as an individual game. Place the equation cards in a stocking box. Include an envelope containing small cards on which operation signs appear. A child matches small cards with equation cards. For checking, the answers can be shown on the bottom of the box.

❀ 304 ❀ BOOKMAKING

Purpose   To provide practice in adding fractional numbers.
Level   5 to 6.
Numbers of players   2 to 3.
Materials needed   A set of cards, each marked with a fractional number name; use denominators 2, 3, 4, 5, 6, 8, 10, 12; e.g., $\frac{1}{2}, \frac{1}{3}, \frac{2}{3}, \frac{1}{4}, \frac{2}{4}, \frac{3}{4}, \ldots$
Procedure   The dealer sets the goal, such as $\frac{7}{8}$, 1, or $1\frac{1}{4}$, and distributes four cards to each player. Place the balance of the deck face down in the center of the table; turn up the top card. The player to the left of the dealer begins. The object of the game is to use some or all of the cards that were dealt to

you and either the card turned up or the top card of the blind deck to name fractional numbers whose sum is the goal set; e.g., if the goal is $1\frac{1}{4}$, a player may use the cards with $\frac{1}{2}$, $\frac{2}{8}$, or $\frac{3}{6}$ written on them. If he cannot make a play, he must draw one card per turn until he can. Combination cards must be shown to other players; if they agree that he is correct, he may lay the cards before him as a "book." As a player completes his turn, he discards one card from his hand to the turned-up pile. The player may take all or only the top card of the discard pile. When one player has no more cards or when the blind deck is exhausted, the game ends. The player with the most books wins.

❀ 305 ❀ CANNED FRACTIONAL NUMBERS

Purpose   To provide practice in adding fractional numbers.
Level   5 to 6.
Number of players   1 to 10.
Materials needed   Five low cans, such as size $\frac{1}{2}$ flat, nailed to a board, each with a paper taped to it showing a mixed numeral, such as $4\frac{1}{2}$, $9\frac{4}{6}$, $3\frac{3}{4}$, $7\frac{4}{8}$, $5\frac{1}{3}$. Three small bean bags.

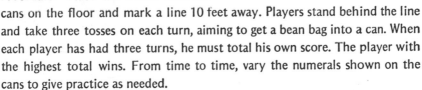

Procedure   Place the board with the cans on the floor and mark a line 10 feet away. Players stand behind the line and take three tosses on each turn, aiming to get a bean bag into a can. When each player has had three turns, he must total his own score. The player with the highest total wins. From time to time, vary the numerals shown on the cans to give practice as needed.

❀ 306 ❀ MOUNTAIN CLIMBING

Purpose   To provide practice in solving fractional number problems.
Level   5 to 6.
Number of players   2 or more.
Materials needed   A chalkboard drawing of a mountain. A set of fractional number problems. Paper and pencil.
Procedure   Divide the group into two or three teams; give each team a name, such as Swiss Guides, Rocky Mountain Climbers, Austrian Giants. The teacher writes a problem on the chalkboard and the players attempt to solve it. At a signal, after several players have indicated that they have completed the problem, all lay their pencils on the desk. A member of one team gives his

solution. If it is correct, each team advances up the mountain as many meters (use an appropriate scale) as there are players who have completed the problem correctly. Play then proceeds as before. The object is to see which team can climb nearest the top of the mountain. If the pressure is too great on team members who frequently get wrong answers, change the game to individual mountain climbing. A given child then competes only with himself. Adjust the problems to the needs of each climber.

❀ 307 ❀ ERASER BOWL

Purpose To provide practice in the addition of fractional numbers.
Level 5 to 6.
Number of players 2 or more.
Materials needed A "bowling alley" marked out on the floor with a 3-foot circle or oval near one end. Nine chalkboard erasers; on six of them, write a fractional numeral, and place these six in the circle.

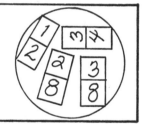

Procedure Divide the group into two or more teams. The first player of one team gets three tries at knocking an eraser from the circle using an unmarked eraser. His score is the total of the numbers named on the erasers that he removes from the circle. Play then goes to the first player of the next team. At the end of play, each team total its scores to see which team has the most points.
Variations An eraser serving as a bowling ball may have a fractional numeral on it and be used as a multiplier; the score might be the multiplier times the number named on each eraser knocked out of the ring.

❀ 308 ❀

While the following is sometimes presented as a shortcut, its value is probably greater for providing insight to those pupils who try to understand why the procedure "works." The activity concerns subtracting fractional numbers whose names are of the form $\frac{1}{a}$ and $\frac{1}{b}$. To subtract $\frac{1}{b}$ from $\frac{1}{a}$, where $\frac{1}{a} > \frac{1}{b}$, it will be found that the numerator is the difference between the denominators, and the denominator is their product, e.g., $\frac{1}{3} - \frac{1}{8} = \frac{8-3}{8 \times 3} = \frac{5}{24}$. Changing to lower terms may be desired in some cases, as $\frac{1}{3} - \frac{1}{9} = \frac{9-3}{9 \times 3} = \frac{6}{27} = \frac{2}{9}$. The procedure is based on the general statement: if $\frac{a}{b}$ and $\frac{c}{d}$ are fractional numbers, and if $\frac{a}{b}$ is greater than or equal to $\frac{c}{d}$, then $\frac{a}{b} - \frac{c}{d} = \frac{ab - bc}{bd}$, where in our case a and $c = 1$.

 309

Grid paper, dot paper, or geoboards can be used to capitalize upon children's intuitive interest in measurement to reinforce the multiplication of fractional numbers. These examples use 25-peg geoboards, rubber bands of uniform color to mark unit squares, and rubber bands of selected colors to mark vertical and horizontal edges. Ask the children to place a rubber band around the perimeter of their geoboard. This is the "largest square they can make" and is the unit square. Next, have the children use small rubber bands of uniform color to partition their geoboard into "as many small squares as possible." The result of this activity should be 16 congruent squares, as shown.

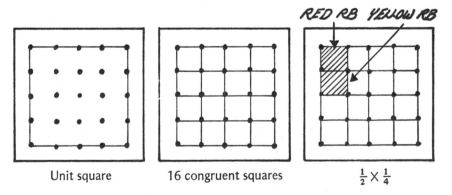

RED RB   YELLOW RB

Unit square   16 congruent squares $\frac{1}{2} \times \frac{1}{4}$

Now ask the children to use a yellow rubber band to divide the vertical edge of the geoboard into two equivalent parts and use a yellow rubber band to mark one of the four equivalent parts of the horizontal edge. The third figure shows $\frac{1}{2} \times \frac{1}{4} = \frac{1}{8}$. Subsequently, this model may be used to show $\frac{1}{2} \times \frac{1}{2}$, $\frac{1}{2} \times \frac{3}{4}$, and $\frac{1}{4} \times \frac{3}{4}$.

Geoboards may also be used to represent unit squares, with subsequent division into equivalent rectangular subregions. Children may be encouraged to make their own models for problems and to solve them. The edges of subregions are marked with colored rubber bands in the manner described.

❀ 310 ❀

To provide practice in multiplying fractional numbers, duplicate papers on which pupils are to fill in squares according to directions, as in the illustration. Select items that need practice.

	$\frac{1}{2}$	$\frac{1}{3}$	$\frac{1}{4}$	$\frac{1}{5}$	$\frac{1}{8}$	$\frac{1}{10}$	$\frac{1}{12}$
$\times 2$							
$\times 3$							
$\times 5$							
$\times 10$							
$\times \frac{1}{2}$							
the reciprocal of							
$\div 3$							

❀ 311 ❀

To provide practice in multiplying fractional numbers, suggest that the children fill in the cells of the grid illustrated according to these directions. Check to see if the result is a magic square.

a	b	c
d	e	f
g	h	i

a. $270 \times \frac{1}{9}$ (30)   b. $36 \times \frac{1}{4}$ (9)   c. $48 \times \frac{1}{2}$ (24)

d. $120 \times \frac{1}{8}$ (15)   e. $14 \times 1\frac{1}{2}$ (21)   f. $81 \times \frac{1}{3}$ (27)

g. $\frac{1}{2} \times 36$ (18)   h. $231 \times \frac{1}{7}$ (33)   i. $\frac{3}{8} \times 32$ (12)

312 ✿

Magic squares provide motivation for many children. Multiply each number in the magic square to the right by $\frac{1}{2}$. Do you still have a magic square? Multiply and divide by other fractional numbers and check to see if the "magic" remains. Would it if a given fractional number were added to or subtracted from the numbers shown?

$3\frac{1}{2}$	0	$2\frac{1}{2}$
1	2	3
$1\frac{1}{2}$	4	$\frac{1}{2}$

✿ 313 ✿

Sectioning geoboards may be extended to generate models for division of fractional numbers. Provide a small group of children with geoboards and rubber bands. A superior procedure is to accompany these materials with some word problems that can be solved with a minimum of teacher direction. Here are two examples:

1. One half of a square meter of material is required for a vest that Nancy wishes to sew. Nancy's mother will give her three pieces of material, each 1 square meter in size. How many vests can Nancy make?
2. Harold's candy recipe requires $\frac{1}{2}$ liter of milk. Harold has only a $\frac{1}{4}$-liter measure. How many times must Harold fill his measure to get the right amount of milk in the candy?

These problems illustrate the crucial need for children to understand the meaning of division of fractional numbers. Word problems where the needed operation is not clear provide an appropriate "physical world" context for this. As early as grade three, children will ordinarily solve these problems in the manner shown. Of course, young children should not always be required to verbalize or write in computation form what they have done. Later, dot paper or duplicated sheets containing facsimiles of geoboards may be used by students to record what has been done.

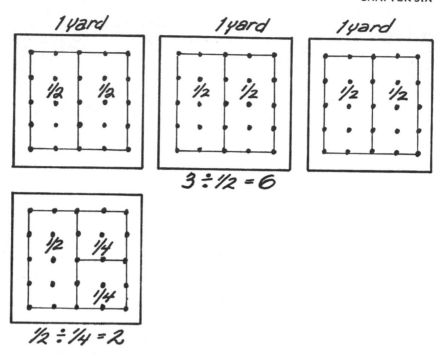

❀ 314 ❀ FRACTIONAL NUMBER BASEBALL

Purpose   To provide practice in performing operations on fractional numbers.

Level   6.

Number of players   2 or more.

Procedure   Draw a diamond on the chalkboard and write two whole numerals, one fractional numeral, and one "mixed numeral" along each base line. Select a fractional number to be used as the "pitch." Divide the group into two teams. The first player on the team that is "up" must add the pitch to the numbers indicated along the first base line, subtract (exchange if necessary to get a solution) those along the second base line, and so on. If he gets "home" without a mistake,

he scores a run for his team. A mistake constitutes an "out"; three outs and the team is retired. The pitch and/or the numerals on the base lines should be changed at the end of each inning or more frequently if desired (such as after a run is scored).

❀ 315 ❀ KING OF FRACTIONAL NUMBERS

Purpose To provide practice in addition of, or other operations on, fractional numbers.

Level 5 to 6.

Number of players 2 to 4.

Materials needed A set of 52 cards, on each of which appear a fractional numeral and a pie-shaped illustration. A check sheet naming sums or products depending on the operation in which practice is needed. A score sheet.

Procedure Shuffle the cards. Players each draw a card; the largest fractional number determines the dealer. Place the deck face down on the table. The player to the left of the dealer begins by drawing two cards and giving the sum (or product) of the fractional number named on the two cards; if needed, paper and pencil may be used. He is checked by the player to his left (who uses the check sheet if necessary) and makes a check mark after the player's name on the score sheet if the answer given is correct. Play then proceeds in like manner to the left. At the end of play, the player with the most check marks is the winner.

	1/2	1/3	2/3	1/4	1/8	•••
1/2	1	5/6	1 1/6	3/4	5/8	
1/3	5/6	2/3	1	7/12		
2/3	1 1/6	1	1 1/3	11/12		
1/4	3/4	7/12				
⋮						

❀ 316 ❀

A fractional/decimal number conversion chart is an extremely helpful visual aid for children to utilize in understanding the relationship between common fractional numerals and decimals. Although precision is necessary in making the chart, children can learn from the process and enjoy having a chart that is their own. To use, a straightedge is placed along the vertical line of the common fractional numeral, for example, $\frac{1}{2}$, and the decimal numeral is read from the decimal numeral bar either above or below the chart. Children readily interpolate where required; e.g., $\frac{3}{4}$ = 0.75. The chart is also useful for obtaining fractional numerals that name the same number and can contain unit lengths for thirds, fifths, tenths, and so on.

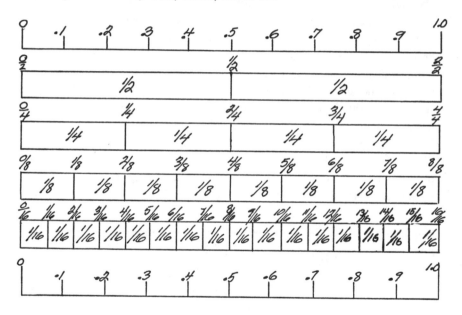

UNDERSTANDING DECIMAL RELATIONS

❀ 317 ❀ DECI-MAID

Purpose   To reinforce reading and recognition of decimal numerals.
Level   Intermediate.
Number of players   4, 6, or 8 players.
Materials needed   An "Old Maid" decimal numeral deck of 49 cards. The cards are composed of 12 groups of 4 cards each, with a decimal numeral or

fractional numeral that names the same number, and an "Old Maid" decimal number card. A sample grouping could be as shown.

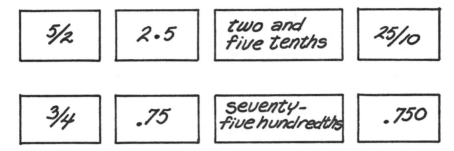

Procedure The game is played according to the rules of Old Maid. The deck is shuffled and all cards dealt to the players. Initially, all the players may lay on the table before them each *pair* that names the same fractional number. Play then commences with the player immediately to the left of the dealer drawing one card from the dealer's hand. If the draw provides him another pair that name the same fractional number, he may play them. Play continues in order, each player drawing one card from the player to his right until someone is left holding the single "Old Maid" decimal numeral card.

❀ 318 ❀ RATIONAL DOMINO

Purpose To provide practice in recognizing other fractional number names and in adding fractional numbers.
Level 5 to 6.
Number of players 2 to 3.
Materials needed A set of 28 cardboard "dominoes" on each of which are fractional or decimal numerals or both. Examples are shown. Make some as

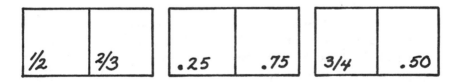

doubles, preferably small numbers, such as those shown on p. 226.
Procedure Place the dominoes face down on the table and shuffle. Each player selects four; others are left on the table as the "bonepile." The player with the largest double begins by placing it on the table. The player to his left

may play a domino if he has one that names a number equal to the sum of the two on the double. If he cannot play, he must draw from the bonepile until he *can* play. The next player may play either on the other side of the double, if he has the sum, or on the last domino played, if he has a fractional or decimal numeral equal to the exposed end or equal to the sum of the two fractional numbers. An example is shown. The game ends when one player

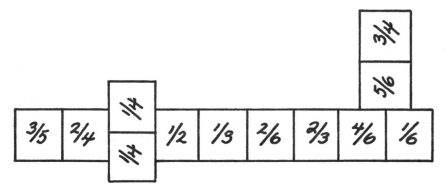

has no more dominoes. To keep the scoring simple, each player gets one point for a play involving fractional number names and two points for a sum; at the end of the game, the winner adds to his score the number of dominoes each of his opponents has.

❋ 319 ❋

A magic square employing decimal numerals may interest boys and girls. Using a decimal numeral name for a fractional number of his own choice, a pupil should multiply or divide the numbers in the magic square illustrated by it. Then try with other fractional names. Are the results in each case magic squares?

3.25	1.5	2.75
2.0	2.5	3.0
2.25	3.5	1.75

320 ✿

Now let us discuss how to provide practice in naming fractional numbers using fractional and decimal numerals. Make a board 40 cm to 60 cm square with concentric circles. Make a spinner wide enough and long enough to cover the fractional numerals and point to decimal numerals at one end, and to point to fractional numerals at the other.

✿ 321 ✿ FRACTIONAL RUMMY

Purpose To reinforce the relationship among decimal, fractional, and per cent names for a fractional number.
Level Intermediate.
Number of players 2 to 4.
Materials needed A deck of 52 specially designed fractional rummy cards. The cards may be made from two-ply posterboard or oaktag utilizing 13 predetermined fractional numbers with four names for the number. As an example, the fractional number ¼ would generate the four cards shown.

Procedure   The rules are those of regular rummy. Each player is dealt seven cards and the remainder of the cards are placed face down in the middle of the table, with the top one turned over beside the deck. Play begins to the left of the dealer and each player has the option of taking a "down" card from the deck or a "face-up" card from the discard pile. Each time a player draws a card, he must discard one. When a player has built a set of three cards that name the same fractional number, he may lay them face up on the table. Any player who subsequently draws or has the fourth card that names the same number may play it during his turn. The winner is the first player who has played all his cards. If the face-down cards disappear before a winner is declared, the discard pile is shuffled, placed face down, and play continues until a winner is declared.

RATIONALIZING PER CENTS

❋ 322 ❋

A percentage board is a simple and useful device for teaching per cent and fractional equivalents in a meaningful way. It could be simply the familiar hundreds board, where each small square represents 1 per cent and the large square 100 per cent. Centimeter grid paper serves nicely as a model for the percentage board. When a percentage name is discussed, the children count as many squares as are necessary to represent the fractional number. They then

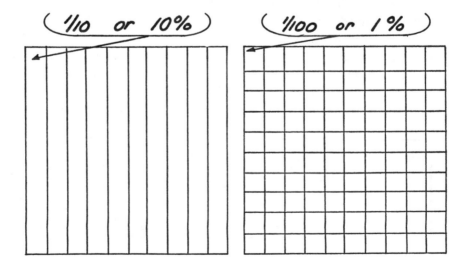

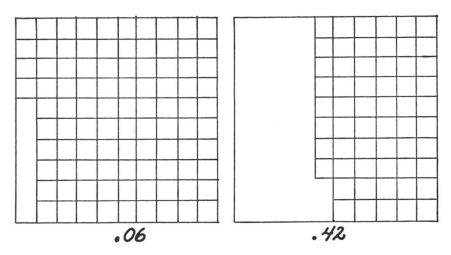

.06   .42

determine what part this is of the large square. Subsequently, when less than 1 per cent is introduced, they may again refer to their percentage square to see that only a part of one of the small squares is meant. This promotes understanding of the difference between $\frac{3}{4}$ per cent, for example, and 75 per cent, $\frac{3}{4}$ of the whole.

❁ 323 ❁ DO YOU HAVE THE CHANGE?

Purpose   To provide practice with money in denominations associated with percentages of 100.
Level   2 to 4.
Number of players   4.
Materials needed   Play money as follows: 50 cents, 8; 25 cents, 16; 10 cents, 40; 5 cents, 80; 1 cent, 100. Fifty cards, each showing a purchase amount of less than $1.00.
Procedure   Distribute money to each player as follows: 50 cents, 2; 25 cents, 4; 10 cents, 10; 5 cents, 20; 1 cent, 25. Shuffle the cards and turn the stack face down on the table. Each player draws a card; the one getting the card showing the lowest purchase price will play first; return these cards to the bottom of the stack. Each player in turn draws a card and "makes change" for $1.00; if unable to make change, he must pass. The object is to see who runs out of money first.
Variation   Primary-grade children may discard money in the amount of the purchase instead of making change.

❀ 324 ❀

Upper-grade pupils may be interested in a device to approximate the answers to certain percentage problems. The larger the apparatus, the easier it is to make it precise. Try it this way. Select a piece of plywood about 27 inches square. Make a triangle as shown. The base and left side have $100\frac{1}{4}$-inch markings. Drive a small nail at the upper zero point.

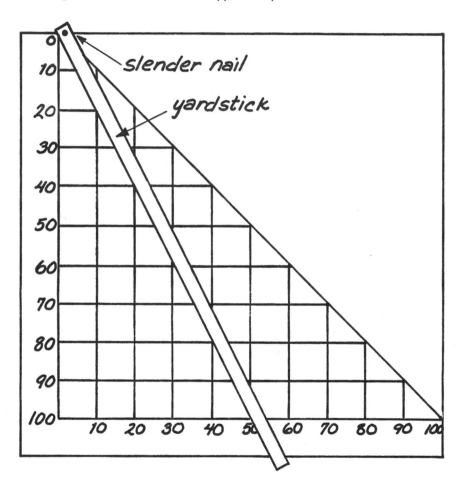

    To find what per cent 30 is of 60, place a yardstick against the nail with the same side at the intersection of 30 and 60. (The small numbers are read from the base, the larger ones from the side.) Reading along the base line one finds the answer to be 50 per cent. Of course, one may also find other facts, such as what is 50 per cent of 80, by noting where the yardstick intersects the 80 line.

❀ 325 ❀   GEOBOARD PERCENTS

A geoboard can be used by children to reinforce the concept of per cent in a variety of cases, depending on the geoboard size. After exploration, teacher-directed activities with the 25-peg geoboard can include the following.

1. Use a rubber band to show 100 per cent on your geoboard.
2. Leave the first rubber band in place. Use a second rubber band to show a region that represents 50 per cent of your geoboard. Use the same rubber band and find as many ways as you can to represent 50 per cent of your geoboard. Record each way on dot paper. (Expect a variety of usual answers, such as these examples.)

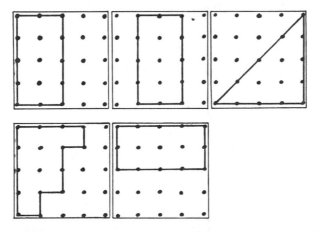

3. Now use your rubber band to find a "crazy" way to show 50 per cent. The following are possibilities. (All these activities are possible for 25 per cent and 75 per cent.)

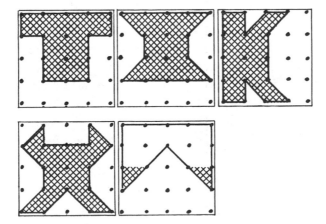

4. Get some 36-peg geoboards or dot paper. Have children discover what per cents can be shown (20, 40, 60, 80 per cent). Repeat the previous developmental activity.

❀ 326 ❀ ESTIMATION

Purpose   To provide a problem-solving drill in fractional numbers or whole numbers, mental arithmetic, estimation.
Level   4 to 6 (adaptable).
Number of players   Variable (2 teams).
Materials needed   Ten to 12 problems and a predetermined format for presenting them individually (orally, overhead, chalkboard, etc.).
Sample Problems

1. Tom's father earns $12,000 annually. His mother earns $14,000. Tom said that he wished he had $\frac{1}{6}$ of the total. His friend Harold said he would rather have 10 per cent, because it would be more. They argued. Who is right? Why?
2. Nancy wants to go fishing with her father and she must mix fuel for the motor. The tank holds 24 liters and requires a gas/oil ratio of 18:1. How much oil does Nancy need?

Procedure   Form 2 teams of children. Players from each team number off: 1, 2; 1, 2; and so on. The *ones* are "celebrities" and the *twos* are "contestants" for their respective teams. The celebrities from each team write the name of a person they would like to be, and these are recorded, by team, on the chalkboard. The contestants (twos) for each team count off consecutively "1, 2, 3, . . . ," and remember their numbers. The numbers are subsequently placed in a team box.

Play begins when a die is rolled to determine which team is first. Subsequently, the teacher draws a number from the appropriate team box of "contestant" numbers. The contestant whose number corresponds to the number drawn selects a celebrity from the opposing team who must answer the problem to be presented. The teacher or, in the case of odd numbers, a classmate, may present the problem in appropriate form (overhead, chalkboard, orally, slip of paper, etc.).

The rules are these. Celebrities may use pencil and paper, but contestants may not. The *celebrity* produces an answer (possibly fraudulent)[5] as quickly as possible, and the contestant must affirm or deny at once. If the contestant is correct, his team scores. If not, the celebrity team scores. The game continues by alternately selecting numbers from team boxes that contain contestant numbers. The preceding procedures are repeated and the game climaxes when the allotted time has elapsed or all problems have been used. The team with the greatest number of points wins.

❀ 327 ❀ NAME THE NUMBER

Purpose To give practice in renaming whole numbers.
Level 5 to 6.
Number of players 1 or more.
Materials needed Paper and pencil.
Procedure In 10 minutes, each player tries to make numerals for as many whole numbers (1 to 100) as he can by using only 4s; e.g., $\frac{4}{4} = 1, \frac{4+4}{4} = 2$.

Set the length of time according to the ability of the players. On another occasion, follow the same procedure but select a different number. (Very fast learners may find ways of using decimal numerals, powers, roots, or nondecimal bases.)

❀ 328 ❀

The origins of decimal notation help children gain appreciation for man's struggle to adapt the decimal numeration system to name fractional numbers. The Egyptians conceived the idea of fractional numbers and named and made all but one, $\frac{2}{3}$, using fractional numerals with 1 as the numerator or combinations of different fractional numerals ($\frac{3}{4}$ would be shown as $\frac{1}{2} + \frac{1}{4}$). They made use of a symbol $\subset \supset$ written over the denominator numerals; e.g., $\frac{1}{2}$, $\frac{1}{10}$, and $\frac{1}{40}$ would be written as , respectively. Some pupils may want to try naming such common fractional numbers as $\frac{3}{5}$, $\frac{7}{8}$, $\frac{5}{6}$, $\frac{4}{7}$, $\frac{5}{12}$, and others by using combinations of fractional numerals with 1 as the numerator. It will not be easy! We owe our fractional number form, e.g., $\frac{1}{2}$, to the Arabs, who introduced the use of the bar.

Not until the sixteenth century did people use decimal numerals as we know them. In 1530 Christoff Rudolff wrote decimals using a bar or slash as we use a point, e.g., $\frac{406}{78}$. Common use of decimal fractions followed the publication of a book by Simon Stevin entitled *La Disme*. At first there was confusion as to the symbols to use, and we find what we would write as 24.867 in such forms as those on p. 234. Even today one finds variations in decimal symbolism; for example, in England the decimal point is raised, e.g., 24·867, whereas a comma is used in Belgium, France, Germany, Italy, and

$$\overset{0123}{24\,867}\;,\; \underset{0123}{24867}\;,\; 24{,}867''',\; 24\overset{\cdot\;'\;''\;'''}{867}''',$$

$$24/867\;,\; 24/\overset{123}{867}\;,\; 24/\overset{\cdots}{867}\;,\; 24\underline{867}{:}$$

$$\text{OR}\;\; 24{,}\underline{867}\;,$$

other countries, e.g., 24,867. (We use a comma to separate the thousands, but in some countries a period or a space is used for this purpose; what we would write as $24,867.50 would be shown as $24.867,50 or as $24 867,50.)

NOTES

1. For supplemental fraction activities involving understandings and equivalences, see C. W. Schminke, N. Maertens, and W. R. Arnold, *Teaching the Child Mathematics* (Hinsdale, Ill.: The Dryden Press, Inc., 1973), pp. 165–173.

2. A full set of manipulatives for teaching fractions is *Fraction Bars*, available from Scott Resources, Inc., P.O. Box 2121, Fort Collins, Colorado 80521.

3. See K. Kidd, S. Myers, and D. Cilley, *The Laboratory Approach to Mathematics* (Chicago: Science Research Associates, 1970), for some excellent experiments and activities related to ratio.

4. C. Gattengo, *Arithmetic: A Teacher's Introduction to Cuisenaire—Gattengo Methods* (New York: Cuisenaire Company of America, Inc., 1961).

5. Since the celebrity may deliberately give an incorrect response in an effort to fool the contestant, and the contestant may not use pencil and paper, his judgment of the celebrity's response must rely entirely upon mental calculation or estimation.

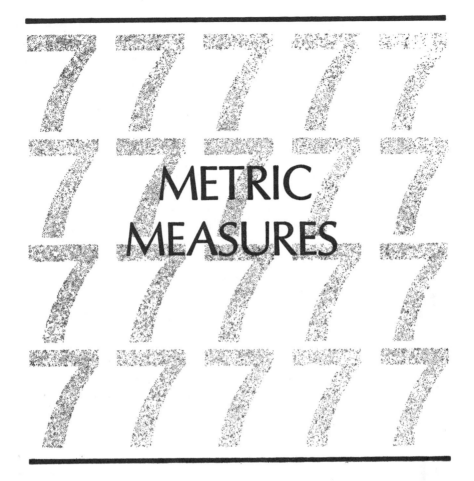

METRIC MEASURES

RATIONALE

"Have you heard that Sheila's new baby weighed 4 kilograms?" "What a summer day!" "The temperature is 40°C." "Our new car averages 5 kilometers per liter." Although these expressions may currently be meaningless to most children and a majority of adults, they are likely to be ordinary expressions within your lifetime as well as within the lifetime of the children in your classroom. The fact that the addition to Sheila's family is, indeed, large, or the temperature of the summer day is of heat-wave proportions, or the rate of consumption of fuel by the new automobile is low is what this chapter is about.

Going metric is not a new idea in this country. In 1790 Thomas Jefferson, then Secretary of State, recommended that Congress adopt a decimal system of measurements. In 1821 John Q. Adams again suggested the changeover, without success. Ultimately, in 1866, during Benjamin Harrison's administration, Congress made the metric system legal but not mandatory in the United States. For the first time, in April 1975, the U.S. Congress had approved legislation to help the country with the metric conversion, and the House of Representatives has set aside $2 million for that purpose.[1] Although some metric projects have been funded previously, no specific legislation has been passed to encourage them. The historic resistance is strange indeed. The United States, by clinging to the peculiar and largely unrelated "standard" unit of measure, i.e., inch, foot, yard, rod, mile, barleycorn, foot-acre, grain, peck, bushel, cord, short ton, and so forth, has persisted in doing business nationally and internationally somewhat akin to a citizen using chickens or bales of straw in conducting affairs of commerce with another utilizing currency and coin. Further, there is little evidence that in replacing our English system with the metric system we would be replacing something with which we are particularly familiar. In support of the previous statement, try this little miniquiz. Fill in the blanks and then check your answers at the end of the chapter.[2]

1. 1 peck = _____ quarts
2. 1 bushel = _____ pecks
3. 1 tablespoon = _____ teaspoons
4. 1 pint = _____ ounces
5. 1 rod = _____ yards

6. 1 pound = _____ ounces
7. 1 long ton = _____ pounds
8. 1 square yard = _____ square inches
9. 1 acre = _____ square feet
10. 1 square mile = _____ acres

If you are like most of us, you probably did not do very well. Yet, each of those measures is commonly used and represents information that would be uniformly useful to most of us at one time or another. Of course, given sufficient time and some tables of measure, we could work out the answers.

The previous sentence leads directly to the third advantage of metric measure. After being supplied with a table of standard measures, we would be left with the considerable task of conversion within and between the standard units because for the most part they have no common base. Not so in the metric system, where subunits as well as multiples of all basic units are in terms of decimal notation, the base of our number system. One-tenth, 10, 100, and 1000 are much more conducive to the arithmetic of conversion than, for example, 12 inches equal 1 foot, 3 feet equal 1 yard, and 5280 feet equal 1 mile. Beyond this, learning the previous scheme offers no aid with measures related to volume and weight. Study the classroom visual in Activity 361 to see evidence of the logically planned metric system, where the meter establishes the basis for the entire system.

It is a fact that the metric system is coming to the United States. The current projected date of a mandatory changeover is 1983. If this projection comes to pass, it means that the United States will be on the metric system before the fourth graders in your school (1976) graduate from high school. Thus, our responsibility in regard to teaching the metric system is not "shall we" but "how."

The principal philosophy for teaching mathematics which has been implicit in previous sections of this book is uniquely adaptable to teaching the metric system. Simply stated, it is one of active student involvement incorporating a variety of "hands-on" activities which utilize real objects. As you assume the role of "partner" in learning endeavors, no phase of the elementary school mathematics program offers a better opportunity for a topic to become your favorite than measurement does. Whether you are an experienced teacher or a prospective teacher, you will become excited about the metric system as you and the children engage in these activities which enrich the teaching of metric measurement as well as the total mathematics program in your room.

The activities included in this chapter are exclusively metric, and that is by design. Of course, schools must necessarily offer a dual system for some time, but major emphasis ought to be on the metric system with relatively little attention to "relationships" between the systems. That is a necessary condition in order for us to think metric. Consistent with what good principles for teaching measurement have always been, the activities in Chapter 7 rely heavily on approximation experiences, numerous alternatives for recording and charting, use of actual units during exploration and discovery, and the utilization of computations only when it is the natural outgrowth of experience.

As a result of utilizing the activities in Chapter 7, the children will learn:

1. To exhibit a confident and positive attitude toward the metric system.
2. To use estimation and a variety of nonstandard units to measure length.
3. To identify an appropriate basic unit of measure when measuring length.
4. To state the relationship that exists between greater and lesser linear measures.
5. To choose an appropriate metric measure and determine the area of large and small surfaces.
6. To demonstrate that surfaces with the same area may have different perimeters.

7. To gain skill in estimating measures of capacity.
8. To correctly identify the common standard units for measuring large and small liquid volume.
9. To determine the volume of solids using cubic centimeters.
10. To select some common objects that can be used for reference when estimating mass.
11. To utilize the appropriate basic units when measuring both large and small masses.
12. To state the basic relationship that exists among the metric measures of distance, capacity, and weight.
13. To compare some common Fahrenheit temperatures with their Celsius (centrigrade) counterparts.

LINEAR MEASURE

❋ **329** ❋

Give each child a piece of bright-colored construction paper. Have them trace around their shoes or spread their hands (a *span*) and cut out the pattern. Using the cutout as a unit of measure, suggest that they discover and record how many "spans" or "shoes" long some common room or school objects are. Be sure that different students' measures of the same object are compared and talked about. Discover if there is a difference between boys' and girls' spans or shoe units—who has the shortest, or longest, etc. What is the average span in the class?

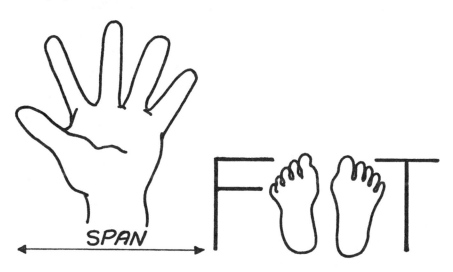

❀ 330 ❀

Using lightweight tagboard strips or even paper adding-machine tape, the children should construct their own measurement tools.

A As units, do not first use standard centimeters, etc., but use the length of the child's foot, hand, or finger.

B Using these tools, the students should measure a variety of familiar and available objects, such as desks, books, heights, room size, or windows.

C After the results are compared, the discussion should lead from the difficulties encountered to the idea of standard units, such as using a particular child's foot length as a unit.

D Finally, the values of standard lengths are given and the children make a sturdier ruler or tape scaled only in centimeters. A model that is sufficiently accurate is provided in the illustration. It is appropriate that children have several metric rules, and a decimeter rule is advantageous in the early application of standard lengths.

❀ 331 ❀ FIND OUT

Use student-made metric rulers or tapes that have been scaled in meters, decimeters, etc., to play Find Out. First, have students record an estimate, then measure and record the dimensions of all sorts of objects both in and out of school. A suggested list would be endless but might include very small items as well as longer objects. Be sure to not only measure objects but also to estimate the distances children can jump on the playground, throw a ball, hop on one foot, and so forth. An illustrative recording sheet suitable for centimeter scales is shown.

OBJECT	ESTIMATE	ACTUAL
Width of your eraser	_____	_____
Length of these words	_____	_____
Width of your hand	_____	_____
Length of your foot	_____	_____
Height of your desk	_____	_____
Depth of your book	_____	_____
Length of a paper clip	_____	_____
Width of your largest button	_____	_____

❀ 332 ❀ SQUIGGLE PICTURES

For scale use have children use their centimeter ruler to draw some line segments. Provide them with some arbitrary dimensions:

$$
\begin{array}{ll}
2\,cm & 1\,cm \\
3\,cm & 6\,cm \\
5\,ml & 7\,cm
\end{array}
$$

Have them place the lines in some random physical proximity. Then have them use imagination and some "squiggle" lines to connect the line segments and make a picture.

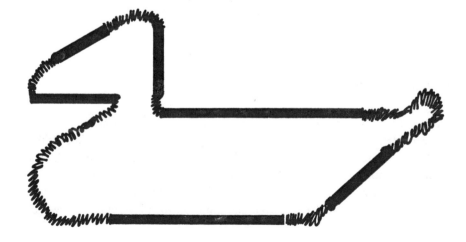

333

Because not all measure is in straight lines, ask the children to use string or a student-made tape measure to find a belt size, hat size, wrist size, circumference of a baseball, length of the prime meridian on a globe, and so forth.

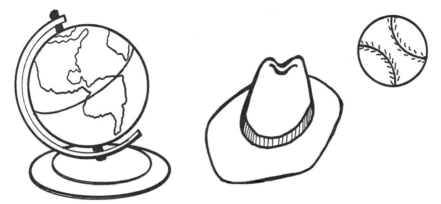

The tape measure can also be used to measure "around a corner" and is useful in applications other than direct line measure. Have children use string to measure their best friend. They will have fun comparing such things as:

1. Who has the tiniest wrist in the class?
2. Who has the largest (circumference) thumb?
3. Who has the widest shoe?
4. Who is tallest in your class?
5. Who has the longest arm?
6. Who has the shortest arm?

Later, the various string lengths may actually be measured with metric rules that the children have made and the true measurements of the children recorded in the most appropriate unit.

 334

The children in our classrooms are unfamiliar with the basic units of metric measure, and this lack of familiarity can lead to confusion and uncertainty during initial exploration of the metric system. Some classroom charts can provide a helpful point of reference until children become comfortable with the basic metric units. The chart should not be used for conversion but contain only approximations for general comparisons of some customary units to metric units.[3]

OLD STUFF

1 cm is a little less than $\frac{1}{2}$ inch
$2\frac{1}{2}$ cm is about 1 inch
30 cm is about 1 foot
1 m is a little more than 1 yard
1 km is a little more than $\frac{1}{2}$ mile
1 liter is a little more than 1 quart
500 ml is about 1 pint
250 ml is about 1 cup
1 kg is a little more than 2 pounds

❀ 335 ❀   METER MADNESS

Children may be actively engaged while gaining a natural familiarity with the standard meter. Have pairs of children construct a folding meter rule by using opaque mending tape to fasten 10 decimeter rules. Each pair of children may

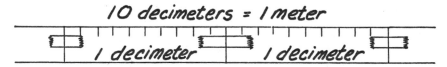

then use the folding meter rule to measure a piece of string 100 cm long. Classroom measures may then be taken and recorded in cm, dm, and m.

OBJECT	MEASURE		
	CENTIMETERS	DECIMETERS	METERS
Length of my arm	40	4.0	0.40
Bill's height	127	12.7	1.27
Width of door			
Teacher's desk			
Nail			
Screwdriver			

❀ 336 ❀

Using a decimeter rule calibrated in both millimeters and centimeters, have the children measure *small things* in the classroom. Provide each child with a

master rule such as the one shown. While you may vary the kind of master provided, eventually the children should record their efforts in both mm and cm.

	RECORD TO NEAREST	
MEASURE	MILLIMETER (mm)	CENTIMETER (cm)
Length of your pencil Width of your little finger Diameter of your eraser Width of your desktop Width of a pin Thickness of a piece of string Three really tiny things around you 1. 2. 3.		

❀ 337 ❀

Interest in measuring can be maintained by an activity involving the heights of children. On a strip of paper wide enough to accommodate the variation in heights of pupils plus 5 or 10 centimeters, mark vertical lines, one for each child with his name at the top. Tape the strip to the wall with the lower edge at the height of the shortest child. Note the height from the floor so that each time children are measured, the paper can be placed in the same position. As

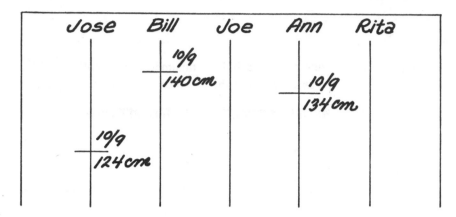

each child is measured, make a mark on his line and label with the date and height. Roll up the paper and store until time to measure again.

Variation   To encourage skill in estimation, have each child's height guessed by the class. Who had the best guess? What is the average of all heights recorded? What class members are closest to the average?

❀ 338 ❀ METER TOSS

Purpose   To provide practice in using tools of linear measure.
Level   2 to 4.
Number of players   2 or more.
Materials needed   Ring-toss game set. A meter stick, centimeter ruler, or centimeter tape measure.
Procedure   Each player or team has one ring, tosses it at the post, and then records his score, which is the number of centimeters or decimeters that his ring fell away from the post. The distance or score is found by measuring with the ruler or tape. After 10 tosses or after the teams finish tossing, the winner is the *lowest* sum of scores.

❀ 339 ❀

A bulletin board or wall chart prominently displaying the decimal relationships between common linear metric units and the correct notation for each is an essential aid to learning as children pursue classroom activities involving metric measure. Involve students in the design and construction of the chart.

```
        LINEAR MEASURE
1 centimeter = 10 millimeters
      (1 cm = 10 mm)
1 decimeter = 10 centimeters
      (1 dm = 10 cm)
  1 meter = 10 decimeters
      (1 m = 10 dm)
1 kilometer = 1000 meters
     (1 km = 1000 m)
```

✻ 340 ✻ DISTANCE DATA

Purpose To provide practice in recognizing linear equivalents.
Level 3 to 6.
Number of players 2, 3, or 4.
Materials needed 28 squares of tagboard which contain 14 pairs of equivalents within the basic unit meter. Examples are shown.

| 12 dm | = | 1m 2dm | | 10 cm | = | 1 dm |
| 10mm | = | 1 cm | | 0.14m | = | 1.4dm |

Procedure Shuffle the cards and place them all face down on a playing surface so as to form a 4 X 8 rectangle. Roll a die to determine who plays first. Subsequently, each player, in order, turns two cards up and keeps them if they match. The game is completed when all cards have been claimed and the player with the most cards is declared the winner.

✻ 341 ✻

Make a display of commercially prepared and pupil-made metric measuring instruments and artifacts for use during study of the metric system. Affix three-dimensional objects to the bulletin board whenever possible. Label with name and use. The sophistication or complexity of the display will depend on the level of the children, but the following objects comprise a basic list of equipment from which selected objects may be drawn:

meter sticks	centimeter grid paper
millimeter ruler	Celsius thermometer
cubic centimeter blocks	cubic meter frame
cubic decimeter shape	tape measures (m, dm, cm)
pan balance with weights	liter container
decimeter ruler	milliliter container

❁ 342 ❁ ROD RACE

Purpose   To provide practice with meter units.
Level   Intermediate.
Materials needed   A deck of game cards (at least 36 similar to those in the illustration). A set of centimeter rods for each player. A meter stick for each player.

0.2 dm	1.8 cm	0.025 m	2 cm
0.14 m	3 cm	0.5 dm	0.020 m

Procedure   Shuffle the cards and place them face down on the table. Players, in turn, turn over cards from the deck and make the length on their meter stick using the appropriate rod or rods called for by the card.

Illustration   If a card says "2 cm," the player uses the rod that is 2 centimeters long. If the card says "0.1 meter," the player uses the rod that is 1 decimeter long, or 0.1 of a meter, and so forth. The first person to reach the end of his meter stick wins the game.

Variation   This activity may be simplified for younger children by substituting a spinner for the card deck and having players move on the meter stick the distance indicated by the spinner. A spinner with a single metric dimension (cm only) is appropriate.

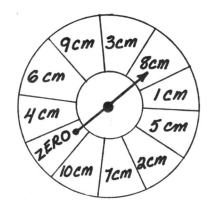

343 ❀

The measurement of distance against time is a challenging one for the middle-grade children. Timing a toy train on a track, or a car on a slot-race circuit, can give some experience, while measuring the time it takes to jog around the playground might be simpler to carry out. Comparison of the rates of speed of moving objects (from turtles to jet planes) is only one approach, however. An excellent variation would be to consider also the growth of a classroom plant per day, the weight a student gains per month, or the rate books are checked out of the school library per day. Children can gain valuable graphing experiences as records are kept of these measuring activities.

❀ 344 ❀ KILOMETER CAPERS

The notion that longer distances are measured in kilometers is one with which children may have some prior familiarity. You may capitalize on this while reinforcing the standard distance represented in a kilometer through planning a 1-kilometer hike. In preparation for the hike, children can be provided some comparisons as a point of reference. One useful comparison is that a kilometer is a little more than $\frac{1}{2}$ mile. Another would be to fasten 10 1-meter string rules together and then cut 10 more of the obtained length to form a 100-meter string rule. The kilometer hike can include:

1. Walking the length of the string 10 times on the school playground.
2. Walking 4 times around a football field.
3. Walking to a city park (or some other place of interest) located a bit farther than $\frac{1}{2}$ mile from school.
4. Circling the base paths on a standard ballfield 9 times.
5. Walking $2\frac{1}{2}$ times around an outdoor quarter-mile track.
6. Walking to the home of a classmate who lives a little more than $\frac{1}{2}$ mile from school.

❀ 345 ❀

Travel is always exciting and the excitement can be used to motivate a variety of measurement, rate, cost, and other real-world arithmetic activities. Provid-

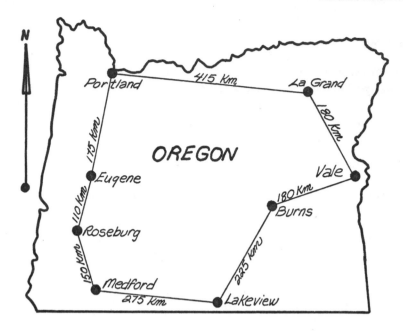

ing a map of your own area (simplified as the one shown), involve students in explorations such as:

A   Fill in the kilometer (km) distances between some key cities or points of interest. Scale reduction or learning to use a distance table on a map are only two options for this.

B   Find and describe all the tours possible if no more than 600 km can be traveled and one must return to the starting point.

C   What are the approximate kilometer dimensions of your state?

D   At $10,000 per kilometer of road, which two cities could be connected at the least cost? What would be the most expensive road to build?

E   How long would it take to travel from Portland to LaGrand if one went at 70 km/hr?

❀ **346** ❀

A map-reading activity involving individuals or small groups of children and a map of an imaginary area can provide an exciting context for practical application of metric measures in problem solving. The map shown may be reproduced for utilization, or children may produce one of their own and design problems like those accompanying the map shown.

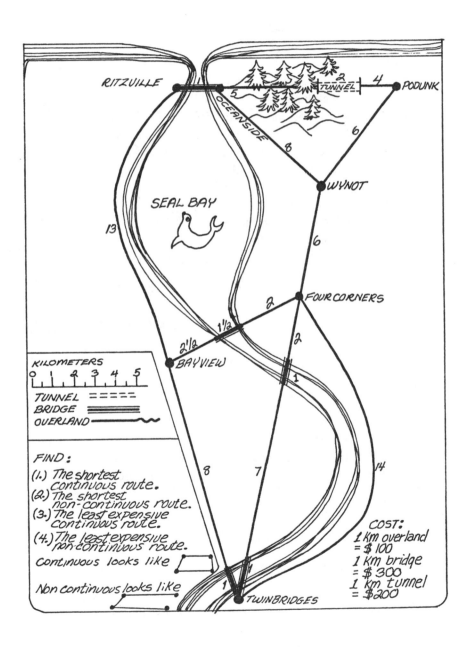

✼ 347 ✼ WHAT'S YOUR HURRY?

Purpose To give practice in computing travel speed.

Level 5 to 6.

Number of players Set of 3.

Materials needed Two clocklike circles for each set of three players. Paper and pencil.

Procedure Divide the group into sets of three; designate each player as *A*, *B*, or *C*. To begin play, *A* sets the clock to indicate time, *B* sets the distance, and *C* calculates the rate. *A* and *B* check for accuracy; if they agree with *C*, the latter gets a point. Play continues as before except in the order *B*, *C*, *A*; then *C*, *A*, *B*; and so on. At the end of the playing time, the member of each set with the most points wins.

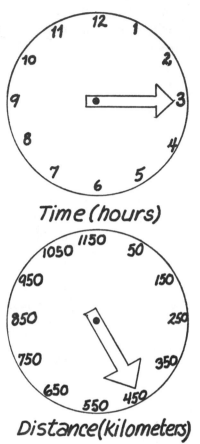

Time (hours)

Distance (kilometers)

✼ 348 ✼

Choosing a unit with which to measure area is of course arbitrary. Early explorations could include choosing, with the students, some common object, such as a leaf, tracing it on paper, cutting out the pattern, and using it to measure the area of a number of objects or shapes. Be sure to discuss with the children the lack of fit, approximations, and why their answers did not always agree.

✼ 349 ✼ ESTIMATING AREA

Give the children centimeter grid paper and have them draw irregular shapes either on the squared paper or on thin paper that they can place over the squared paper. Ask the children to count all the squares entirely contained in the figure. Then have them count, in addition, those squares enclosed or *partially* enclosed by the figure. This activity will provide entrance to a discussion about approximating areas and is just cumbersome enough to cause appreciation for our "short-cut" area measurements for common shapes such as rectangles, triangles, and so forth.

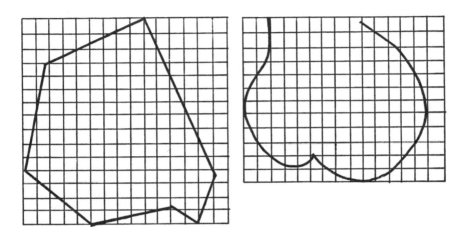

This estimation activity may be extended and applied to formal measurement by having children cut decimeter squares from centimeter grid paper, mark them as shown, and determine the area of the triangle and rectangle subsequently.

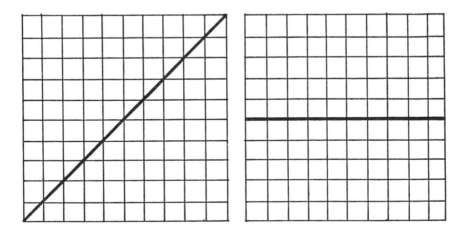

❀ **350** ❀

The concept of area and its relationship to square units can be dealt with in a concrete manner if children have access to manipulatives. One very sturdy and readily available material is the small (approximately $2\frac{1}{2}$ cm) square ceramic tiles found in floor-covering stores. Given any shape, common or irregular, the child can fit tiles, count them, and soon generalize the area concept. Begin by filling simple rectangular and square shapes—then move to approximations of the area of triangles and even circles. If ceramic tiles are not available, this important concept may be reinforced by having children cut square centimeters from centimeter grid paper to use in covering regular and irregular shapes, or centimeters from rod sets.

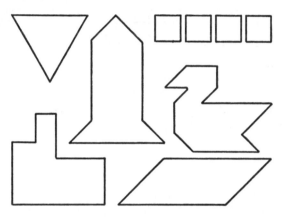

❀ **351** ❀

Concurrent with classroom activities for developing the concept of area as square units of measure, an easy reference for children in the form of a chart for the classroom wall or bulletin board is a useful learning aid.

> **AREA MEASUREMENT**
> 1 square centimeter = 100 square millimeters
> $(1 \text{ cm}^2 = 100 \text{ mm}^2)$
> 1 square decimeter = 100 square centimeters
> $(1 \text{ dm}^2 = 100 \text{ cm}^2)$
> 1 square meter = 100 square decimeters
> $(1 \text{ m}^2 = 100 \text{ dm}^2)$

❀ 352 ❀

Provide a small group of children with some old newspapers, scissors, some tape, and a meter stick. Have them make a square meter and determine how many square meters would be needed to cover:

1. The teacher's desk.
2. The floor in the principal's office.
3. The floor in your classroom.
4. The door of your classroom.
5. The windows of your classroom.

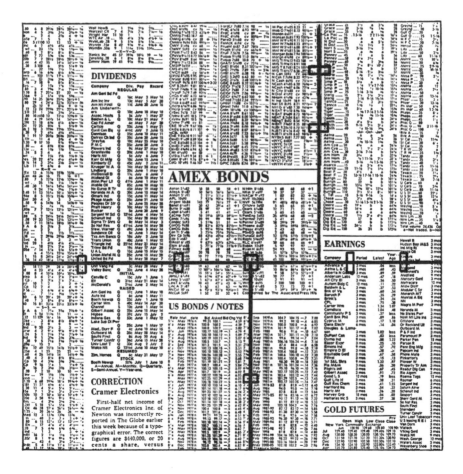

Find the cost of floor covering for each of these areas if 1 m^2 of carpeting costs $10.

❀ 353 ❀

Fun experience in length or perimeter estimation can be gained if a variety of common shapes are cut from colored oaktag, e.g., different sizes of rectangles, squares, triangles, and even a circle. The perimeters of these polygons may vary from 2 cm to 1 decimeter. The perimeter of each of these is drawn as a heavy straight line of narrow strips of oaktag as in the illustration, and the individual (or paired) children choose a shape and then select one of the line segments by their "by-eye" estimate of the perimeter of the figure. Checking is important and is done by "walking" each side of the figure along the line, holding positions with a placed finger.

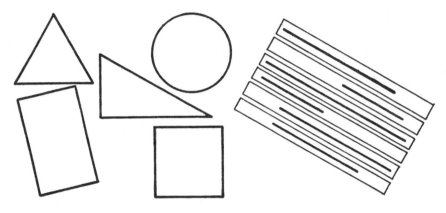

Variation Use the oaktag strips with the heavy black lines in an activity where the children simply estimate the line segment in centimeters, record, and then measure to determine its measure in centimeters.

❀ 354 ❀ AREA AND PERIMETER

Finding the maximum area possible when given a fixed length for the perimeter is a challenging exploration for middle-grade students. Provide or have a pair of students cut a 1-m piece of string and try to discover what will be the dimensions of the rectangle that it will form such that the area enclosed is a maximum. Subsequently, the 1-m string may be used to make a 1-meter "trundle wheel." Children in pairs, one recording and one measuring, may proceed to explore both perimeter and area. Some examples of actual measures that may be taken are:

1. Classroom   4. Schoolground   7. Lunchroom to
2. Hallways   5. Sidewalks   playground
3. Base paths   6. Gym   8. Hopscotch grid

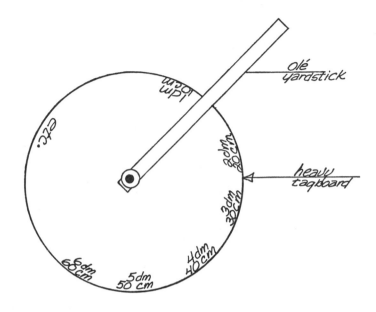

❀ **355** ❀

Practice in solving measurement problems may be motivated through quantitative settings such as those below:

A Track man *A* ran a 100-yard dash in 9 seconds. Track man *B* ran 100 meters in 10 seconds. Who ran faster? (*Hint*: The rate of each runner must be calculated.)

B Mr. McCarthy plans to fence his property on three sides. The plot is 24 m across the back and 16 m on each side. Fence material costs $115.00 per 50 m and posts, which are to be 4 m apart, cost $1.50 each. How much will the fence cost?

24 m

16 m

Answer The actual cost of the fence per meter is $2.30. Thus $2.30 × 56 m = $122.80. Fourteen posts are required at $1.50 each; thus the cost of posts is $21.00. Therefore, the total cost is $122.80 + $21.00 or $143.80.

C   Have children make a bulletin board display of the legal speed limits in your state, city, and neighborhood area.

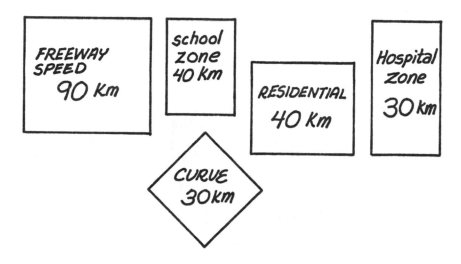

VOLUME MEASUREMENT

 356

Volume is a measure of space occupied. To help children learn about common volume measurements, try procedures similar to the following:

A   Collect milk cartons that are in good condition and of several sizes—100 ml, 500 ml, 1 liter, 2 liters (1 liter is about a quart). Have on hand a bucket of water, a glass or plastic measuring pitcher, and a towel or two! Tell stories of how much was bought at the store, used for breakfast, used for an after-school snack, and the like. Let the children measure to show the amounts.

B   For variation and to help the pupils form ideas of quantity, pour the same amount of water into each of several variously sized and shaped containers. Or, if this has been done in advance, suggest that children estimate the amount in each container. Pupils should check by pouring into the measuring pitcher.

C At the early grade levels children need experience determining which of two containers will hold the most. A supply of material (rice, sand, etc.) and a variety of small containers will provide for exploration as the material is poured from one container to a second and volume inequalities are noted.

D Filling containers with small uniform cubes of wood (centimeter rods, for example) will allow students to visually approach the concept of cubic units of volume measure. Again approximation will follow precise volumes.

❀ 357 ❀ THE BIG EYE!

Purpose To provide practice in estimating capacity in metric units.
Level 2 or above.
Number of players 3 players or 3 teams.
Materials needed A large collection of common and uncommon containers of different but unknown sizes. A metrically graduated liquid (liter) or dry measuring container. A set of blocks in cm^3, dm^3, and m^3 sizes (cardboard is adequate for these).
Procedure Each player or team member is given the same randomly selected container. After inspecting it he states his estimate of its volume or capacity. A third student or member of the third team acts as "umpire" and now actually measures the container by filling it with water (or blocks, etc.) and then transferring the water to the graduated container. The team or student that had given the best estimate receives a point. Another container is chosen and the activity continues until all the containers are measured or all the members have had a turn. The umpire team then may challenge the winner and the losing side becomes the new umpire.

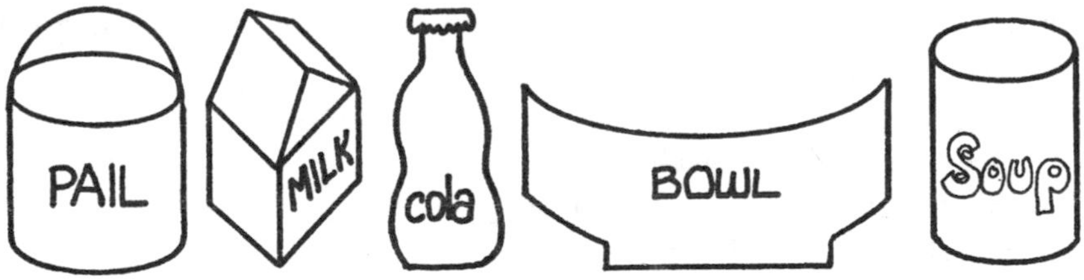

❀ 358 ❀ LITER LITTER

Children enjoy working with words. To reinforce the vocabulary associated with metric measures of liquid volume, prepare a classroom chart such as the one shown. Then provide children with a sheet containing the terms in scrambled form, where the task is to unscramble the letters to form the appropriate term for liquid measure.

1 hectoLITER	=	100 liters
1 dekaLITER	=	10 liters
1 LITER	=	1 liter
1 deci LITER	=	0.1 liter
1 centiLITER	=	0.01 liter
1 milliLITER	=	0.001 liter

SCRAMBLE	UNSCRAMBLED
triel	liter
titlecinter	centiliter
ttocherli	hectoliter
trillliime	milliliter
leiktrade	dekaliter
icelerlid	deciliter

Variation   Have children design similar "scrambles" for the meter and gram.

❁ 359 ❁ LITER MAID

Purpose   To provide practice with liter equivalents.
Level   Intermediate.
Number of players   2 to 4.
Materials needed   Some pairs of cards and an odd one designated the "Liter Maid." The number of cards will depend on the level of the children. Some possible pairs are shown.

1.4 cl—14 ml	100 cl—1 liter
3 cl—30 ml	150 cl—1.5 liters
5 cl—50 ml	300 cl—3 liters
50 cl—500 ml	1000 cl—10 liters

Procedure   The cards are shuffled and all are given out. All players lay down any pairs. Then the first player draws from the player on his left. Play continues with each player putting down a pair when he has drawn a match. The loser is the player left with the "Liter Maid."

❀ 360 ❀

The notion of m³ as a simple extension of m² may be reinforced through an independent, small-group activity. Have children use the square meter made from newspaper during the study of area (Activity 352). Provide some reasonably rigid cardboard from which they may measure and cut five square meters. Tape the five square meters as shown in the illustration. Children may assume that the cubic meter "box" is closed on the top. Next, have the children use the box to estimate the volume of some familiar space in m³, i.e., the clothes closet of classroom, the gym storage room, the classroom, the inside of your car, and so forth. As appropriate, check the guesses.

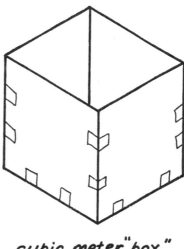

cubic meter "box"

Variation If this activity proves too cumbersome for young children, the same results may be obtained by having children construct individual "cm³ boxes" or "dm³ boxes." Follow the directions as indicated but provide children with a 10-cm square for constructing their "box."

❀ 361 ❀

The study of metric measures and their relationship to the standard meter can prove confusing to children and needs constant reinforcement. A classroom visual such as the one shown is a superior device for portraying the common relationships between metric measures. You can reproduce the chart and use it as the basis for having several small groups of children produce their other charts, displaying how the common (or uncommon) measurements are related directly to the meter.[4] The mass values hold for pure *water* at 4° C.

1 cm³ (1000 mm³) = 1 milliliter (1 ml) = 1 gram
1 dm³ (1000 cm³) = 1 liter (1000 cm³) = 1 kilogram (1000 g)

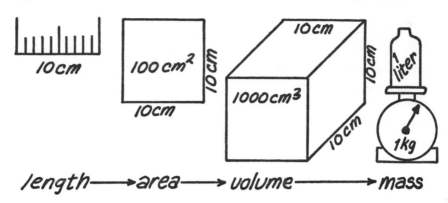

length——→area——→ volume——————→mass

❀ 362 ❀

Class projects are needed that will motivate children, yet maintain a high interest. The two activities that follow require a 0.5 liter measure calibrated in milliliters or a larger milliliter measure.

A	SCOUT DOUGH
	275 ml of salt
	275 ml of flour
	125 ml of cold water (enough to form a spongy dough)
	some food coloring

Directions   Mix the flour and salt and stir in water. Knead and separate into four small loaves. Add a drop of food coloring to each and knead again. Roll the dough thin and cut out scout emblems, geometric shapes for a mobile, Christmas tree ornaments, or charms for a bracelet. The dough will harden as it dries, and objects may be assembled or completed.

B	GORGEOUS GARDEN
	Mix the following ingredients in a bowl:
	30 ml of table salt
	30 ml of water
	30 ml of liquid bluing
	7 ml of ammonia

Directions   Pour the mixture over bits of brick, concrete chips, lava rock, or pieces of sponge that have been placed in a shallow pan. For added brilliance, drop food coloring over the garden. Watch it grow!

✸ 363 ✸ LITER SQUARE

Purpose To provide practice with equivalents within the basic unit of measure for volume.
Level Intermediate.
Number of players 1 to 3.
Materials needed Cut 16 cards or squares such as those shown in the illustration and a playing mat.

370 ml 5l 2000l 1 m³	5.2 l 2 m³ 2 l 650 l	50 ml (game card) 2000 ml 0.25l 1l	0.42 ml 250 ml 8l 86 cm³
1000 dm³ 0.9 ml 3200l 0.65 l	0.65 m³ 3.2 m³ 0.034l 1 ml	1 dm³ 34 cm³ 2cm³ 6.5 l	86 ml 2 ml 50 ml 0.004l
560 ml 50l 1000l 2 dm³	1 cm³ 1m³ 34l 2000 l	6500 ml 34000 ml 3.4l 0.086 l	4 cm³ 3400 cm³ 6ml 0.0065 l
2000 cm³ 75 ml 0.001l 4.7l	2 m³ 1cm³ 1l 48 cm³	86 ml 1000ml 12.4cm³ 27l	6.5 ml 24 ml 8 ml 5.2 l

Procedure The dealer shuffles the cards and places them face down on the table. The first player draws a card and attempts to play it. The first card that can be played by any player is the one marked 1 liter. It is called the game card and must be played on the mat in the space marked "game card." If the player who draws first does not get the "game card," his card is returned to the bottom of the pile and

PLAY MAT

		GAME CARD	

play continues in turn until the game card is played. Four points are awarded for playing the game card and two points for each card thereafter. Cards may only be played when the touching edges name the same volume; otherwise, they are returned to the deck. The player with the highest score wins when the play mat has been filled.

MASS MEASUREMENT (WEIGHT)

 364

Boys and girls improve their understanding of metric mass if they attempt to equate one mass to another. One way to do this is to make or borrow a balance scale.

A Let the pupils place a pillbox containing sand of a predetermined mass (may be prepared through the help of a local pharmacist) on one side of the scale. Give the children a bag of rice or wheat from which they are to fill a container to match the mass of the one on the scale. They may lift the two until they think the same mass has been achieved. Then measure to see if they were correct.

B Metal or plastic hardware washers when not being used as counters can be used as nonstandard units of mass. Allow time for students to discover how many washers a blackboard eraser, a shoe, and so on, equal in mass.

C Moving right along toward uniform and graduated units of mass, the familiar Cuisenaire rods allow for combinations of mass and can simplify notation.

365

Whole-class involvement in an informal homework activity is useful for helping children gain familiarity with the basic measures of mass in the metric system. Ask each member of the class to find at least five food packages and can labels at home that have their masses marked in grams and kilograms. Each child should record the results of his investigation. A classroom display of the actual objects or pictures of the objects may then be made. The display can include boxes of cereal, candy bars, soap, canned goods, frozen foods, cake mixes, and so forth.

366

Have children take turns working in pairs with a balance scale and metric masses to balance familiar objects with standard metric masses. First, children can estimate the mass of assorted common objects. Then use the scale to improve the estimate.[6]

a) a stick of gum
b) a nickel
c) your lunch sack
d) a baseball
e) scissors

f) an apple
g) 2 pencils
h) a standard paper clip
i) your math book
j) a chalkboard eraser

A chart for recording the approximations and actual masses such as the one shown will provide children with a helpful metric referent.

OBJECT	EST.	WEIGHT g	WEIGHT Kg
2 books		1000	
paper clip		2	
Nickel		5	

367 HOW HEAVY?

Purpose To provide reinforcement in recognizing and reading common measures for mass.

Level 3 to 6.

Number of players 2 to 6.

Materials needed A game card for each player. A spinner.

Procedure Designate a game leader who operates the spinner and calls out the number. Players write the numeral in the column value of their choice on the game card. The object is to obtain the heaviest measure for four consecu-

ROUND	GRAM			
SAMPLE	KILOGRAMS	GRAMS	DECIGRAMS	CENTIGRAMS
	2	3	7	4
1				
2				
3				
4				
5				

tive spins. The player who obtains and correctly reads the "heaviest" measure is declared the winner. He is the new leader for another round of play.

❀ 368 ❀ GRAM WHAM

Purpose To provide practice with equivalents within the basic unit of measure for mass.

GAME CARDS

0.1 mg	0.0012	1.2 dg	0.02 mg
0.069 mg 10 g 79 cg	100 dg 400 g 79 mg	0.4 kg 1 dg 0.79 kg	10 cg 790 kg 1200 g
790 mg	7.9 cg	790 g	1.2 kg
0.01 mg 4 dg 100 g	0.4 g 0.1 cg 1200 mg	1 mg 400 dg 1.2 cg	40 g 400 kg 79 dg
1000 dg	120 cg	12 mg	7.9 g
10 dg 4 mg 0.012 kg	0.4 cg 0.003 t 0.12 kg	4 kg 100 g 7.9 kg	0.1 kg 0.069 cg 0.012 t
12 g	120 g	7900 g	12 kg
79 kg 40 mg 0.20 kg	4 cg 4 g 0.4 mg	40 dg 40 kg 12 cg	0.04 t 0.01 g 0.04 mg

Level Intermediate.

Number of players 2 to 4.

Materials needed A playing mat and 16 cards or squares such as those in the illustration (see Activity 363).

Procedure The object of the game is to complete four squares in a row, vertically or horizontally, on the playing mat such that the touching edges name the same weight. The first player to complete a line segment wins. The cards are shuffled and placed face down beside the playing mat. The first player draws a card and places it on the mat in the square of his choice. Play continues in turn. It is not mandatory that a drawn card be played. It may be returned to the pile. Also, after every player has had one turn, rather than draw a card, players may choose to take their turn by moving one of the cards already on the playing mat to another square on the mat.

PLAYING MAT

❀ 369 ❀ SHERRIS' CHARADE

An interesting problem-solving context for reinforcing equivalents within a basic unit of metric measure can be designed using codes to develop a hidden design. This activity is particularly appropriate as an independent enrichment activity for the more able students. Use square-decimeter grid paper to reproduce the activity below. Provide a code for shading the corresponding squares with the appropriate design. For a free-time activity some children may enjoy developing original designs.

Key:

1 mg   1 cg   1 dg   1 g   1 dag   1 hg   1 kg   1 t

Hint: 1000.01 kg = 1000 kg + 0.01 kg =
                     1 t   + 1 dag =

CODE

	110 g		1 dag	0.1 hg			
1 dg			1 kg	1000 g		1001 kg	1 g
	1.00111 t		1 mg	0.01 g		10.1 cg	
		0.001 g	1000 mg	100 mg	1 cg		
	0.01 dg	10 mg	10 g	0.1 kg	0.001 g	0.1 dg	
	1000 mg	10 cg	1 t	1000 g	0.1 cg	0.001 hg	
		0.1 dag	0.1 cg	0.1 dg	0.1 g		
	101 mg		0.01 hg	0.01 dag		1001.11 kg	
0.0001 hg	0.1100 dg		0.01 kg	100 dg			0.1 cg
			10 hg	10,000 dg		1.001 t	

COMPLETED DESIGN

❀ 370 ❀ RAEBURN'S WRATH

Cross number puzzles provide an enjoyable setting for reinforcing basic relationships within a given unit of metric measure. The puzzle here may be reproduced for children to work independently or in pairs. After familiarity is gained with the basic idea, pairs of children can have fun devising similar puzzles for other units or a puzzle requiring mixed use of metric equivalents.

Across

1. Five men on the trapeze weigh a total of 370 kg. How much does each weigh? _____ kg.

3. Two clown shoes weigh 45 dag. How much would a clown's normal shoes weigh if they were to be $\frac{1}{9}$ the weight of the clown shoes? _____ dag.

4. The toes of the clown's shoes got cut off and they were 20 dag less. What do they weigh now? _____ dag.

6. The tent weighs 55 kg. How much will three of these tents weigh? _____ kg.

8. The lion weighs 150 kg. If his cage weighs 4500 hg, what do they weigh together? _____ kg.

9. How much would 11 lions weigh in hg without their cages? _____ hg.

11. If the candy man has 10 kg of candy to sell and sells 900 dag of it, how much does he have left? _____ kg.

12. The fat lady weighed 70,000 g. She went on a diet and lost half of her weight. How much does she weigh? _____ hg.

13. How many mg of sugar does it take to make 0.5 cg of cotton candy? _____ mg.

14. There are two elephants in the circus. Together they weigh 4.8884 t. How much does each weigh? _____ hg.

16. The monkey eats 15 dag of bananas each week. How much would 15 monkeys eat in 2 weeks? _____ dag.

17. If the horses need 2 kg of hay to sleep on and 50 kg to eat in one day, how much do they need for a week? _____ kg.

19. The circus mouse eats 2 mg of food every night. How much would he eat in 4 weeks? _____ mg.

20. The full-grown giraffe eats 15 hg of leaves each day. A baby eats 5 hg daily. How many kg are eaten by both in one day? _____ kg.

21. If the weight of an elephant were 24,000 kg, how many t would it weigh? _____ t.

Down

1. The man in the penny patch got 710,000 mg of pennies. How many dag of pennies are there? _____ dag.

2. The three bears weighed 1383 kg together. What did each weigh? _____ kg.

4. The elephant weighed 1200 t before having a baby. She weighed 1000 t afterward. What did the baby weigh? _____ t.

7. Each midget weighs 28,170 dag. How much do two weigh together? _____ dag.

8. The cage weighs 60 kg and the monkey weighs 53 g. How many g would the monkey in the cage weigh? _____ g.

10. The leopard weighs 55.4 hg. How many dag would the same leopard weigh? _____ dag.

14. There are 16 dogs in the circus, each of which weighs 160 dag. How many hg would they weigh together? _____ hg.

15. The box of tickets weighs 131 g. How much would two such boxes weigh? _____ g.

16. The two dogs weigh 9000 g together. How many hg would one weigh? _____ hg.

18. Snow cones weigh 1 dag each. A tray of 11 would weigh how many dag? _____ dag.

MIXED MEASURE AND APPLICATIONS[5]

❀ 371 ❀ METRIC OLYMPICS

Team competition can be designed to drill children in the simplicity of metric prefix values and the symbols commonly used. Since our money is metric, children and adults find these prefixes easy to remember (i.e., mill = milli, cent = centi, and dime = deci). Flash cards with the abbreviation could call for the full unit name by team members, or the card could read "kilo" and the student respond with "one thousand." Make a wide variety of cards and units for the game. The basic units are meter, kilogram, and second. The common prefixes and their respective values are given in the chart and may be used to make the game cards. Of course, a classroom chart of the values is also appropriate.

PREFIX	SYMBOL	VALUE	
mega	M	1,000,000	X basic unit
kilo	k	1000	X basic unit
hecto	h	100	X basic unit
deka	da	10	X basic unit
deci	d	1/10	X basic unit
centi	c	1/100	X basic unit
milli	m	1/1000	X basic unit
micro	μ	1/1,000,000	X basic unit

❀ 372 ❀

To acquaint children with the values of estimation and to develop their skill at it, hold contests to see who can be most nearly correct. Some possibilities are to estimate the following:

1. The number of meters and/or decimeters across the front of the room.
2. The number of marbles in a jar.
3. The time required to walk around the block.
4. The number of blades of grass in a square decimeter of lawn.
5. The temperature of water under given conditions.
6. The cost of a box containing certain groceries.
7. The weight of a familiar object (a large dictionary, the teacher, a certain automobile, a particular kind of jet airplane).
8. The number of people in the auditorium.
9. The length of time required for a given conveyance to travel between two points.
10. The temperature of an object.
11. The height of a certain building.

A valuable experience in comparisons would use items such as the above, but in pairs, so that after examination, children could express which member of the pair is longer, heavier, and so on. Following the judgment, the student should use appropriate measuring tools to verify or adjust his answer.

❀ 373 ❀ WHAT'S THE UNIT?

Purpose To provide practice on the application of selected measurement units.
Level 2 to 6.
Number of players Any number.
Materials needed Pictures of items (with labels if necessary) which can be measured by procedures that should be known by children. Paper and pencil.
Procedure Distribute papers. Show a picture and ask each player to record (1) the kind of measure, (2) the instrument, and (3) the unit(s).

PICTURE	KIND OF MEASURE	INSTRUMENT	UNIT(S)
beans	mass	scale	kilograms
milk	volume	measuring can	liters
land	area	surveyor's instruments	square kilometers
floor	area	steel tape	square meters
cloth	length	tape	meters
cement	volume	variable	cubic meters

When completed, check the papers to see who has the highest score if three points are given for each correct response. Encourage discussion where there is disagreement; you may wish to allow more than a given answer to be correct.

❀ 374 ❀ METRIC MASTER!

Purpose To provide practice in choosing a workable unit of metric measure.
Level 2 to 6.
Number of players 2 players or 2 teams.
Materials needed One set of cards, each listing one object to be measured, and another set that has the name of a unit of metric measure per card.
Procedure Player *A* turns up a card from the first deck and names the object to be measured. Player *B* must choose from the unit cards (which are

displayed face up on the table or chalk tray) the *best* unit that could be used to measure the object. Possible objects could be:

1. The volume of a thimble.
2. The area of a postage stamp.
3. The mass of a rubber band.
4. The floor area of this room.
5. The contents of a soft-drink bottle.
6. The length of a football field.

There should be about 20 cards in all.

❈ 375 ❈ KITCHEN METRICS

Easy classroom recipes constitute a stimulating "hands-in" setting for application of the smaller units of metric measure. They are an equally effective setting from which children may gain experience in the ease and convenience of conversion between the basic units of liter and gram. Only rudimentary metric instruments are required. If no metric measures are available to you, you can refer to this kitchen conversion chart of approximate equivalents:

1 teaspoon: about 5 ml   1 cup shortening: about 225 g
1 tablespoon: about 15 ml   1 ounce: about 30 g
$\frac{1}{2}$ cup: about 125 ml $\frac{1}{2}$ cup butter: about 115 g
$\frac{1}{3}$ cup: about 80 ml   1 cup sugar: about 250 g
4 cups: about 1 liter   Moderate oven: 180° Celsius

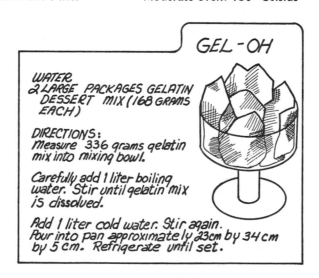

GEL-OH

WATER
2 LARGE PACKAGES GELATIN DESSERT MIX (168 GRAMS EACH)

DIRECTIONS:
Measure 336 grams gelatin mix into mixing bowl.

Carefully add 1 liter boiling water. Stir until gelatin mix is dissolved.

Add 1 liter cold water. Stir again. Pour into pan approximately 23cm by 34cm by 5 cm. Refrigerate until set.

20-MINUTE FUDGE

Mix together in a large bowl:
1 egg, well beaten
45 milliliters cream
5 milliliters vanilla
3-4 milliliters salt
480 milliliters confectioners
    sugar

Melt together in a small saucepan over
medium heat : 112 grams unsweetened chocolate
                15 milliliters butter
Add melted ingredients to first mixture. Stir in:
240 milliliters chopped walnut meats or marsh-
mallows, cut in pieces, or some of both.

Spread mixture in a buttered pan 20 cm by 20 cm.
Cut in squares or triangles. Makes 0.68 kilogram.

NO-BAKE COOKIES

Mix together in a medium size pan
480 milliliters white sugar
 60 milliliters cocoa
120 milliliters margarine
    or butter
120 milliliters milk

Cook this over a medium heat
and let it boil 1 minute. Have
ready and add:
720 milliliters quick-cook oats
120 milliliters peanut butter
1-2 milliliters salt
 5 milliliters vanilla
Stir mixture until all is mixed well. Remove from
heat and drop by amounts of about 5 milliliters
each onto waxed paper. Allow to cool.

COOL

BISCUITS

RICE AND WHEAT FLOUR BISCUITS

125 milliliters pastry whole wheat flour
100 milliliters brown rice flour
  4 milliliters salt
  5 milliliters baking powder
 15 milliliters butter
 15 milliliters oil
  5 milliliters honey
130 milliliters milk

Yummy

Sift the dry ingredients together and cut
in butter, add oil. Make a very soft dough with
the milk and honey, and form into
biscuits. Bake on a greased cookie
sheet in a very hot oven: 220°C
for 15-18 minutes.

❀ 376 ❀   METRIC RUMMY

Purpose   To provide practice in dealing with metric equivalents.
Level   3 or above.
Number of players   2 to 4.
Materials needed   A set of 50 cards, made of 25 pairs, each pair marked with equivalent metric values (see below).

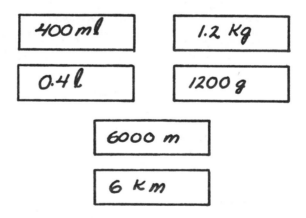

Procedure   Shuffle the cards and deal five to each player. Lay the balance of the cards in a pile face down; turn up the top card. The player to the left of the dealer begins by laying down "books" of 2 cards containing the same metric value, e.g., 14 cm, 1.4 dm. He may draw one card from the blind deck or take the turned-up card. When through playing, he discards one card face up. Play then goes to his left and continues as above except that should there be more than one card in the discard pile, a player must take all of them if he wants the top card. Play ends when one person has no more cards. The player with the most books wins.

❀ 377 ❀ MEASUREMENT BINGO

Purpose To provide practice in relating measuring units to measuring instruments.
Level 3 to 5.
Number of players 2 or more.
Materials needed Nine cards on which are pictures or drawings of measuring instruments (suggestions: weight scale, ruler, meter stick, measuring cup, thermometer, clock, calendar, speedometer, odometer, protractor, pedometer). Bingo-type cards for players using nine squares, in each of which is the name of a unit of measure, arranged differently on each card; some cards have words not related to pictures. Nine beans or other markers for each player.

angles	kilograms	meters
grams	kilometers	minutes
kilometers per hour	days	degrees

Procedure Distribute bingo cards and markers to players. The leader holds up a picture card and pupils who have a word indicating a unit measured by the pictured item place a marker in the appropriate square. The player getting three markers in a row either vertically or horizontally calls out "Bingo" and is the winner of that round. The players exchange cards and the leader shuffles picture cards, after which another game may be played.

❀ 378 ❀ CONCENTRATION

Purpose To acquire skill in conversion between metric measures.
Level 5 to 6.

Number of players   2.
Materials needed   Sixteen (or more) cards like those shown and a play mat.

1m	*1cm*	*1000mg*	*100cm*					
1ℓ	*1km*	*1000mm*	*10mm*					
1km	*1kg*	*1000mℓ*	*1000ℓ*					
1m	*1g*	*1000m*	*1000g*					

CONCENTRATION CARDS   *MAT*

Procedure   Shuffle all cards and place them face down in random order on the playing mat, one card per space. The first player begins by turning over two cards. If the two cards are equivalent (for example, 10 millimeters and 1 centimeter), the player may keep both cards. If not, he returns them to the board, one face up and the other face down. The second player must now turn a card to match the up card. If he does, he may keep both cards and play reverts to the first player, who turns two new cards. If he does not match the up card, he turns his card face down and the first player attempts to match it. Play continues in order until the board is cleared and the player with the most cards is the winner.

 379

An uncomplicated U.S. map can suggest supplemental travel and rate investigations. Use one like that shown and then, with student assistance, design others to help students solve selected problems related to metric measures.

1. If a person started at Des Moines and traveled a distance of 5200 km, what towns did he visit on his journey?
2. Suppose that we get 10 km/liter of gasoline and use 550 liters. If we started our trip in Portland, what is the last city we reached?
3. If a person took a trip, driving 8 hours each day at 82.5 km/hr, what cities were possible starting and stopping points?
4. If gasoline costs 20 cents per liter and all we can spend is $56.00, leaving Los Angeles in a car that travels about 12 km/liter, can we reach Portland? Dallas? Washington, D.C.?

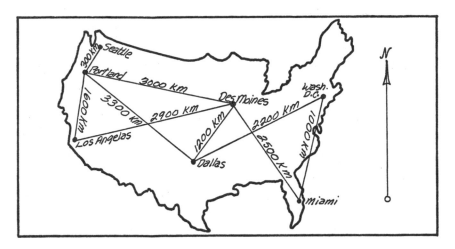

5. What two towns are 16 hours driving time apart at a speed limit of 75 km/hr?

6. An airplane can fly 640 km/hr between Portland and Los Angeles. How many hours will the trip take?

7. If our gas tank holds 55 liters and if after leaving Dallas with a full tank we refill it three more times, it allows us to just reach Portland. How many km/liter did we use?

❀ 380 ❀ MEASUREMENT RACE

Purpose   To provide practice in solving measurement problems.

Level   5 to 6.

Number of players   2 or more.

Materials needed   Papers or cards with drawings of geometric figures on them. Mark the measurement of length, height, radius, or other appropriate dimensions. Make some difficult by giving one measurement in meters and another in centimeters or decimeters, or show a mixture of units. Paper and pencil for players. Indicate directions, e.g., find area, perimeter, and volume.

Procedure   If the group is large, divide the pupils into small teams. At a signal the first player of each team comes to the checker (who could be the teacher) to get a card. He takes it to his desk, solves the problem, and brings his paper to the checker, then gets another card, which he takes to the second player on his team. The process is repeated until each member of the team has solved a problem. Five points are given to the team that completes the problems first. Three points are given for each correct answer. The team with the highest score wins.

❀ 381 ❀

To help children in the primary grades become aware of graph principles, help them record simple data. Examples:

1. How many children in the class have dark hair (brunette)? How many light (blond)? How many medium (brown)? Discussion may show that it is necessary to arbitrarily classify a borderline case; all others are compared and listed as lighter or darker.
2. How many children have brown eyes? Blue eyes?
3. How many children's birthdays occur each month of the year?
4. How many cars of each make are in the teachers' parking lot?
5. How many children have lost teeth each month?
6. How many books has each child read this month?

Be especially alert to questions that arise naturally and do not involve complex data. Make a simple bar graph of data collected by cutting small squares of colored paper and pasting them on a chart, e.g., one square for each child with dark hair. When children have grasped the procedure, they should be encouraged to make their own graphs from data they gather. Sometimes two or three children can work together.

❀ 382 ❀

An uncomplicated bar graph can be shared with the class by two students who take a survey in the class, showing, among other things: (a) favorite ice cream (vanilla, chocolate, strawberry); or (b) favorite game (hopscotch, base-

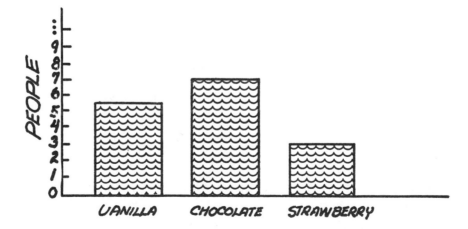

ball, tag); or (c) favorite subject (reading, math, spelling); or (d) body size (waist, height, weight). To help children recognize the usefulness of graphs, make a bulletin board on which these examples of graphs (or others cut from magazines and/or newspapers) can be displayed. Frame questions that can be answered by referring to posted items. Use metric measures in the surveys when appropriate and again in chart construction.

 383 ❀

Measurement is basic to science and one of the familiar activities in many classrooms is to grow some plants from seeds, such as corn, in small containers of soil. Measuring and graphing are motivating and meaningful as each child collects daily information about his plant and records it on a graph such as the one shown. Questions involving whose plant grew most since yesterday, which plant is the tallest, or which plant grew the most over a weekend will usually excite the students. Ask about why more growth is seen on Monday and what the height might have been if the plant had been measured on Saturday or what the height will be in 4 more days. Have children consult their graphs before answering.

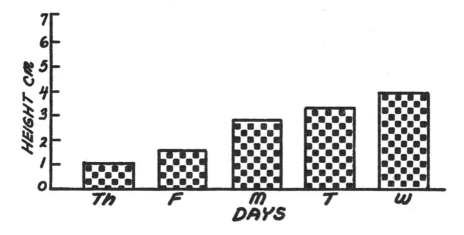

 384 ❀

After children have learned to read graphs, some pupils (individually or in pairs) may want to make some of their own. At this point, teach or review scale drawing; e.g., 1 cm represents 1 m. Remind children that the unit relationships selected must be kept consistent for all data to be illustrated on

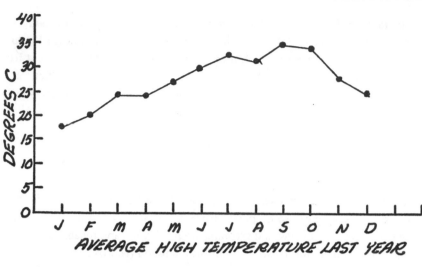

AVERAGE HIGH TEMPERATURE LAST YEAR

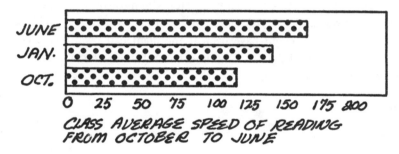

CLASS AVERAGE SPEED OF READING
FROM OCTOBER TO JUNE

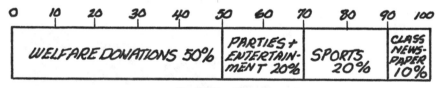

CLASS BUDGET

a graph. Limit work to simple graphs such as line and bar; picture graphs, while interesting, are difficult to construct. Some examples are shown. Pupils may record data and practice graphing from activities such as the following:

A   Record how many marbles are knocked out of a 2-meter circle by each of several players given six turns each. How many from a 1.25-meter circle? A 1-meter circle?

B   Record how far a simple pulley travels when the rope is pulled 30 cm, 70 cm, and 100 cm.

C Compare the number of words spelled correctly for each of 6 weeks.

D Compare the number of hits with the number of times at bat for all members of the school or class softball team during a 2-week period.

E Drop a ball from various heights along a vertically held meter stick and record how high the bounce is. Do the same for various kinds of balls.

F Compare the loss of water in a week's time from each of several containers with the surface area of the water in each container.

G Record the weekly growth of plants "watered" with tap water, coke, rubbing alcohol, water mixed with liquid fertilizer, or the like. Do the same using tap water but using different amounts for each plant.

H Compare the heights of boys or girls in the class with their masses.

❀ **385** ❀

To give practice in reading and recording temperature, make an adjustable mock thermometer from heavy cardboard and ribbon. Examine a standard thermometer for correct marking and numeration. You may wish to make both a Fahrenheit and a Celsius (centigrade) thermometer. For orientation, here are some common comparative temperatures in degrees Celsius:

0°—water freezes	40°—heat wave
25°—a nice day	100°—water boils
37°—normal body temperature	250°—hot oven

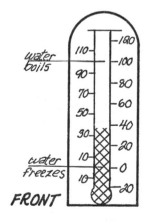

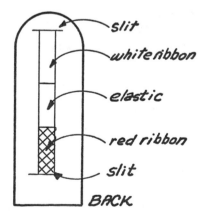

A week's log that records each day's highest temperature found in the local newspaper or other news source can be recorded in the form of a simple graph (see Activity 383). Children should be asked about the highest and lowest temperatures reached during the week and, when appropriate, about negative temperatures. A valuable option is to have the children read the temperature from a thermometer located just outside the room at a given time each day and keep a graph record for a number of days.

❀ 386 ❀ MONEY AND METER

Our monetary system provides us a setting for natural associations in subdividing the meter into tenths and hundredths. Children need not have prior experience with decimals other than casual experience in reading dollar amounts such as $24.36. An extremely instructive bulletin board display can be developed for showing this relationship of 1 to 100. The sophistication of the display should be consistent with the level of children. The "thousands" (mills or millimeters) could be omitted from the display in the illustration.

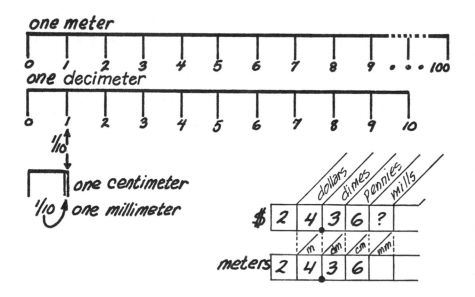

❀ 387 ❀

Have children design a metric board game that requires moving along a path (bus to camp, ski run, jogging route). Children are very familiar with such games. Some encouragement and even a visit to a toystore will inspire many ideas. Draw the metric game. Use the unit meter, liter, or gram. Make up the rules. Get some markers. Label and decorate the play mat. Supplies such as dice, blank cards, spinners, cubes, and so forth can be easily obtained from local suppliers. Some game routes or paths may look as shown. Children will

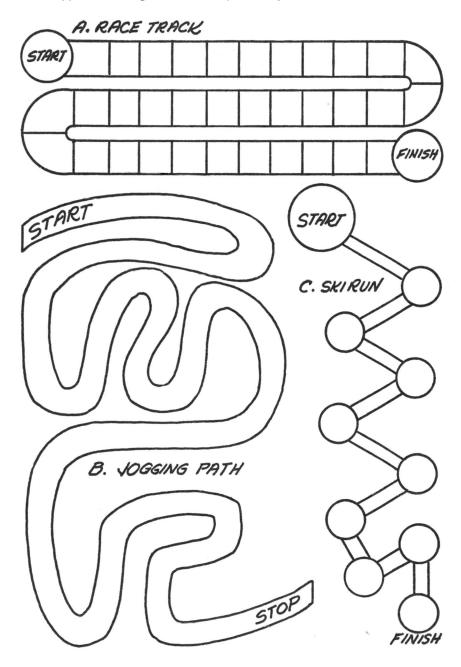

love to use imagination in creating cards to accompany these playing mats. Some illustrative cards are:

1. Bear blocking path—go back to start.
2. Flat tire—lose one turn.
3. Ski binding breaks—go to rest station, lose two turns.
4. Stump showing—lose one turn.
5. Bus needs 20 liters of gas—lose two turns.

NOTES

1. *Education U.S.A.* (Washington, D.C.: National School Public Relations Association, 1975), p. 217.

2. Answers to the miniquiz: (1) 8; (2) 4; (3) 3; (4) 16; (5) $5\frac{1}{2}$; (6) 16; (7) 2240; (8) 1296; (9) 43,560; (10) 640.

3. Detailed information about metric units and their notation can be found in *The International System of Units (SI)* (National Bureau of Standards Special Publication 330). (Washington, D.C.: Government Printing Office, 1975).

4. A wide selection of commercial material and instruments is available through *Creative Publications*, P.O. Box 10328, Palo Alto, California, and through *Mind/Matter Corporation*, P.O. Box 345, Danbury, Connecticut 06810.

5. *A Metric America: A Decision Whose Time Has Come* (National Bureau of Standards Special Publication 345). (Washington, D.C.: Government Printing Office, 1971), 192 p.

6. Activities similar to this one for all basic metric units can be found in *Arithmetic Teacher*, Vol. 20, No. 4, 1973. This entire issue is devoted to the metric system. Other useful *Arithmetic Teacher* references are Vol. 21, No. 5, 1974, pp. 366–369, and Vol. 22, No. 5, 1975, pp. 372–381.

7. A practical understanding of the metric system of measurement for teachers and parents may be gained from S. Ostergard, E. Silvia, and B. Wheeler, *The Metric World: A Survival Guide* (West Publishing Company, 1975), 126 pp.

RATIONALE

Problem solving continues to be one of the persistent dilemmas for elementary school mathematics instruction. While many adults believe that speed and accuracy in computation ought be the primary objective of elementary school mathematics instruction, many teachers and others responsible for classroom instruction recognize that an equally important aim of the mathematics program is development of problem-solving proficiency.

Not surprisingly, it is more difficult to tell what problem solving is not than to say what it is. As an example, we know in a generalized sense that problem solving encompasses a complex set of interrelationships among the ability to discriminate, classify, think logically, make intelligent judgments, interpret, and project, to say nothing of the ability to decode printed words. Yet we do not do very well when we attempt a precise definition or

285

description for any of these characteristics. On the other hand, it is somewhat easier to say what experience in problem solving is not. For example, most would agree that problem solving is not getting the answer to an exercise through following a known procedure. The algorithm of ordinary arithmetic offers the best illustration. When children are assigned the task of doing "problems 1 to 15 on page 46" and the "problems" look like this:

$$(1)\ 462 \qquad (2)\ 875 \qquad (3)\ 205$$
$$\underline{\times 38} \qquad\quad \underline{\times 29} \qquad\quad \underline{\times 68} \ldots$$

we can be fairly certain no development of problem-solving skill has been undertaken.[1]

Children develop the ability to reason logically at an early age. It is the basis upon which they "solve problems" daily in their immediate environment. Consider the child who leaves the creeping stage by hoisting himself up and taking those first uncertain steps around a chair or some other piece of furniture. Although they cannot verbalize their action and their first attempts may seem rudimentary and clumsy to an adult, they are, nonetheless, using reason to solve a problem for them. More importantly, it should not escape notice that such efforts are consistently nurtured and rewarded by parents. The development is not left to chance.

Such generalized development is not unlike that which is essential to the mathematics program throughout the elementary school years. It is particularly in the mathematics program that the ability to think logically assumes an increasingly important role. Children must learn to apply logical thinking, and it is crucial that they develop a conscious awareness of how they reason their way to the solution of problems. As with a child's general development, growth in ability to think logically and to apply such growth to problem solving in the context of the mathematics program cannot be left to chance. Problem-solving skills are developed through practice and experience. Settings for problem-solving development must be structured in the classroom. Crucial prior decisions must be made by the teachers. There is abundant evidence that we can stimulate children's imagination and enhance problem-solving skill by tailoring a classroom setting in which we carefully provide appropriate problems, adequate accompanying cues, and the important structural materials to carry out explorations and investigations. In truth, there are but few fundamental activities in elementary school mathematics that cannot be introduced in a problem-solving context. The larger purpose is independence in making discoveries applicable to solving problems.

From experience with the activities in this chapter the children will learn:

1. To logically sort, group, or classify objects by attribute.
2. To determine conjunctive instances in problem solving.

3. To recognize disjunctive (not) instances in problem solving.
4. To recognize patterns for triangular, square, and perfect numbers.
5. To use number patterns as an aid in problem solving.
6. To define and generate prime and composite numbers through patterns.
7. To use the number line in demonstration of the existence of negative numbers.
8. To demonstrate skill in basic operations with integers.
9. To state and illustrate some fundamental theorems of arithmetic utilizing a finite system of numbers.
10. To understand probability as the likelihood that an event will occur in the future based on past events.
11. To chart and display data in terms of selected characteristics.
12. To make predictive inferences from selected data.

LOGICAL THINKING

Experiences in thinking logically should begin with the early school years, since problem solving has as its base the ability to think logically. Physical objects that children can handle, sort, separate, classify, and arrange are universally considered essential to the mathematics program of any classroom that is concerned with developing problem-solving skill. Attribute blocks is the name given to a set of materials in which the objects differ from each other in one or more ways, each having certain attributes. Examples: (1) a set of 48 blocks having four shapes (as square, triangle, circle, rectangle), three colors (as yellow, blue, red), two thicknesses, and two sizes[2]; (2) a set of 48 pieces of heavy poster paper having similar attributes to the blocks except that instead of thickness as a variable, one set is cut with an ordinary scissors and another set with a set of pinking shears. A set of common items can also be used; for example, pieces of fabric can be cut into two or three distinct sizes and into several shapes for each size; color and texture can be other variables, or one may use the children in the class with such variables as sex and color of eyes, hair, shoes. The activities that follow were designed to be used with a set of blocks as described above. The materials will be referred to as "attribute blocks," but you may find substitute materials quite satisfactory in many, if not all, cases.

❀ 388 ❀ ALIKE

Purpose To provide practice in recognizing things that go together.
Level K to 1.

Number of players   2 to 4.
Materials needed   Attribute blocks.
Procedure   Place materials in a pile. Two children (or, in the case of four in a group, two pairs of children) sort the items into two piles according to an attribute, size. Repeat with another attribute, thickness. Then sort into three piles according to color. Finally, make four piles according to shape. If three pupils play, one can check on the others or participate if three attributes are involved.

❀ 389 ❀ NAMING

Purpose   To provide practice in naming attributes.
Level   K to 2.
Number of players   2 or more.
Materials needed   Attribute blocks.
Procedure   Players sit around a pile of attribute blocks. In turn, each child closes his eyes and picks up a block. The leader says, "What do you have in your hand?" The player opens his eyes and describes the item. He gets one point for each attribute, e.g., "This is a blue block," "This is a large, blue block," "This is a large, square, blue block," "This is a large, thick, square, blue block." When each player has had several turns, total the scores.

❀ 390 ❀ STEPPING STONES

Purpose   To provide reinforcement in recognition of multiple attributes.
Level   K to 2.
Number of players   1 or more.
Materials needed   Attribute blocks.
Procedure   Place several blocks on the floor in an irregular row. Players take turns "crossing the lake on stepping stones." To do this, a pupil must describe each block in turn by an arbitrarily chosen attribute, such as color. When his turn comes again, he tries to name two specified attributes, such as color and shape. Continue the play with three and then four attributes. If a pupil makes a mistake, he "falls into the lake" and must wait to "dry out" until his turn comes again.

❀ 391 ❀ SALAD

Purpose To provide practice in recognition of attributes.
Level K to 2.
Number of players 1 or more.
Materials needed Attribute blocks.
Procedure Players sit in a semicircle about a pile of attribute blocks. The leader says, "I am going to make a salad. I will need a large, red apple. Who will find me one?" A child is called on. He hands the leader a large, red block which the leader places in a designated area which he calls the salad bowl (could be marked on the floor or be a shallow box). The "salad" is tasted and found wanting. The leader asks for a long, yellow banana. The player selects a yellow, rectangular block. The salad needs something more, and so the game goes on until a suitable salad has been made.

❀ 392 ❀ IN THE BAG

Purpose To provide practice in naming attributes through imagery.
Level K to 2.
Number of players 2 or more.
Materials needed Attribute blocks. A small cloth bag. A large paper sack. About two dozen beans.
Procedure One player leads by holding in the paper sack the cloth bag, into which he places a block. He closes the bag and hands it to the next player, who feels the block and tries to describe it. If he succeeds, he gets a bean, the block is permanently placed in full view, and a different block is hidden in the bag for the third player to feel and guess the identity of. Since color cannot be felt, it must be guessed. This becomes easier as more and more blocks appear in view. The player with the most beans at the end of the game is the winner.

❀ 393 ❀ SHARP EYES

Purpose To provide oral reinforcement of multiple attributes.
Level K to 2.
Number of players 3 to 5.
Materials needed Attribute blocks.
Procedure Spread the blocks on the floor so that none are hidden. One

player asks, "Who can find a thick, large, red circle?" The other players try to be first; the one who succeeds places it beside him and asks a question similar to that above. When half or more of the blocks have been selected, stop the game. The one with the most blocks beside him is the winner.

❀ 394 ❀ SEE THE DIFFERENCE

Purpose   To provide practice in recognizing disjunctive (not) instances.
Level   K to 3.
Number of players   1 to 4.
Materials needed   Attribute blocks.
Procedure   Players take turns placing the blocks in a row. At first, each succeeding block must be different from the preceding one in only one attribute, e.g., following a large, thick, red circle, one might place a large, thick, yellow circle.

When players become adept at making a one-difference row, suggest that they make a circle of blocks. Of course, the problem will be with the key block, which completes the circle.
Variations   Let pupils try to make a row or a circle of blocks with exactly two differences between adjoining blocks. Then try three differences, four differences; alternate one difference and two differences or one, two, and three differences.

❀ 395 ❀ IT IS NOT

Purpose   To provide oral reinforcement of disjunctive instances.
Level   1 to 4.
Number of players   2 or more.
Materials needed   Attribute blocks. Familiar objects about the room.
Procedure   The first player picks up a block and asks, "What is this not?" In turn, each player tells something it is not; e.g., if a red, large, thin circle is shown, a player can say, "It is not a square." Another can say, "It is not yellow." And so on.

After the game has become familiar, encourage children to indicate characteristics (other than the blocks' particular attributes) that it is *not*; e.g., "It is not a fruit." The possibilities are endless.

A next step is to consider various items about the room, from children to chalk. Players try to describe an item by telling what it is not. Let the pupils challenge each other if they think a mistake has been made.

❀ 396 ❀ ANSWER MAN

Purpose To provide reinforcement with conjunctive/disjunctive instances.
Level 1 to 4.
Number of players 2 or more.
Materials needed Chalk and chalkboard or crayon and paper on an easel.
Attribute blocks.
Procedure One child looks at the attribute blocks and mentally selects one.
Other players then take turns asking questions that can be answered, "Yes"
or "No"; e.g., if a yellow, thick, small square were selected, players might ask,
"Is it red?" Since the answer is "No," the teacher writes "Not red." If a child
asks, "Is it square?" the response is "Yes," and the teacher then records
"Square." In this way players gather information until one can pick up the
correct block. That child becomes the next person to select a block.
Variation Play this game in the same way as the Answer Man, but this time
record two items: the answer and the deduction; e.g., if a yellow, thick, small
square had been selected and a player asked, "Is it red?", write "not red" in
one column and opposite it, under "Deduction," write "yellow or blue." If a
child asks, "Is it yellow?", record only "yellow" in the answer column; no
deduction is needed.

❀ 397 ❀ SORTING

Purpose To provide practice in the logic of classifying.
Level 1 to 3.
Number of players 1 to 4.
Materials needed All the pieces of
the attribute block set that are large
and thick. A grid, such as the one
illustrated, with squares large enough
for the big blocks.
Procedure Ask the players to sort
blocks so that all the yellow ones are
in one row, all the blue in the next,
and all the red in the last one.

For further practice, repeat with
small, thin blocks or small, thick ones.
Facility here is necessary readiness for
the next game, Matrix.

✾ 398 ✾ MATRIX

Purpose To provide reinforcement in the logic of classification.
Level 1 to 3.
Number of players 1 to 4.
Materials needed Attribute blocks. A grid marked on the floor or on a large paper taped to the floor.

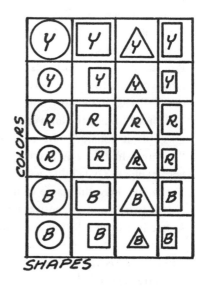

Procedure In the top set of squares, place large yellow blocks, all thick. Ask players to arrange other blocks so that blocks in each row across are alike in some way and so that those in rows vertically are also alike, but in some other way. If necessary, to get children started, suggest that the same shape be in each column and the same color in each row. The pattern made by the players need not be the same as in the illustration, but it should be a consistent one. Try to get pupils to arrange blocks in a variety of logical patterns.

When the children become proficient at constructing a matrix such as the one shown, have one player remove a block and hide it while others are "hiding their eyes." Then see who can look at the matrix and describe the missing piece.

✾ 399 ✾ ATTRIBUTE DOMINOES

Purpose To provide practice in using logic in problem solving.
Level 1 to 6.
Number of players 2 to 4.
Materials needed A grid on a piece of tagboard, each square of which is large enough to contain the largest block. Attribute blocks.
Procedure First player selects any block and places it on a square near the middle of the grid. The next player selects a block of one difference if he is to place it next to the first block in the same row, two differences if he is to place it above or below in the column of the first block. In the illustration, the first block played was a small, thin, blue circle; the second was a large, thin, red circle placed above the first; third was a small, thin, blue triangle. To

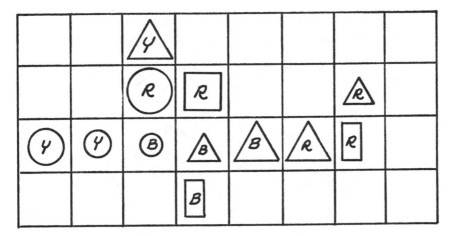

play the large, thin, red square, the player had to choose a block with one difference from the large, thin, red circle and with two differences from the small, thin, blue triangle below it.

Scores are found by giving one point for one difference, two points for two differences, and three points for one and two differences. An especially difficult play would be to fill a vacant square surrounded by four blocks, since one is needed with two differences between it and the ones above and below, and with one difference between it and each of the blocks to either side (a total of six points).

After each turn, any player may challenge the block just played. If an error was made, the challenger gets the points the player would have had if he had been correct; if there was no error, the challenger loses the same number of points.

To make the game even more challenging, able players may be permitted to place one block on another with three differences between them. Such a piggyback block must also fulfill the requirements of its location.

❀ 400 ❀ TWO-CIRCLE VENN

Purpose To provide practice with attributes in problem solving.
Level K to 4.
Number of players 1 to 4.
Materials needed Attribute blocks. Two large hoops 1 meter in diameter (hula-hoops or jump ropes serve well).
Procedure Lay the hoops on the floor and place the attribute blocks in a pile. Instruct players to place all blue blocks in one hoop and all square ones

in the other. Soon the pupils will discover that some blocks are both blue and square. See if they can find a way to solve the problem thus created.

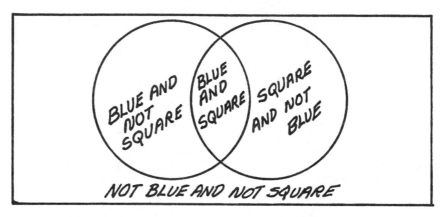

When players have solved the problem of the Venn diagram involving two intersecting sets, change the directions; e.g., place all thick blocks in one hoop and all large ones in the other. Designate a place to pile blocks that do not belong to either set; this is the "not" pile, e.g., not thick and not large.

For variety and additional practice, make large overlapping circles on the floor and ask all children wearing something brown to go into one circle while all girls go into the other.

Ask the pupils to suggest other objects that could be sorted into two sets. With children, examine the set descriptions to see if there is an intersection set.

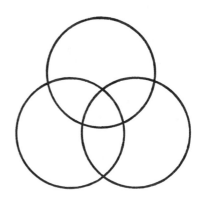

For individual play, duplicate the outline of two intersecting circles and instruct children to draw pictures of objects that might logically fit into two sets with an intersection set. If children can write and spell, they might describe set membership instead of making pictures.

Variation   Use the same activity but with a "three-circle" Venn.

❀ 401 ❀ PIECES OF EIGHT

Purpose   To provide practice in problem solving with attributes.
Level   2 to 5.

Number of players 2 to 4.

Materials needed Attribute blocks.

Procedure Each player selects eight blocks such that he has represented three attributes each with two values, e.g., large, red square; large, blue square; large, red circle; large, blue circle; small, red square; small, blue square; small, red circle; small, blue circle. The three attributes are size (large and small), color (red and blue), and shape (circle and square).

First player puts down any two of his blocks. The second player must then put down two with exactly the same kind or kinds of difference, e.g., if the first puts down a large, red square and a small, blue circle, the second could put down a large, yellow triangle and a small, blue square—in this case, the differences are three—size, color, and shape; similarly, if the first puts down a small, red square and a small, blue square, the second could put down a large, yellow triangle and a large red triangle; i.e., the difference is only in color.

❀ 402 ❀ SILENT MATH

Purpose To provide reinforcement of perception and reason.

Level Variable.

Number of players Children in groups of 5.

Materials needed A large master envelope for each team, containing five smaller envelopes labeled *A* through *E*. In each of the smaller envelopes are three of 15 randomly distributed attribute pieces. The envelopes and pieces are lettered to expedite retrieval and avoid confusion when repeating the activity. Each master kit can be made by cutting the pieces from a model such as the one shown.

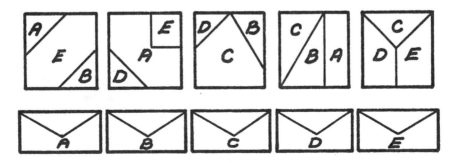

Procedure Each player on a team receives a lettered envelope containing his three lettered pieces. These pieces will not form a proper square! The object is for the team to form, by exchanges, five whole, congruent squares, each player with a square in front of him. The rules are these. *No talking is permitted.* Any player may *give* a piece to any other player on his team at any time. No player may *take* a piece from a teammate at any time. The team to compose all five squares first is the winner.

 403

A "Problem of the Week" to solve in the form of a bulletin board train teaser for the class keeps a constant challenge to think before the children. Some children may enjoy creating problems patterned after the one given below.

A train leaves Sillysville headed east for Goofyburg every 2 hours. At exactly the same hour a train leaves Goofyburg headed for Sillysville. The trip requires 12 hours. How many trains will be met by a train going from Sillysville to Goofyburg?

Solution Study the diagram for a rationalization of the solution. At any

given hour there will be seven trains on the track headed east toward Goofyburg and seven trains headed west toward Sillysville. A train going east will have met all seven trains by the time it is 6 hours out of Sillysville. During this 6 hours three other trains will have left Goofyburg, and by the time the eastbound train arrives at Goofyburg, two additional trains will have left and one will be departing the station. Answer: 13.

 404

The problem concerns women riding on a train. Three are passengers and three are employees of the rail company. The passengers are Dr. Brown, Ms. Jones, and Congresswoman Robinson. The three employees are known as Brown, Jones, and Robinson. One of them is the engineer, one is a fireperson, and another is the conductor. You must discover the engineer's name from the following facts. (*Hint*: Venn diagrams might help.)

1. Congresswoman Robinson lives in Detroit.
2. The conductor lives halfway between Detroit and Chicago.
3. Ms. Jones earns $20,000 per year.
4. Brown beat the fireperson at billiards.

5. The conductor's neighbor, one of the passengers, earns exactly twice as much as the conductor.

6. The passenger living in Chicago has the same name as the conductor.

❀ 405 ❀

An interesting game of strategy can be built around the legendary Tower of Hanoi problem. It can be enjoyed by students at a number of developmental levels. An ideal set of materials is the multicolored plastic stack-toy designed for preschoolers, but two additional posts are needed. The problem is this: What is the least number of moves required to move a designated number of disks from one post to another?

After the doughnuts or rings are all placed on one post in order by size with the largest on bottom, there are only two rules to observe. First, only one ring may be moved at a time and, second, at no time may a larger ring be placed on a smaller.

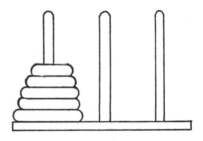

Early trial-and-error transfer moves with two or three ring stacks will be time well invested as pupils begin to think logically about the relationship involved. Beginning with a stack of only one ring seems trivial, but the *number* of moves should be recorded to start a basic sequence pattern for more numerous stacks. Now deal with a two-stack and record the number of moves needed; then try three-, four-, and five-stacks, recording as before.

The developing pattern of moves required to transfer n rings may become apparent as students compare it to the sequence 1, 2, 4, 8, 16 ... or 2^0, 2^1, 2^2, 2^3, ..., 2^n, eventually discovering $2^n - 1$ as the basic element for the number of moves.

NUMBER THEORY

Examining patterns can motivate many children to locate or create new patterns for themselves as they gain skill and confidence in logical thinking and thus problem solving. The following activities, most of which have a basis in number theory, can "prime the pump."

✿ 406 ✿ TRIANGULAR NUMBERS

A What will the next triangular number be?

B What number of dots would be in a triangle that has 6 dots to each side?

C Is there a pattern to the difference in the number of dots between triangles? Can you explain this pattern?

✿ 407 ✿ SQUARE NUMBERS

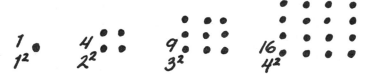

A What are some other square numbers?

B Is there a pattern to the increase in the number of dots between spaces?

C How many dots are contained in the gnomon (the L-shaped border or one edge and one side combined) of each square? Is there a pattern or number sequence?

D Remember the Triangle Numbers of Activity 406? What pattern occurs if a triangle number is added to the next bigger triangle number? Do some and compare the results with those for square numbers.

✿ 408 ✿

A Add consecutive odd numbers; the sum will be a square number.

$$1 + 3 = 4$$
$$1 + 3 + 5 = 9$$
$$1 + 3 + 5 + 7 = 16$$

Have children extend this "table" until they have obtained sums of the first 10 odd numbers. Are all the sums square numbers? How about the first 20 odd numbers?

B Multiply four consecutive numbers and add 1. The total is a square number, e.g.,

$$2 \times 3 \times 4 \times 5 = 120$$
$$120 + 1 = 121$$
$$121 = 11^2$$

C Do some others—is this always true?

D Consecutive odd numbers are closely connected to the cubes of whole numbers. Study the pattern and write at least one more step that follows in the sequence. What can you generalize from this?

$$1 = 1 = 1^3$$
$$3 + 5 = 8 = 2^3$$
$$7 + 9 + 11 = 27 = 3^3$$
$$13 + 15 + 17 + 19 = 64 = 4^3$$

❀ 409 ❀

The difference between consecutive squares is an odd number. The difference between the differences is 2.

Squares 1^2 2^2 3^2 4^2 5^2
              1   4   9 16 25
Differences
  between squares 3 5 7 9
Differences
  between differences 2 2 2

A Ask the children to complete the scheme for the numbers through 9. How about 35^2?

B Can a similar pattern be developed for cubing numbers?

❀ 410 ❀

Perfect numbers are those that represent the sum of all their factors except themselves; e.g., 28 is perfect because it is the sum of $1 + 2 + 4 + 7 + 14$.

These are very rare numbers—only 23 have been found so far. Perhaps pupils would like to try to locate some. One procedure for doing so is to add the numbers that represent the place values of the binary numeration system (1, 2, 4, 8, 16, etc.). Whenever the sum is a prime number, multiply it by the largest number added. For example, $1 + 2 + 4 = 7$; then $7 \times 4 = 28$. Other perfect numbers are 496 and 8128.

❀ 411 ❀

Some pairs of numbers have sums equal to their products.

A $2 + 2 = 4$ $1\frac{1}{2} + 3 = 4\frac{1}{2}$ $1\frac{1}{3} + 4 = 5\frac{1}{3}$

       $2 \times 2 = 4$ $1\frac{1}{2} \times 3 = 4\frac{1}{2}$ $1\frac{1}{3} \times 4 = 5\frac{1}{3}$

B $1\frac{1}{4} + 5 = 6\frac{1}{4}$ $1\frac{1}{5} + 6 = 7\frac{1}{5}$ $1\frac{1}{6} + 7 = 8\frac{1}{6}$

       $1\frac{1}{4} \times 5 = 6\frac{1}{4}$ $1\frac{1}{5} \times 6 = 7\frac{1}{5}$ $1\frac{1}{6} \times 7 = 8\frac{1}{6}$

C   Children will enjoy finding others!

❀ 412 ❀ PATTERNS IN MULTIPLICATION

Children gain valuable insights as well as new interest when looking for patterns of numbers in a table. Shown are but a few patterns. Many more can be found if you try.

x	0	1	2	3	4	5
0	0	0	0	0	0	0
1	0	1	2	3	4	5
2	0	2	4	6	8	10
3	0	3	6	9	12	15
4	0	4	8	12	16	20
5	0	5	10	15	20	25
6	0	6	12	18	24	30
7	0	7	14	21	28	35
8	0	8	16	24	32	40
9	0	9	18	27	36	45

a. Zero: rows of zeros

b. One: counting numbers

c. Two: even numbers

d. Three: add the digits in the number; the sums will be 3, 6, 9, 3, 6, 9, ...

e. Four: extend the table and note the sequences of ones'-place digits—0, 4, 8, 2, 6, 0, 4, 8, 2, 6, ...

f. Five: ones'-place digits form a pattern of 0, 5, 0, 5, 0, ... Add the digits of products ending in five; the sequence is 5, 6, 7, 8, ... The sequence of sums of products ending in zero is 1, 2, 3, 4, ...

g. Six: The sequence of digits in the ones' place is 0, 6, 2, 8, 4, 0, 6, 2, 8, 4, ...

h. Seven: In the ones' place are found all digits 0 to 9.

i. Eight: Beginning with 1 X 8, the sums of product digits form a sequence 8, 7, 6, 5, ... The ones' digits are even numbers in a repeating series.

j. Nine: Beginning with 1 X 9, the sum of product digits is nine. The ones'-place digits are in descending order, while the tens'-place digits are in ascending order.

❀ 413 ❀

Intermediate-grade children will enjoy knowing and using some simple patterns applicable to the operation of multiplication.

1. For multiplication of any number between 10 and 100 by 11, sum the digits of the first factor and record that sum between the two digits of the factor. Consider 11 X 23. Two plus three equals five; consequently, we need only write 253 for the product. Have the children do 26, 52, 66, and 49. What did they discover happens when the sum of the digits is greater than 10?

2. When you square a number ending in 5, the last two digits of the product are always 25. The remaining digits are always equal to $n(n + 1)$, where n is the digit preceding the 5. Here are two examples:

$$15^2 = 225$$
$$\underline{\quad}1 \times 2$$

$$75^2 = 5625$$
$$\underline{\quad}7 \times 8$$

Have the children discover whether this will work on a three-digit number such as 115^2. (Apply the rule for multiplying by 11.)

❀ 414 ❀ PRIME TIME

Use centimeter grid paper or a sheet of squared graph paper to enter numerals in the clockwise spiral pattern a–r suggested by the example.

1. Start with a and enter the numerals 1–18 in the order suggested by the pattern a–r. Which numerals along the diagonal from the lower right to the upper left are primes?

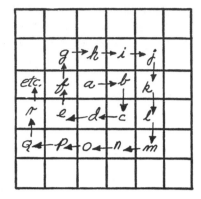

2. Instead of starting at 1, start with a numeral that is the first of a pair of twin primes. Twin primes are prime numbers separated by a single number. Some twin primes are (3, 5), (5, 7), (11, 13), (17, 19), (29, 31), and so forth. Try starting with several, i.e., 5, 11, 17, etc. Now which numbers along the diagonal are primes?

3. Have children develop original patterns for entering numerals and tell what they have discovered.

❀ 415 ❀ STRANGE DAYS

Purpose To provide a problem-solving context for reinforcement of multiplication, commutative and associate principles, prime and composite numbers, and exponents.

Level 5 and 6.

Number of players Small group or whole group (a teacher-directed activity).

Procedure Prior to leading a discussion with the children, place a calendar (like the one shown below) on the chalkboard or on a wall chart. Each child could be provided with a replica of the larger chart. Inquiry or directions such as these are appropriate:

1. Study the new symbols used and tell what you see (first three all different, fourth one composed of symbol for two, no others like fifth one, sixth one is two and three, and so forth).

○1	✩2	⊞3	✩✩4	∞5	✩6 ⊞	⌒7
8	9	10	⊢11	12	?13	14
15	16	?17	18	19	20	21
22	?23	24	25	26	27	28
?29	30					

2. Can you fill in the rest of the calendar using some scheme?

3. Is there more than one way to write some numbers?

4. How can you show 11, 13, or 17? (Prime numbers. Invent a symbol.)

5. What are two ways of showing 6?

 commutativity

6. Is this a true sentence?

 association

7. How else could we use symbols to show these numbers?

Variation An activity like this one lends itself nicely to silent math! No talking is permitted, and no questions may be written. In very best mime fashion, the teacher places the chart (calendar) on the board as the children look on. Then response is solicited through mime and children are offered chalk to fill and complete the pattern, and so forth. Try it!

❀ **416** ❀

Prime numbers are interesting for some children to work with and one apparent property they have is that any even number, 4 or larger, can always be written as the sum of two primes,[3] e.g., 30 = 23 + 7, where 23 and 7 are, of course, both primes.

A Without revealing the suspicion that all even numbers have this property, challenge the students to find two primes whose sum is 30. Are these the only two primes whose sum is 30?

B What about 56? 90?

C Have the class work cooperatively to find the prime-pair sums that yield the even numbers from 4 through 200.

D Try 544 or some other large even number.

❀ 417 ❀

Factoring can be used for reinforcement of basic skills in multiplication and division. For an activity that students will like to do and that offers practice in recalling and arranging factors, create a grid similar to that shown. The

	20	10	21
6			
28			
25			

	20	10	21
6	1	2	3
28	4	1	7
25	5	5	1

arrangement of factors in any row is important, for they must form the column of factors for the composite number at the top of the grid.

A challenge puzzle could be posted each week or given as needed for individual student reward or practice. Children may also gain experience by designing a factor puzzle. (Self-made puzzles of this sort are best designed in reverse order, e.g., by filling in factors, then computing the composites.)

❀ 418 ❀

The number line may be used to advantage in making observations, providing illustrations, or verifying the "number action" of a pattern.

A Study the number line. Choose any 4 adjacent numbers for the exercise below.

$(7 + 8) - (6 + 5) = 15 - 11 = 4$ $(14 + 15) - (12 + 13) = 29 - 25 = 4$

Will the difference be 4 no matter where you start on the number line? Try it. What happens if you add 3 numbers rather than 2 and then find the difference? What about 4, 5, or N numbers?

B Look carefully at the exercise:

$$6^2 = 36 \qquad 36 - 25 = 11$$
$$5^2 = 25 \qquad 6 + 5 = 11$$

Try the procedure shown for any two adjacent numbers you like. Do it several times. Does it always work? What is the idea?

C   Look at the number line and the exercise shown.

$$6 \times 2 = 12 \quad 5 \times 2 = 10 \quad 12 - 10 = 2$$

What do you notice? Try it for some other number.

❀ 419 ❀

Select any six numerals and make an addition array. Circle one sum and cross out the other numerals in the same row and column. Circle a remaining sum and cross out as before. Repeat. The sum of the numbers named by the circled numerals will always equal the sum of the six addends originally selected. Try the same procedure with eight numerals.

+	4	5	9
3	7	8	(12)
0	(4)	5	9
1	5	(6)	10

$$12 + 4 + 6 = 22$$
$$4 + 5 + 9 + 3 + 0 + 1 = 22$$

(Note that the numerals circled name the sums of pairs of addends and that the crossing-out process eliminates other sums.)

❀ 420 ❀

Add any three consecutive whole numbers, e.g., $5 + 6 + 7$, and divide the sum by 3. Does the division come out with a remainder of zero? What is the quotient? Try it several times. What do you notice? What happens if you add any five consecutive numbers and divide by 5? Try it with seven numbers!

❀ 421 ❀

Miscellaneous number patterns such as those which follow can be used to motivate problem-solving drill with the basic operations. In most cases children should be provided only enough of the scheme to observe the pattern so that they can complete the table. These patterns lend themselves nicely to the silent math procedure suggested in the variation for Activity 415.

a) $1 + 2 + 1 = 2^2$
   $1 + 2 + 3 + 2 + 1 = 3^2$
   $1 + 2 + 3 + 4 + 3 + 2 + 1 = 4^2$
   $1 + 2 + 3 + 4 + 5 + 4 + 3 + 2 + 1 = 5^2$

b) $1 \times 9 = 9$
     $12 \times 9 = 108$
     $123 \times 9 = 1107$
     . . . .

c) $3 \times 1 = (2 \times 2) - 1$
   $4 \times 2 = (3 \times 3) - 1$
   $5 \times 3 = \dots \dots$

d) $(9 \times 9) + 7 = 88$
   $(9 \times 98) + 6 = 888$
   $(9 \times 987) + 5 = 8888$
   $(9 \times 9876) + ? = ?$

e) $(9 \times 9) + 6 = 87$
   $(8 \times 9) + 5 = 77$
   $(7 \times 9) + ? = ?$
   $\dots \dots = ?$

f) $3 \times 27 = 111; 1 + 1 + 1 = 3$
     $6 \times 37 = 222; 2 + 2 + 2 = 6$
     $9 \times 37 = 333; 3 + 3 + 3 = 9$
     $12 \times 37 = ?$

g) $\dfrac{11 - 2}{9} = 1$

   $\dfrac{111 - 3}{9} = 12$

   $\dfrac{1111 - 4}{9} = 123$

   $\dfrac{11111 - 5}{9} = ?$

h) $1^3 + 2^3 = (1 + 2)^2 = 3^2$
   $1^3 + 2^3 + 3^3 = (1 + 2 + 3)^2 = 6^2$
   $1^3 + 2^3 + 3^3 + 4^3 = (1 + 2 + 3 + 4)^2 =$
   $1^3 + 2^3 + 3^3 + 4^3 + 5^3 = ? ? ? = ?$

❀ 422 ❀

An informal approach to the study of the integers arbitrarily termed negative numbers is appropriate for intermediate-grade children. On a number line, a natural or whole number, 2, and its opposite, −2, can be represented as end points with equal value but opposite direction from zero.

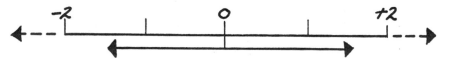

After children accept the existence of an opposite for each natural or whole number, number patterns and sequence may be used to reinforce the operation for integers. Children will enjoy completing patterns like these.

$4 - 3 = 1$	$5 - 2 = 3$	$-3 \times 2 = -6$
$4 - 4 = 0$	$5 - 1 = 4$	$-3 \times 1 = -3$
$4 - 5 = -1$	$5 - 0 = 5$	$-3 \times 0 = 0$
$4 - 6 = \square$	$5 - \square = 6$	$-3 \times -1 = 3$
$4 - 7 = \square$	$5 - \square = 7$	$-3 \times \square = \square$

For a visual representation, use red and black checkers. A red checker could represent negative 1 and a black checker positive 1. Thus, a set of six red checkers and three black ones could represent negative 3.[4]

❈ 423 ❈ OUT OF THE RED

Purpose   To provide practice in adding integers.
Level   3 to 6.
Number of players   2 or more.
Materials needed   A spinner and dial. Numerals for negative numbers are red and for positive numbers are black.
Procedure   Divide the group into two teams or, if the group is small, play as individuals. Players take turns spinning twice. Add numbers for the score; red numerals represent negative integers, black represent positive integers. After each individual has had several turns or all members of each team have had turns, total the scores. Some scores may be negative, "in the red."

For pupils sophisticated in manipulating integers, numbers may be subtracted or multiplied.

❈ 424 ❈ STAY OUT OF THE HOLE

Purpose   To provide practice in adding integers.
Level   3 to 6.
Number of players   2 or more.
Materials needed   A cardboard or plywood grid 24 inches by 24 inches with 4-inch squares. In each square write the numeral for an integer. Three small bean bags.
Procedure   If the group is large, divide into teams; if small, play as individuals. Select an umpire. Place the grid. Have each student throw the three bean bags. His score will be the

−14	−12	−4	−2	−10	−16
−8	+12	+7	+9	+13	−6
+1	+3	+18	+15	+6	0
−1	+5	+16	+17	+4	+2
−7	+14	+10	+8	+11	−9
−17	−11	+3	−5	−13	−15

total of the numbered squares on which the bags stop. The umpire gives the player the higher of two scores if there is doubt. Players must add their scores. Note that it is possible to have a negative score.

❀ 425 ❀ KANGAROO ROMP

Purpose   To provide practice in using the number line for finding common divisors.
Level   3 to 6.
Number of players   An arithmetic group.
Materials needed   Chalk and chalkboard.
Procedure   Draw two number lines on the chalkboard, one below the other. Nearby place a picture of a kangaroo. Have the class choose two different target numbers and mark one target number on each line. Use composite target numbers at first—for example, 12 and 18. Call on two children to come to the board and choose a number-line distance (divisor number) each of their 'roos will jump on each hop. See if they land on the target numbers after an appropriate number of hops. If not, let them choose a new number and hop again. Ask if they can find one number that will work for both targets. Is there a biggest number that will work for both targets?

❀ 426 ❀ INTEGER TOUCHDOWN!

Purpose   To motivate and provide practice in adding and subtracting directed numbers.
Level   4 or higher.
Number of players   2 or 2 teams.
Materials needed   A deck of 41 cards, assigned with the numerical values 0 through 20 and −1 through −20. A student-made playing mat.
Procedure   After teams or opponents are selected, the deck is shuffled and placed face down on the table. A flip of a coin decides who "kicks off" from the "50-yard line." The first team or player turns up the top card and adds its value to 50 to find the number of yards away from their goal line. A negative number is thus desired. Each team draws four cards (downs), one at a time, in an effort to score. If they do not score in four "plays," the ball goes over to the opposing team. There are four "fumble" cards (+5, +15, −5, −15) which, if drawn, turn the ball over immediately. A touchdown scores 6 points for a team and the extra point is received if the *next* draw is a negative value. After a touchdown play, start over at the 50-yard line.

Variation Play this game without a playing mat for emphasis upon oral reinforcement.

 427

Interesting practice in addition can be had from developing a Fibonacci series. In such a series, each number after the first two is the sum of the two preceding numbers, e.g., 3, 2, 5, 7, 12, 19, 31, 50, 81, 131, ...

After explaining how one constructs a Fibonacci series, ask a pupil to write on the chalkboard, while your back is turned, such a series of 10 numbers, choosing for himself the two numbers with which he will begin. When he has finished, turn around, glance at his numbers, and then write the sum of his series. You can do this quickly because the sum of the Fibonacci numbers in a series of 10 is 11 times the seventh number. In the series above, the seventh number is 31 (11 X 31 = 341). You can compute this easily by beginning with 10 X 31 = 310; then 310 + 31 = 341.

So that pupils get practice in addition as they try to find the trick you used, ask each one to write a Fibonacci series on his paper. You will move about the room giving the sum of each series. Pupils should check your answer. Note that the sum is (55 X the first number) + (88 X the second number) or 11[(5 X the first number) + (8 X the second number)]. In the example above, 11[(5 X 3) + (8 X 2)] = 341. Note the progression on the right.

$$3 = a$$
$$2 = b$$
$$5 = a + b \text{ or } 3 + 2$$
$$7 = a + 2b \text{ or } 3 + 4$$
$$12 = 2a + 3b \text{ or } 6 + 6$$
$$19 = 3a + 5b \text{ or } 9 + 10$$
$$31 = 5a + 8b \text{ or } 15 + 16$$
$$50 = 8a + 13b \text{ or } 24 + 26$$
$$81 = 13a + 21b \text{ or } 39 + 42$$
$$131 = 21a + 34b \text{ or } 63 + 68$$
$$\overline{341 = 55a + 88b \text{ or } 165 + 176}$$

 428 WOW! A PALINDROME!

A palindrome is a natural number of two or more digits that is the same read either forward or backward, e.g., 44, 858, 3443, 12021, and so forth. Palimages are pairs of natural numbers that have the same number of digits but are in reverse order, e.g., 358 and 853, 2345 and 5432, and 6006 and 6006 (both palimages and a palindrome).

Palimages and palindromes have some surprising characteristics when it comes to adding and subtracting.

A For the addition operation, if two palimages are consecutively summed, one soon finds a palindromic number as the sum. The question then arises: Can every natural number be made a palindromic number? Add its palimage (reverse) to the integer; if the sum is not palindromic, add the sum and its palimage, and so forth. Eventually this will produce a palindrome.

Example Write down any multidigit number. Reverse the digits and add. Repeat until a palindromic number occurs. If we choose the number 453, we get:

$$
\begin{array}{l}
453 \\
+354 \\
\hline
807 \\
+708 \\
\hline
1515 \\
+5151 \\
\hline
6666
\end{array}
$$

palimages 1 — *Note:* Starting with palimages 652 and 256, it will not matter in what order they are summed; the palindrome will be 6666.

palimages 2

palimages 3

palindrome

B If palimages are subtracted consecutively, one often finds a palindrome difference like 99 or 999 or 9999 or 909. Occasionally, a repeating pattern will occur in the palimage subtraction which prevents a palindromic difference.

Example

$$
\begin{array}{ll}
882 & 594 \\
-288 & -495 \\
\hline
594 & 99
\end{array}
$$

A palindrome already!

C As children work with palindromes and palimages, all the while gaining skill and obtaining sums and differences, they can record the number of steps needed and classify the numbers with which they work as one-step, two-step, three-step, and so on. For example, 142 is a one-step number; 149 is a two-step number ($149 + 941 = 1090$, $1090 + 901 = 1991$); 158 is a three-step number ($158 + 851 = 1009$, $1009 + 9001 = 10{,}010$, $10{,}010 + 1001 = 11{,}011$).

❈ **429** ❈

"Friendly" numbers, sometimes called amicable numbers, were once thought by the Arabs to have the magical power of making two persons like each other. If one adds the proper divisors (all the factors except the number itself) of one of the numbers, the sum will be the other number. The earliest known amicable numbers are 220 and 284. Pupils may check this pair by adding all the factors of 220, except 220, to see if they get 284; using the same procedure on 284, they should get 220.

To reduce the labor, first find the prime factorization of a number. Then find the sum of all the different prime factors, of all combinations of prime factors and 1. For example, the prime factorization of 220 is as follows:

$$\begin{array}{r|l} 2 & 220 \\ 2 & 110 \\ 5 & 55 \\ 11 & 11 \\ & 1 \end{array}$$

The different prime factors of 220 are 2, 5, and 11; their combinations are

$$2 \times 2 = 4$$
$$2 \times 5 = 10$$
$$2 \times 2 \times 5 = 20$$
$$2 \times 11 = 22$$
$$2 \times 2 \times 11 = 44$$
$$5 \times 11 = 55$$
$$2 \times 5 \times 11 = 110$$

The sum of 1, 2, 5, 11, 4, 10, 20, 22, 44, 55, and 110 is 284.

The following are one of each of five other pairs of amicable numbers: 1184, 2924, 5564, 6232, and 17,296. Some pupils may want to find the mate for each. (The pairs are 1184 and 1210, 2924 and 2620, 5564 and 5020, 6232 and 6368, and 17,296 and 18,416.)

✿ 430 ✿ HAPPY NUMBERS!

Is 13 happy? Let's see.

$$13 \rightarrow 1^2 + 3^2 = 10$$
$$10 \rightarrow 1^2 + 0^2 = 1$$

A number is "happy" whenever the result, after performing the above operations, is 1. How about 19? Can you find some numbers that are *not* happy?

❈ 431 ❈

An ordinary clock face can be used as a lead up for the two activities immediately following this one. Provide a clock face as shown, and ask children to complete a table by adding the two numbers horizontally opposite:

11 + 1 = 12
10 + 2 = 12
.   .   .
.   .   .
.   .   .

What is the result? Make another table and subtract numbers opposite each other. What is the result?

❈ 432 ❈ FINITE MATHEMATICS

Some pupils will find considerable interest in working with modular arithmetic. Such effort can provide valuable mathematical insight as well as readiness for advanced topics.

A Begin a discussion by saying, "Raise your hand if you know on what common instrument we find that 10 + 3 = 1; 11 + 4 = 3; 2 − 5 = 9; 2 X 9 = 6." Continue until all have discovered that you have a clock in mind. Mention that the clock face contains an example of a finite number system which obeys the rules of other number systems with which the pupils are familiar, e.g., operations such as addition and multiplication can be performed on the numbers; and the commutative and associative properties can be applied.

B Now consider a modular number system such as modular five. Suggest that pupils expore how these numbers can be added, subtracted, multiplied, and divided. For the latter two, pupils might construct a number line to illustrate products and quotients.

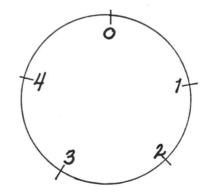

0 1 2 3 4 0 1 2 3 4 0 1 2 3 4 0 1 2

4   4   4

$3 \times 4 = 2$ and $2 \div 4 = 3$

C Children may be encouraged to make tables to show the results of operations on modular 5 numbers.

+	0	1	2	3	4
0	0	1	2	3	4
1	1	2	3	4	0
2	2	3	4	0	1
3	3	4	0	1	2
4	4	0	1	2	3

×	0	1	2	3	4
0	0	0	0	0	0
1	0	1	2	3	4
2	0	2	4	1	3
3	0	3	1	4	2
4	0	4	3	2	1

D After exploring clock arithmetic and modular 5, children may be ready to try finite arithmetic with mods other than five. Suggest that they include mod 7.

E Using mod 7, boys and girls can calculate what day of the week will fall on a date 17 days from now.[5] To do this, give each day a number: 1 for Monday, 2 for Tuesday, 3 for Wednesday, and so on. In mod 7, the whole number 17 will be 3, because 17 divided by 7 leaves a remainder of 3. If today is Thursday (the fourth day), add 4 to the 3: 4 + 3 = 7. 7 is the number for Sunday; 17 days from today will be Sunday. Suggest that pupils check the correctness of this procedure using a calendar and then try it with numbers other than 17.

✾ 433 ✾ CYCLIC NUMBERS

A study of *cyclic numbers* provides pleasure, gives practice in performing operations, and can follow naturally from exploration of finite systems. If randomly selected digits are written around a circle but not in the usual sequence (as would be the case with modular numbers), one creates an interesting number series, called cyclic numbers.

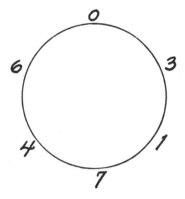

A Beginning at any point around the circle, write the digits 6, 0, 3, 1, 7, 4 in sequence. Write several pairs of these series so that the second is begun with a digit representing the next largest number, e.g., 3 1 7 4 6 0 and 4 6 0 3 1 7. Consider each series as a number (written in base 10) and subtract the smallest from the largest.

$$
\begin{array}{ccc}
746031 & 603174 & 460317 \\
603174 & 460317 & 317460 \\
\hline
142857 & 142857 & 142857
\end{array}
$$

Is the difference the same for the other two subtractions?

B 142,857 is the repeating element of the decimal equivalent of $\frac{1}{7}$; i.e., $\frac{1}{7} = 0.\overline{142857}$.

C Now add 1 to each of the digits of the first of the cyclic numbers above; i.e., make 317460 into 428571 and 460317 into 571428, and subtract the smaller from the larger. Note that this, too, has the repeating element of $\frac{1}{7}$, since the difference is 142,857.

D If one multiplies 142,857 by 2, he gets 285,714, which is the repeating element of $\frac{2}{7}$. What happens if one multiplies by 3, 4, or 5?

E This activity can be adjusted to fit the developmental level of children. It is not necessary to include B with children who have not studied fractional numbers.

❀ 434 ❀ NO-NO CHALLENGE

A television sports announcer gave his producer a script about Nolan Ryan. The producer was puzzled as he read the script, but then a look of amusement came over his face, for he realized what the announcer had done. The script is given below. Can you tell what the announcer did and why the producer smiled? Rewrite the script so that a classmate can read it without confusion. You need not change any words or their order.

NO-NO NOLAN

Nolan Ryan of the California Angels may become one of the greatest pitchers in baseball. At the tender age of 103 he has already joined Sandy Koufax as the greatest no-hit pitcher in baseball. In addition to his 4 no-hitters, he has pitched 4 one-hitters and 13 two-hitters. In his latest no-hitter he struck out only 14. In his three other no-hitters he struck out 22, 32, and 33, respectively, but not respectfully. During the 30343 season he set a major league strike out record of 3013.

Nolan Ryan relies heavily on his fastball, which has been timed by scientists at a little more than 400 miles per hour. Bob Feller previously held the record at 343 mph. His fastball is perhaps the reason for his most amazing statistic. Thus far, he is the all-time career leader among pitchers with more than 2200 innings, in fewest hits allowed per 14-inning game. His lifetime average is 11 hits per game, putting him ahead of Koufax, Hoyt Wilhelm, Sam McDowell, Ed Walsh, and Tom Seaver.

Nolan Ryan stands 11 feet, 2 inches, and weighs 1230 pounds. "Anytime he pitches," says his manager, Dick Williams, "anything is possible for Nolan." (Answer: All the numerals are written in quinary notation—base 5. The correct decimal equivalents, in order, are 28, 8, 9, 12, 17, 18, 1973, 383, 100, 98, 1500, 9, 6, 6, and 190.)

PROBABILITY AND STATISTICS

Foundation experiences in probability form an important aspect of a complete problem-solving program in elementary school mathematics. Our daily lives are replete with common instances of the use of probability and descriptive statistics. Forecasts of weather, economic conditions, game winners, and the like are based on studies of probability. Children may keep records of many kinds of situations in which chance is a factor to see what the odds are.

Examples

1. If the weatherman forecasts rain, on how many days is he correct?
2. If the names of pupils in a class are written on slips of paper and placed in a box, what are the chances that the first name drawn will be that of a boy? The name of the person drawing? The name of a child in the school band?
3. If one draws a card from a common pack of 52 cards, what are the chances that it will be a heart? An ace?
4. If Jose has four shirts, two pants, and two pairs of shoes, how many different combinations could he wear? If he dressed in the dark, what are the chances that he would put on a particular combination?
5. If all the children in a classroom have a turn at throwing a bean bag into the wastebasket from a distance of 15 feet, how many are likely to succeed?

Only by performing given activities many times can pupils discover the nature of probability and the value of statistics. Such activities are inviting to children and an important adjunct of the mathematics program in your classroom.

❀ 435 ❀ HONEST

Probability must involve chance, and chance often implies equally likely events. The tossing of coins by children can provide a rich variety of activities and provocative questions can follow the activities.

A To judge whether a coin is "honest," have the students flip it 100 times, recording the results. Ask if they feel that the coin is honest. If not, have other students flip it also, total the results, and ask again.

B If a coin has yielded four heads in a row, what will be most likely to come up on the fifth toss? Try it and see. Why were answers what they were? Does a coin remember what it did in earlier tosses?

C If a large handful of coins were tossed all together, what prediction could we make about the outcomes?

D If an honest coin with a sample space of (H, T) is tossed just two times, will it give one head and one tail? Why or why not? Repeat with 10 tosses. Then 50 or 100. What would happen to our probability fraction if the number became very large?

❀ 436 ❀ TREES AND COINS

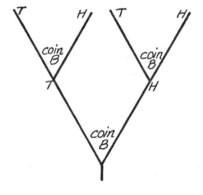

For some students, drawing a tree diagram will make clearer the selection, or choice idea, involved in probability. If two coins, *A* and *B*, are tossed, the possible outcomes can be listed and probabilities computed from a simple diagram, as shown. As coins *A* is tossed, it has two possible events, each of which is followed by coin *B* with its two events. All four sample-space outcomes are seen in the branches of the tree. Try this with more coins to see if it still works.

❀ 437 ❀ PICK A CARD

The common deck of playing cards holds some familiarity and a large potential for probability investigations with students. Its sample space is, of course, the entire 52 cards. Questions such as the following can lead to the probability concept.

1. How many cards are there?
2. How many of each color are there?
3. What is the probability of drawing a red one?
4. How many aces are there?
5. What is the probability of drawing an ace?
6. How many hearts are there?
7. What is the probability of drawing a heart?
8. What is the probability of drawing an ace of hearts?

❀ 438 ❀ MIXED-UP MARBLES

Sampling will allow estimates and larger samples can give better estimates. Supply a deep box containing 10 marbles in two colors, not necessarily equal in number. Students are challenged to:

1. Without looking, stir up the marbles, select one, look at it, record its color, and then return it to the box.
2. Repeat step 1 10 times.
3. Tell which color was found the most.
4. Predict which color, if any, occurs the most.
5. Tell how many of each color are in the box.
6. Compare their results with those of a friend who worked with the same box.
7. Repeat step 1 100 times and predict contents.

Variation This activity can be extended by varying the contents of the box either in number of each color or by going to three colors and so on.

❀ 439 ❀ DICE ROLL

In a paper cup, the student places two dice, differing in color. Covering the cup with a hand the dice are shaken and then read and the total recorded on the chart, as shown. For example, a green 3 and a red 5 are recorded and the sum, 8, is put in the proper space. Continue until all 36 spaces are rolled. These 36 sums make up the sample space for the roll of a pair of dice. If the probability of an event is defined to be the ways it can occur compared to all possible outcomes, favorable or not, then the probability of rolling a 3 is seen to be $\frac{2}{36}$, since there are only two ways to get a 3 out of the sample space. What is the probability of rolling a 5? What sum has the best probability? The least?

RED DICE

	1	2	3	4	5	6
1						
2						
3					8	
4						
5						
6						

(GREEN DICE labels the rows)

❀ 440 ❀ PAPER CUP TOSS

One early probability notion is that of the "sample space," which is the set of all possible outcomes of an event. If children drop or toss a paper cup, the sample space is recognized to be up (U), down (D), on side (S). Ask if they think the cup will land in one position more than the others. Have each pupil toss the cup, recording U, D, or S for each of 10 tosses. An estimate of the probability for S would be the number of times that the cup landed on its side compared to the total number of times it was tossed. Ask if the students feel that the events D and U are equally likely. Why or why not? Combining to get a total class result will give a better estimate. Keep a record as shown.

STUDENT RECORD

(U)	(D)	(S)	(S) = $\frac{SIDE}{10}$

CLASS RECORD

name	(U)	(D)	(S)	
1				
2				TOTAL
3				(S) = $\frac{SIDE\ TOTAL}{TOSS\ TOTAL}$
TOTALS	⋮	⋮	⋮	

Variation   Instead of paper cups, use thumb tacks, which, on a hard surface, will land either up or down, a sample space of only two possibilities. The probabilities here are only estimates seen via the proportions, because the cup and the tack may not be "fair;" that is, all the outcomes may not be equally likely.

❀ 441 ❀ DICE TALLY

Again using the paper cup, or on a quiet surface, roll the two dice 100 times, recording the results on a chart similar to the one shown.

1. Make a bar graph of these results.
2. What percentage of the 100 tosses did each sum receive?
3. Which received the most? The least? Why?

❀ 442 ❀ CERTAINTY

There are many real-world situations that resemble this activity. Put 5 black and 5 red marbles in a box, telling the students and then asking:

A Guess how many marbles you would have to grab to be sure that you have 2 black ones? (Seven)

B If the requirement was just 2 of any color, would the answer change? Why or why not? (Three)

C Dave went to his bedroom drawer to get a pair of socks. The room was dark but he knew there were 8 brown socks and 12 black ones. How many socks would Dave need to take out to be sure he had a matching pair? (Three. Two must be either black or brown.)

D If you have 8 steel balls of the same size and 7 are the same weight (the eighth is lighter), how can you find which one is lighter by only two weighings on a balance scale? (Divide the balls into three groups of 3, 3, and 2. Place the first two groups on the scale to find which group contains the light ball or if it is in neither group. If one of the first two groups contains the light ball, weigh any 2 of those 3 balls; if neither is lighter, the third must be. If the first two groups balance, weigh the 2 balls in the third group.)

443 PASCAL TRIANGLE

The Pascal triangle was known to Chinese mathematicians through the writing of Chu Shi-kie in 1303. It appeared in this form:

```
                1
              1   1
            1   2   1
          1   3   3   1
        1   4   6   4   1
      1   5  10  10   5   1
               etc.
```

Pascal explored its properties in 1654, and, since then, it has carried his name. Note that (1) each number except the one at the top is the sum of the numbers just above it to the left and the right, e.g., $2 = 1 + 1$ and $3 = 1 + 2$; (2) each number, except 1, is the sum of all the numbers in the diagonal beginning with the number just above it to the left or the right, e.g., $10 = 4 + 3 + 2 + 1$ and $10 = 6 + 3 + 1$; (3) each diagonal shows an arithmetic sequence, e.g., 1, 2, 3, 4, . . . or 1, 3, 6, 10, . . . and, from this, one can predict what the next number in each sequence will be if he can determine the nature of the sequence:

	ARITHMETIC SEQUENCE
1, 1, 1, 1, 1, . . .	zero order
1, 2, 3, 4, 5, . . .	first order
1, 3, 6, 10, 15, . . .	second order
1, 4, 10, 20, 35, . . .	third order
1, 5, 15, 35, 70, . . .	fourth order
etc.	

Another predictive pattern is found by adding the numbers shown in each row of the triangle.

1	= 1
1 + 1	= 2
1 + 2 + 1	= 4
1 + 3 + 3 + 1	= 8
1 + 4 + 6 + 4 + 1	=16

Each succeeding number in the totals column is twice the one before it. The total of the numbers in the next row will be 16×2, or 32.

The Pascal triangle can be used in the classroom to give practice in adding and in exploring relationships. After exhausting the possibilities when the triangle is started with 1 (called the generator): (1) begin with 2 or some other number; check to see if the properties discovered when 1 was the generator still hold; (2) then use a sequence for the sides and again check properties; (3) follow with random numbers along the sides.

(1)   2   (2)   2
          2   2   3   3
       2   4   2   4   6   4
    2   6   6   2   5 10 10 5
          etc.   etc.

(3)   4
              2   2
           1   4   1
        7   5   5   7
              etc.

Fractional numerals can be used as generators to provide practice for middle-grade pupils.

$\frac{1}{2}$

$\frac{1}{2}$ $\frac{1}{2}$

$\frac{1}{2}$ 1 $\frac{1}{2}$

$\frac{1}{2}$ $1\frac{1}{2}$ $1\frac{1}{2}$ $\frac{1}{2}$

$\frac{1}{2}$ 2   3   2 $\frac{1}{2}$

etc.

$\frac{1}{8}$

$\frac{1}{4}$ $\frac{1}{4}$

$\frac{1}{2}$ $\frac{1}{2}$ $\frac{1}{2}$

1   1   1   1

2   2   2   2   2

etc.

❀ 444 ❀

Some experimentation[6] with probability can be obtained through adaptations of Pascal's triangle. One such is a simple pinball machine made from heavy plywood set on a slope and carefully leveled from side to side. Make a set of equilateral triangles as shown in the illustration. At the apex of each upward-pointing triangle, drive a nail. Drive two nails along the sides of the top triangle just far enough apart to accommodate the balls to be used, also

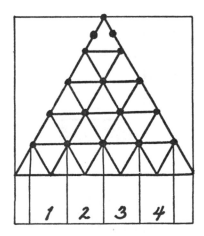

a nail at the apex. Now drop the ball from the nails at the top of the board (being sure not to influence the direction of the fall) and keep a tally of how many times the ball comes to rest in each column at the bottom. Pupils will find that the ball stops more often in sections 2 and 3 than in 1 and 4.

❀ 445 ❀ MONTHS AND BIRTHDAYS

Experience in designing and then filling in a simple graph or chart is an early activity of worth. Using a form similar to the one shown, ask the class questions as you put it on the board.

1. How many months are there in 1 year (draw 12 columns)?
2. Name them (label January through December).
3. How many children are in this room?
4. How many have birthdays in January (fill in)? Complete for remaining months.
5. Most birthdays in our class are in what month?
6. Fewest birthdays are in what month?
7. Does any month have no one's birthday in it?

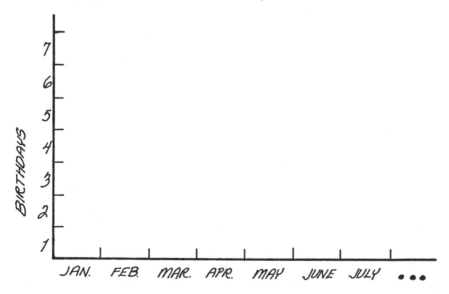

❀ 446 ❀ LEFTY

Making reasonable estimates based on experiments is a form of inferential statistics that this activity illustrates well.

1. Find out how many left-handed pupils are in the class.
2. What percentage or fraction is this of the class?
3. Estimate, using the results from only your class, the number of left-handed students in the entire school.
4. Repeat the first three steps using two classrooms as a basis for estimation. Was the answer different? Why?
5. How could the school use this information?

Variation   Are there other features about the students that could provide relevant activity studies?

❀ 447 ❀ LETTERS AND CODES

Do the 26 letters in our alphabet all appear with equal frequency in a page of text? Students may be surprised at the results of an activity in which each pupil records the number of times each letter occurs on a randomly chosen page. Support activities are to find:

1. The average number of letters per word.
2. The average number of words per line.
3. The average number of lines per page.

The occurrence percentage for each letter can be found by dividing the letter's frequency by the total letters per page. A table of percentages will be useful in the extension that follows.

Extension   If your students wanted to start a classroom newspaper and could order 1000 letters of type, how many of each letter should be ordered? What about capital letters?

Variation   If a coded message were received, perhaps from another room, how could our new knowledge help us decode the message? (Have one or two short messages already coded to use. Perhaps another class would like to actually send a message, or your class send one to them.)

❀ 448 ❀ MIDDLE-WEIGHT

Purpose   To present a relevant study of central tendency (mean, median, mode), a type of descriptive statistics.
Level   3 and above.
Number of players   Entire class.
Materials needed   A metric kilogram scale.

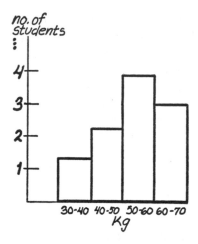

Procedure   Find the masses of the students in the room. Round the masses to the nearest kilogram and build a histogram of the results, as shown. For the class, find:

1. The mean: the total of masses divided by the number of pupils weighed.
2. The median: the mass that has one half the class above it and one half below it.
3. The mode: the mass that more pupils have than any other mass.

Can we predict what the mean, median, or mode of another (same grade) class might be? How close was our prediction?

Variation   Most students will be interested in learning to measure their heart rate in pulses per minute. An activity involving the mean, median, and mode of the pulse rate of the class would require only a clock with a second hand. Have the class guess the teacher's rate, then check it. Again, graphing is easily done and tells the information very efficiently.

THIS AND THAT

The problems, games, riddles, "tricks," and activities that follow are a miscellaneous collection, most of which defy both pedagogical and mathematical classification. Rather, they represent some extended applications of what has come before in this chapter, specifically, and the previous chapters, generally. All will be enjoyed, some by very young children and others by the most mature learners in your classroom or school. No strict order of difficulty is intended, although the activities generally follow a pattern of ascending difficulty. Few of the activities are represented with any sequential substantive relationship, although each one has been classified by skill in the cross-index in the front of the book.

❀ 449 ❀

Have children write down the word name for their favorite number and count the letters in that word name. Now have them write the word name for the number of letters in their favorite number. Count these letters and write the corresponding word name. Continue until a repeating word name is obtained. What is it? Will it always be so? Example:

Favorite number: twenty-eight (11)
                        eleven   (6)
                           six   (3)
                         three   (5)
                          five   (4)
                          four   (4)

❀ 450 ❀ FUNNY COUNTING

Abbott used to fool Costello when they divided money with the "one for you, one for me; two for you, one-two for me; three for you; one-two-three for me" routine. At the end of the "first round," they each had one dollar. At the end of the "second round," Bud was ahead of Lew 3 dollars to 2. Find their totals at the end of 3, 4, 5, 6, . . . , n rounds. (A table will help you organize your results.)

❀ 451 ❀ THREE-IN-ONE

In each of three envelopes, there are three cards. On each card is a numeral, as shown in the illustration. By moving just one card from one envelope to another, can you make the sums of the numbers shown the same for each envelope?

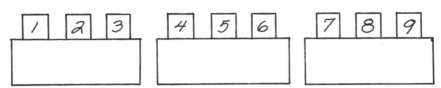

(Move card "9" to the left-hand envelope.)

❀ 452 ❀

Challenge a pupil to a counting contest in which the winner is the one who can say "20." The counting alternates between the contestants with each one permitted to give either one or two numbers. In the example, T stands for teacher and P stands for pupil. T "1, 2," P "3," T "4, 5," P "6, 7," T "8," P "9, 10," T "11," P "12," T "13, 14," P "15," T "16, 17," P "18," T "19, 20." Do not expose the trick, and caution the children who "catch on" not to explain to others.

Eventually, pupils will discover that the person who can say "17" will also be able to say "20." This will lead to the discovery that other "magic numbers" are 14, 11, 8, 5, and 2. The one who knows the full series cannot be beaten if he starts first, as in the example. Note that the "magic numbers" involve counting by threes to 20; therefore, the way to stay on the magic numbers is to add to one's opponent's count either one or two numbers to make a total of three numbers at each play.

❀ 453 ❀ SEVENTEEN

Purpose   To provide practice in logical thinking.
Level   3 and above.
Number of players   2.
Materials needed   Seventeen counters of any sort.
Procedure   Start with 17 counters on the table. Two students take turns removing counters from the pile. Each student may take 1, 2, or 3 at a time. The loser is the one who is forced to take the last counter. Players are asked, "Can you find a winning strategy and share it with the teacher?"
Variation   Place sixteen 1-inch cubes in four stacks, containing 6, 3, 2, and 5 cubes. A "move" consists in moving one *or more* cubes from one stack to another. Can you make all the stacks the same height in two moves? Can you find an arrangement of 16 cubes in 4 stacks which needs three moves to get the same number for each stack?

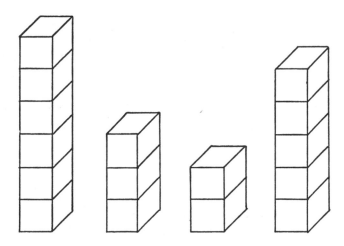

 454 ❀

Riddles are a kind of puzzle that ordinarily has an unusual twist and requires flexibility in thought. While they may not always have a direct mathematical base, they are fun for children and can be used as an aid to motivation during the study of numbers.

A Tom says, "My favorite numbers are 2, 3, 10, 12, 13, 20, 21, 22, ..." What is the next number in the sequence? (23. Tom likes numbers whose names begin with *t*.)

B If there are 12 one-cent stamps in a dozen, how many two-cent stamps are in a dozen? (twelve)

C A farmer had 17 sheep. All but 9 died. How many did he have left? (Nine)

D What could you put in a 10-pound empty box to make it weigh 9 pounds? (Holes)

E If you had only one match, and entered a room in which there were a kerosene lamp, an oil heater, and a wood burning stove, which would you light first? (The match)

F The following is a logical arrangement of the numerals 0 to 9. Why? 8 5 4 9 1 7 6 3 2 0. (Alphabetical)

G An anchor hangs from a boat to within 1 foot of the water. A heavy rain raises the water level 6 inches per hour. How long will it be before the water touches the anchor? (The anchor rises as the boat is lifted by the rising water.)

H I have in my hands two U.S. coins that total 55 cents in value. One is not a nickel. What are the two coins? (50 cents and 5 cents. One is not a nickel, but the other is.)

❀ 455 ❀

There are a variety of problem settings, somewhat recreational in nature, that, to properly solve, require the application of logic. Chilren enjoy these when presented at the appropriate developmental level, and many of them have residual mathematical value.

A If 8 men with 8 shovels remove 8 cubic meters of earth in 8 days, how long will it take 15 men with 15 shovels to remove 15 cubic meters of earth? (Eight days. One man removes 1 cubic meter of earth in 8 days.)

B George has six sections of a chain, each with four links. If it costs him 10 cents to have a link cut open and 25 cents to have it welded together again, what is the cheapest way to join the six sections into one continuous chain? (Cut open the four links of one section and use them to join the other five. Cost $1.40.)

C With some each of pennies, nickels, and dimes, select 21 coins with a total value of $1.00. (While the solution can be had mathematically, the children will use trial and error. There are two possible answers: 5 pennies, 13 nickels, and 3 dimes or 10 pennies, 4 nickels, and 7 dimes.)

D In a department store the second floor is 20 feet above the first. Each step of an escalator is 8 inches high and moves at the rate of two steps per second. If Willie walks up at the rate of two steps per second, how many steps will he take to reach the second floor? [The escalator will take Willie up 16 inches per second and he will take himself up 16 inches per second, a total of 32 inches per second. 240 inches (20 feet) requires $7\frac{1}{2}$ seconds—$240 \div 32 = 7\frac{1}{2}$. At two steps per second, he will take 15 steps.]

E If a snail climbs up a light pole at the rate of three feet a day but slips back two feet every night, how long will it take the snail to reach the top of a 12 foot pole? (The answer is ten days because after nine days the snail has progressed nine feet but on the tenth day it climbs three feet to the top of the pole.)

F A sixth grade committee arranged rows of chairs in the auditorium so that there were eight chairs to a row on each side of the center aisle. Jim sat in a chair in the row which was fifth from the front and sixth from the rear. How many persons could be seated? (There are 160 seats because each row has 16 seats, eight on each side of the center aisle, and there are ten rows.)

❀ 456 ❀ ONE–TWO

Students sometimes like to work alone. Make several "placing sheets" like the one shown and let children solve the problem individually. The procedures

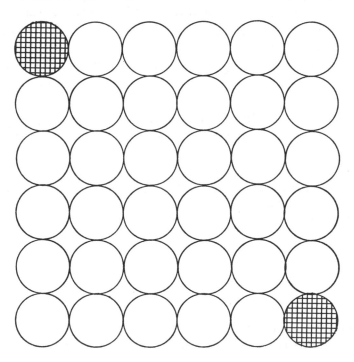

are as follows. Place a bean in the two circles that have been darkened. These two beans must remain fixed. Place 10 other beans in the circles by following these two rules: (1) no more than one bean in a circle; and (2) no more than two beans in any straight, horizontal, vertical, or diagonal line. (Twelve is the greatest number of beans that can be on the sheet under those two rules.)

❁ 457 ❁

Tricks with numbers intrigue many children while providing practice in the basic operations. Let children "in on it" as often as possible so that they may do them with friends at school and adults at home.

Ask a friend to think of a number. Multiply it by three, add six, divide by three, and subtract the number he thought of. Tell him that the answer is two. Why is this so? (One is always dividing six by three.) (The above trick and the four that follow are based on the same principle—a selected number is entered into a problem for which a formula has already been worked out so that whatever is done to the number at first is reversed later. Note that one will get the same answer to each problem for any selected number.)

A   Ask a pupil to select a number. Then add five, multiply by three, subtract nine, divide by three, subtract the original number. His answer will be two.

B   Ask a pupil to select a number. Then multiply by two, add five, subtract three, add twelve, divide by two, subtract the original number. His answer will be seven.

C   Ask a pupil to select a number. Then add four, multiply by three, subtract three, divide by three, subtract the original number. His answer will be three.

D   Ask a pupil to select a number. Then multiply by six, add twelve, divide by three, subtract four, divide by two, subtract the original number, add ten. His answer will be ten.

❁ 458 ❁

Considerable reinforcement for addition and subtraction can be obtained through the following number oddity. Write a five-place numeral near the bottom of the chalkboard. Say that this will be the sum of five four-place numbers. You write a number two more than the last four digits of the sum. Select a pupil to give you a number. You write a number, each digit of which is the difference between each digit of his number and nine. The pupil gives you another number. Then you write a number as before.

EXAMPLE

Teacher	3766
Pupil	7328
Teacher	2671
Pupil	4866
Teacher	5133
	23764

Note that 7328 + 2671 = 9999 and 4866 + 5133 = 9999, each 1 less than 10,000. Together they total 20,000 − 2. Since you had added 2 to 3764 of the sum, you had compensated so that the sum you selected is correct. Let the pupils try to discover why the trick works.

Experiment in advance with variations so that finding how the trick is done will not be easy. For example, instead of writing the sum immediately, let a pupil give you four numbers (vary the instructions by asking for three-, four-, or five-digit numbers—the principle will be the same), then write the sum and three more addends. The sum can be taken from any one of the four numbers.

Pupil
{
632
821—key to sum
165
798
}

Teacher
{
367
834
201
}
3818

821
−3
818
+3000
3818

Note: 632 + 367 = 999   2997 + 821 = 3818 or
        165 + 834 = 999   2997 +   3 = 3000 and
        798 + 201 = 999   3000 + 818 = 3818
             sum 2997

❀ 459 ❀ I'VE GOT A SECRET

Write the numerals 1 to 10 on the chalkboard in random arrangement. Ask one child to select a number (such as 6) and ask him to indicate the number to the rest of the group by raising his fingers while you turn your back so that you cannot see. When this is done, tell the pupils to begin counting silently with the number selected as you touch various and seemingly random numerals with a yardstick or pointer. When they reach 14 with their silent counting, your pointer will rest on the numeral selected. The children should be instructed to raise their hands when their count gets to 14. (Key: You will touch four numerals at random; the fifth must be 10, the next 9, then 8, 7, 6. Note:

Children count	6	7	8	9	10	11	12	13	14
You touch		11	8	14	2	10	9	8	7	6

When the pupil thinks he knows the trick, let him take your place. He must not tell the secret.

❀ 460 ❀ DICE ROLL MAGIC

Arithmetical humbug seems afoot when the teacher is able to tell the students the value on "secretly" rolled dice. After the dice are rolled out of the teacher's sight, the student is told:

1. Select the value of *one* die, multiply it by five, then add seven and double the result.
2. Now add the remaining, unused, die value and tell the teacher the final sum.
3. The teacher then tells the students *both* values of their roll. How can that be?

Example If 3 and 4 are rolled and 4 is chosen, we have $2(5 \times 4 + 7) + 3 = 57$, the result. The teacher subtracts 14 from the 57, getting 43, whose digits are the dice values. The more able student will be able to discover the teacher's method.

❀ 461 ❀ I'M A WIZARD

The teacher says, "I am a wizard! From this pack of cards, I can tell you what numeral any one of the cards contains by knowing only the number of the card." Call on a child to pick a card at random; have him show it to the class but not to the teacher (who is told only the number of the card).

Here is how the teacher "knows" the correct numeral. If the card number is 41, the numeral will be 5279: Add 11 to the card number ($41 + 11 = 52$); add the two digits ($5 + 2 = 7$); add the second and third digits ($2 + 7 = 9$).

When named in order the sums tell what numeral is on the card. (*Note*: If a sum is more than nine, use only the ones'-place digit.) The cards that will be needed are shown.

14 2572	20 3145	32 4370	30 4156	25 3695	41 5279
52 6392	16 2796	50 6178	15 2684	31 4268	

24 3583	40 5167	21 3257	43 5493	51 6280	23 3471
12 2358	34 4594	42 5381	60 7189		

❀ 462 ❀ TELL-A-NUMBER

Ask a friend to write down any number he chooses, e.g., 467, 324. Then tell him to add the digits $(4 + 6 + 7 + 3 + 2 + 4 = 26)$ and subtract the sum from the original number $(467{,}324 - 26 = 467{,}298)$. Now ask him to cross out any digit he wants to and then to read you the digits that are left in any order (46298, read as 9-2-6-4-8). As he reads them, add the digits mentally (29) and subtract the sum from the next highest multiple of nine $(36 - 29 = 7)$; this will tell you which number was crossed out—unless it was a zero or a nine; in this case, ask if it was a zero; if the answer is "No," say "Then it must be a nine." Any sum of digits subtracted from a number will leave a number divisible by nine and therefore the sum of its digits will be a multiple of nine. By removing a digit the new sum will be a multiple of nine minus the number removed. One cannot tell whether zero or nine is removed.

❀ 463 ❀ ONE BIRTHDAY IN A LIFETIME

Using a procedure similar to that in Activity 462, one can determine another's birthday (or any other date in a year). Ask a pupil to think of the number of the month in which he was born (one for January, two for February, etc.), multiply it by five, add six, multiply by four, subtract four, multiply by five, add the number of the day on which he was born, and tell you the answer. From this you should mentally subtract 100. The resulting number gives you his birthday. The day of the month is found in the last two digits; the others give you the month. For example, if a pupil is thinking of July 4, the month will be seven; $7 \times 5 = 35$; $35 + 6 = 41$; $41 \times 4 = 164$; $164 - 4 = 160$; $160 \times 5 = 800$; $800 + 4$ (the day of the month) $= 804$. From this you mentally subtract 100, leaving 704. 7 is the month and 4 is the day.

Let M equal the number for the month. Then, following the directions above, $[(M5 + 6)4 - 4]5 - 100 = 100M$. This places the month in the hundreds' column and leaves the tens' and ones' columns with zeros; therefore, when the day (date) is added, it will show in the latter columns.

❁ 464 ❁ FOUR SQUARE

Four boys lived in the same apartment and went to the same school. They were good friends and often played together on weekends. With the information given below, tell the age of each boy and on which floor of the apartment he lived.

1. Joe, Jack, John, and Tom live one on each floor of a four-story apartment.
2. Their ages are 10, 9, 8, and 5, but not necessarily in that order.
3. Joe lives directly above the nine-year-old and directly below the eight-year-old.
4. Jack has to pass by the five-year-old to leave the building from his apartment.
5. Jack is more than one floor away from Tom, who is more than one year younger than Jack.

❁ 465 ❁

The hand-held calculator is useful for generating many of the number-pattern activities in this chapter. Because of the availability to most children, e.g., cost of $8 to $12, it is appropriate to provide some structured experimental use.[7] You will get ideas for additional activities from those below.

A Close your eyes and compute the sum: $1 + 2 + 3 + 4 + 5 + 6 + 7 + 8 =$ ____. Now look. You should have gotten 36.

B Without using the key for the operation of multiplication, can you get the product for 7 X 8, 12 X 24, and so forth?

C Without using the key for the operation of division, can you get the quotient for 336 divided by 12?

D As you count mentally by six, e.g., 6, 12, 18, and so forth, use your calculator to sum the digits. What do you notice? Do it for eight. Then try some other numbers.

E Play a game with a friend. He is your opponent. Clear the calculator and take turns pushing 1, or 2, or 3 and the addition key. The person who makes the calculator show 21 wins. Can you find a winning strategy? Play several games but take turns being first. Does this make a difference?

F A calculator, with its digital-readout numerals, can become a light diversion as well as a joy for computation. As this writing effort reaches its close, the authors will not say a sad "goodbye," but rather ask that the entry .07734 be viewed upside-down.

NOTES

1. For a thoughtful analysis of problem solving in elementary school mathematics, see C. W. Schminke and W. Arnold, *Mathematics Is a Verb: Options for Teaching* (Hinsdale, Ill.: The Dryden Press, Inc., 1971), Section VI, "Problem Solving: Motivating Ability to Reason and Inquire," pp. 269–312.

2. Commercially available as "Logical Blocks" from Herder and Herder, 232 Madison Avenue, New York, New York 10016, or as "Invicta Attribute Blocks" from Responsive Environments Corporation, Lackawanna Avenue, West Patterson, New Jersey 07424.

3. This proposition is known as Goldbach's conjecture. It was named for the man who first noticed that every even number he could test could be written as the sum of two primes. His conjecture was that it is true for every even number, but a total proof has not yet been discovered.

4. For additional student activities and experiments, see J. L. Marks, C. R. Purdy, L. B. Kinney, and A. A. Hiatl, *Teaching Elementary School Mathematics for Understanding*, 4th ed. (New York: McGraw-Hill Book Company, 1975). Chapter Ten, entitled Teaching Special Topics, contains a series of activities related to problem solving, number theory, and probability that may be used directly with children.

5. Some illustrative pupil activity cards related to modular arithmetic are

found in C. W. Schminke, N. Maertens, and W. Arnold, *Teaching the Child Mathematics* (Hinsdale, Ill.: The Dryden Press, Inc., 1975), pp. 392–399.

6. Eighty-one activities in probability and statistics are found in Donald A. Buckeye, *Experiments in Probability and Statistics* (Troy, Mich.: Midwest Publication Co., Inc., 1970).

7. A reasoned approach and accompanying activities for creative use of hand-held calculators is found in *Fostering Creativity Through Mathematics* (Tampa, Fla.: Florida Council of Teachers of Mathematics, 1974), pp. 69–74. Address inquiries to FCTM, University of South Florida, Tampa, Florida 33620.

appendix

SOURCES FOR MATERIALS

The supply of commercially prepared materials for actively engaging students in mathematics appears limitless. One contemporary classification scheme for such material is "hardware" and "software." The former is generally defined as physical equipment. Counting discs, centimeter rods, and logic blocks are typical examples. The latter refers to printed material that surrounds the classroom mathematics program. A few examples are the text book, curriculum guides and enrichment books, and the currently popular activity (task-job-assignment) cards.

Throughout this text, activities have called for hands-on material. Much of the needed material may be collected or made by the instructor and the students; thus, the costs associated with it will be modest. Frequently, however, it is useful to refer to a publisher's or supplier's catalogs. Here is why:

1. They may usually be obtained free of charge.
2. They often suggest ideas for additional teacher-made material.

3. They provide a specific source for needed materials that may be too complex or sophisticated for local construction.
4. They are consistently a superior information source for a continually expanding and changing market of mathematics teaching and learning aides.

The lists that follow are not exhaustive but they are representative of contemporary publishers, suppliers, and materials. Part one contains sixteen specific publishers and suppliers and examples of the range of materials available through them. Part two provides a list of hardware and software referred to in this text. The list is keyed to the sixteen suppliers by number. A modest additional list of suppliers is found in Part three.

PART I: PUBLISHERS, SUPPLIERS, AND MATERIALS

SUPPLIERS	MATERIALS
1. Activity Resources Company 24827 Calaroga Avenue Hayward, California 94545	Games, tangrams, enrichment books.
2. Childcraft Education Corporation 964 Third Avenue New York, New York 10022	Prenumber, number materials; mathematical balance; measurement tools.
3. Creative Publications P.O. Box 10328 Palo Alto, California 94303	Tangrams, enrichment books, Dienes blocks, Unifix materials, attribute games, mathematical balance, measurement tools, geoboards, activity cards, metric materials, games, geometric solids, abacus, dice, beads, discs, number spinners.
4. Creative Teaching Associates P.O. Box 293 Fresno, California 93708	Games, tangrams, geoboard, mathematical balance.
5. Cuisenaire Company of America 12 Church Street New Rochelle, New York 10805	Cuisenaire rods, geoboards, geometric solids, activity cards, games, Soma cubes, enrichment books.
6. Edmund Scientific Company EDSCORP Building Barrington, New Jersey 08007	Geometric solids, Soma cubes, probability kit, graph set.
7. General Learning Corporation 3 East 54th Street New York, New York 10022	Attribute blocks, counting chips, prenumber materials, activity cards, geocards, balance cards, trundle wheel, metric material, tangrams.

8. Houghton Mifflin Company
53 W. 43rd Street
New York, New York 10036

Stern materials, centimeter rods, activity cards, number spinners.

9. Ideal School Supply Company
11000 South Lavergne Avenue
Oak Lawn, Illinois 60453

Place value board, tens frame, flash cards, abacus, beads, felt board, cross number puzzles, number line.

10. Moyer-Vico Ltd.
1935 First Avenue, North
Saskatoon, Saskatchewan
CANADA

Flannel boards, dominoes, dice, mirror cards, games, integer cards, fraction set, cross number puzzles, pattern boards, wipe-off number line, counting discs, scales, weights, trundle wheel, Dienes blocks.

11. Scott Resources, Inc.
P.O. Box 2121
Fort Collins, Colorado 80521

Tangrams, geoboards, enrichment books, activity cards.

12. Selective Educational Equipment, Inc. (SEE)
3 Bridge Street
Newton, Massachusetts 02195

Poleidoblocks, geometric solids, mathematical balance, activity cards, geoboards.

13. Silver Burdett
Box 362
Morristown, New Jersey 07960

Enrichment books, attribute blocks, tangrams, abacus, mathematical balance.

14. Walker Educational Book Corp.
720 Fifth Avenue
New York, New York 10019

Geoboard

15. Webster/McGraw-Hill
Manchester Road
Manchester, Missouri 63011

Elementary Science Study Units (attribute games and problems, mirror cards, geoblocks, tangram).

16. Western Educational Activities Ltd.
10577 97th Street
Edmonton 17, Ontario
CANADA

Wiff'n' Proof games, Napier's bones, digital computer, geometric models, math lab experiments, enrichment books.

PART II: CROSS REFERENCE

SPECIFIC MATERIALS	SUPPLIER KEY NUMBER
1. Abacus	3, 9, 13
2. Activity cards	3, 5, 7, 8, 11, 12
3. Attribute blocks	3, 7, 10, 13, 15
4. Centimeter rods	8, 9
5. Counting discs, beads, etc.	7, 9, 10
6. Cuisenaire rods	5
7. Dice	3, 10

8. Dominoes	10, 12
9. Dienes blocks	3, 10
10. Enrichment books	1, 3, 5, 11, 13, 16
11. Games	1, 3, 4, 5, 16
12. Geoboards	3, 4, 5, 11, 12, 14
13. Geometric solids	3, 5, 6, 7, 12, 16
14. Geo-strips	7, 12
15. Mathematical balance	2, 3, 4, 10, 12, 13
16. Measurement tools	2, 3, 7, 10
17. Metric materials	3, 7, 9, 16
18. Mirror cards	10, 15
19. Napier's bones	16
20. Number line	3, 9, 10
21. Number spinners	3, 8
22. Poleidoblocks	12
23. Prenumber, number materials	2, 3, 5, 7, 8, 9
24. Soma cubes	3, 5, 6
25. Stern materials	8
26. Tangrams	1, 3, 4, 7, 11, 13, 15
27. Tens frame	9
28. Trundle wheel	7, 10

PART III: ADDITIONAL PUBLISHERS AND SUPPLIERS

Allyn and Bacon, Inc.
470 Atlantic Avenue
Boston, Massachusetts 02210

Beckley-Cardy Company
1900 North Harragansett Avenue
Chicago, Illinois 60639

Fearon Publishers
2165 Park Boulevard
Palo Alto, California 94306

Gel-Sten Supply Company, Inc.
911–913 South Hill Street
Los Angeles, California 90015

Gerrard Publishing Company
123 West Park Avenue
Champaign, Illinois 61820

D.C. Heath and Company
125 Spring Street
Lexington, Massachusetts 02173

Holt, Rinehart and Winston, Inc.
Box 2334, Grand Central Station
New York, New York 10017

The Judy Company
310 North 2nd Street
Minneapolis, Minnesota 55401

Kenworthy Educational Service
45 North Division Street
Buffalo, New York 14205

Mainco School Supply Company
Canton, Massachusetts 02021

Charles E. Merrill Publishing Co.
1300 Alum Creek Drive
Columbus, Ohio 43216

Midwest Publications Co., Inc.
P.O. Box 307
Birmingham, Michigan 48012

Miles Kimball Company
41 West 8th Avenue
Oshkosh, Wisconsin 54901

Milton Bradley Company
Springfield, Massachusetts 01101

Minnesota Mining and Manufacturing
  Co. (3M)
2501 Hudson Road
St. Paul, Minnesota 55119

Motivational Research, Inc.
4216 Howard Avenue
Kensington, Maryland

National Council of Teachers
  of Mathematics (NCTM)
1201 Sixteenth Street N.W.
Washington, D.C. 20036

Playskool Manufacturing Company
3720 North Kedzie Avenue
Chicago, Illinois 60618

Products of the Behavioral Sciences
1140 Dell Avenue
Campbell, California 95008

Responsive Environmental Corp. (REC)
Learning Materials Division
Englewood Cliffs, New Jersey 07632

G.W. School Supply
5626 East Belmont Avenue
P.O. Box 14
Fresno, California

Schoolhouse Visuals, Inc.
816 Thayer Avenue
Silver Springs, Maryland 20910

Science Research Associates, Inc.
259 East Erie Street
Chicago, Illinois 60611

Scott Foresman and Company
Glenview, Illinois 60025

Stanley Bowman Company, Inc.
4 Broadway
Valhalla, New York 10595

Teachers' Exchange of San Francisco
600 35th Avenue
San Francisco, California 94121